KNOCK WOOD

CANDICE BERGEN

Simon & Schuster Paperbacks

New York   London   Toronto   Sydney   New Delhi

Simon & Schuster
1230 Avenue of the Americas
New York, NY 10020

This Simon & Schuster trade paperback edition July 2014

SIMON & SCHUSTER and colophon are registered trademarks of Simon & Schuster, Inc.

For information about special discounts for bulk purchases, please contact Simon & Schuster Special Sales at 1-866-506-1949 or business@simonandschuster.com.

The Simon & Schuster Speakers Bureau can bring authors to your live event. For more information or to book an event, contact the Simon & Schuster Speakers Bureau at 1-866-248-3049 or visit our website at www.simonspeakers.com.

Interior design by Akasha Archer
Cover Photograph by Mary Ellen Mark

Manufactured in the United States of America

10   9   8   7   6   5   4   3

Library of Congress Cataloging-in-Publication Data:

Bergen, Candice.
Knock wood.
1. Bergen, Candice. 2. Moving-picture actors and actresses—United States—biography. I. title.
pn2287.b434a34 1984 791.43'028'0924 [b] 83-25139

ISBN 978-1-4767-7013-0
ISBN 978-1-4516-5174-4 (ebook)

For my family

ACKNOWLEDGMENTS

Thanks to my friends for their help and generosity: Luis San Jurjo, Rusty Unger, Mary Ellen Mark, Connie Freiberg, John Calley, and, in particular, Henry Jaglom, who encouraged me to begin this book and stuck fast for years to make sure he saw its end. Thanks also to my publisher, Joni Evans, and my editor, Marjorie Williams, for their attention and persistent prodding, and to my agent, Lynn Nesbit.

I am especially grateful to my mother for her friendship and support, and most of all to my husband for giving me a happy ending.

PROLOGUE

1952

"We are gathered here today to say farewell to our little turtle, Toby, who is now departed. He was a brave, good little turtle and he died—*How* did he die, Candy?"

A pause. "He was supposed to get food once a week and he didn't get it at all."

"I see, he died because you forgot to feed him and so he has gone to turtle heaven, and we will say a prayer for him today. Candy?"

"Dear God, please bless my turtle, Toby, and keep him safe and please forgive me for not feeding him. Amen."

It is the morning of the turtle funeral. I am six. We are standing in the rose garden; a light rain is falling. The day is pale and gray. My mother, eyes respectfully downcast, is wrapped in a trench coat and carries a calla lily; I wear a hat, veil and shawl over jeans and sneakers and carry a toffee tin containing the deceased. Dena, my governess, wears a coat over her uniform, and clusters with Kay, the cook, who holds an umbrella. Mickey, the gardener, his head bowed, stands silently by with a tiny hoe and shovel to break the earth. There is a man shooting 16 mm sound and another shooting stills. They are filming my father, splendid and somber in top hat and overcoat, who holds the Northwestern telephone directory, from which he pretends to read the eulogy.

Though it is a solemn occasion, my father is making us all

laugh, and I am trying hard to keep a straight face. I am also trying to remember the words to my song; my father has arranged
that I will sing at the service and I am nervous at the thought. It
is not so much the singing itself that makes me nervous, nor the
presence of the cameras; I am used to appearing with my parents
in public, accustomed to cameras. I am nervous about performing well for my father. More than anything, I want to please my
father.

In the elaborate, frenzied preparations and excitement of the
funeral, the turtle has all but been forgotten. In my preoccupation
with performing well, Toby has almost slipped my mind.

My governess and I plucked him from the seething turtle tank
at the Farmers' Market. Hundreds of turtles writhed and squirmed
in the tank, some whose backs were covered with brightly colored
decals of beach scenes and hula girls. Those with the decals died
quickly, Dena explained (though ours died fast enough), unable to
breathe through the tropical scenes on their shells, so we chose a
traditional green one and then selected a home. We settled on a
custom turtle dish with an island in its center, shaded by a curving
plastic palm, to which we added a Chinese bridge and a porcelain
pagoda.

It was a policy at our house that people took responsibility for
their pets—a policy pointedly aimed at me, as I was the only one
who wanted them. But a turtle was a kind of "para" pet, resembling
a pet only in that it moved from time to time and required scant
quantities of food. So scant was the amount required, in fact, that
in no time I forgot his food completely. As turtles are the lowest and
most sedentary form of pet—popular only for that reason—death
does not come to them dramatically, and days went by before anyone realized that Toby had passed on.

"Candy, do you have a song you'd like to sing for Toby?"

"Yes."

"What song is that?"

" 'The Tennessee Waltz.' "

"Go ahead then. And project."

I give it all I have:

> *I was dancin' with my loved one*
> *As the music was playin'*
> *When an old friend I happened to see . . .*

"I think the turtle's turning over now," my father says, peering into the tin.

Doggedly, I continue:

> *I introduced her to my darlin'*
> *And while they were swayin'*
> *My friend stole my sweetheart from me . . .*

"Well, if the turtle's not dead yet," my father chuckles, "I'm sure that would really kill him."

But I can see that my father is pleased. The funeral has gone well. My father is happy; I am happy. Toby is put to rest in the rose garden. The photographs run in the *Saturday Evening Post*.

1978

It is the morning of the funeral. I am thirty-two. The day is brilliant, warm and sunny. My mother is weeping and wears a pearl-gray suit. My brother, blond head bent, is weeping too. I am wearing a dark-green dress; I do not weep. I am composed, controlled, and I perceive the events as if from a great distance. There are hundreds of people attending the funeral. It is covered by all the press.

I am used to appearing with my family in public, accustomed to cameras. I smile at them as I enter the church; it is an unexpected gesture. I am nervous. Once again, I am performing for my father. Wanting more than anything to please. But it is the morning of his funeral, and I will never know if I succeed.

Charlie's Sister

1

My dad and I would spend Sunday mornings in the breakfast room. Me and my dad: it was our time together and usually it was just the two of us. And occasionally Charlie.

There we'd be, in the gentle morning light, with the sun slipping through the colored circles in the bottle-glass windows, tossing brilliant spots of blues and greens across the gleaming oakwood floor. From the kitchen floated whiffs of waffles, smells of sausage and, on Sundays, Swedish pancakes heaped with lingonberries twinkling like rubies. My father was a lifelong Swedish loyalist, and the Swedish pancakes arrived in the hands of Simon, the Swedish houseman, hot off the griddle of Aina, the Swedish cook.

Life was good for me and my dad in that breakfast room: big, blond people moving softly, reassuringly through a string of golden mornings. And there we were, in our secret Scandinavia, just like a perfect couple, you know, unless Charlie or someone was there.

When Charlie was there, my dad would sit him on one knee and me on the other and he'd put a hand on both our necks, and when he squeezed my neck, I'd move my mouth, and when he squeezed Charlie's neck, he'd move his. As Charlie and I yammered away at each other across my father, mouths flapping soundlessly, behind us, smiling politely, sat my dad, happily speaking for both of us.

And whether or not Charlie was there, my father would often spend these Sunday mornings talking—rhapsodizing, really—about vaudeville. About the "Chautauqua circuit," about "playing the Palace." His face would fill with light and his eyes would dance, and though I had no idea what vaudeville was and cared less, the way he looked when he talked about those days, like a man remembering a first love, made me think vaudeville was something special. Certainly it was to him.

Vaudeville: *vau de vire, voix de ville*. Music halls and minstrel shows, circuses and showboats. In 1903, when my father was born, vaudeville was about to reach its fullest flower, its shining hour. It would be America's Golden Age too, and for a time the two grew up in tandem—the unself-conscious, wild and woolly spectacle of vaudeville a perfect mirror for the country's most expansive, sprawling era.

Theodore Roosevelt cried out against "the malefactors of great wealth" as vast fortunes formed in flashes and huge empires were built overnight by Rockefellers, Fricks and Carnegies—ruthless, iron-fisted, adventurous Americans who knew the knack of spinning straw into gold.

Vaudeville's features were as flamboyant as those fortunes: Madame Chester and her Educated Statue Dog; Babu Abdulle— the Hindu Conjurer; Herr Strassel and his Wonder Seals; Isham's Octaroons—Colored Singers; and W. C. Fields—Unique Comedy Juggler.

In vaudeville, there were big-time circuits and small-time circuits. The big-time, or "first," circuits showcased the hot acts, two shows a day, and the small-time, or "second," circuits three shows a day with entertainment geared to the rural, unsophisticated mentality of the farmer and his family in America's middle.

At the turn of the century, much of midwest America was settled by Scandinavians; they headed straight for those parts of the country that resembled most closely their own and duplicated communities of fair-haired crisp efficiency on the lush, rich land so scarce at home.

Towns of towheads with bright blue eyes were strung across new states like Michigan and Minnesota, Wisconsin and Illinois. These were people from the land of Ibsen and Strindberg, Munch and Grieg—tall, pale people, stern and strong. Without so much as a backward glance at the fjords and the midnight sun, they resumed the productive severity of their spare and structured lives. Weathering the sub-zero winters in gleaming kitchens by wood-burning stoves, patiently waiting till spring to turn spotless cows out into tidy green pastures, they were a race of industrious introverts, controlled and uncomplaining.

It was people like these who were my grandparents, Nell and John Berggren, who left their life in Sweden for America's Midwest, bought a dairy farm in Michigan and raised two boys, Clarence and Edgar.

And it was people like Nell and John Berggren who made up the audience out in front of the stage under the tents of vaudeville: hardworking, religious farmers and their families, who wanted their entertainment cheap and wanted it clean. And it was these shows, these second-circuit stops for the hicks and rubes in the heartland, that Edgar Berggren and his brother went to see—sometimes sneaking in under the crackling canvas of the tent, sometimes paying a nickel for a seat on the splintered benches inside to watch, with wide eyes, the world of vaudeville.

From 1875 to 1925—for half a century—vaudeville was America's favorite form of entertainment and a vital part of the middle-class life. Then, perhaps more than at any other time, America was a land of magic. Hocus-pocus, razzle-dazzle. It was ragtime, the Jazz Age, when everything was believed possible and its people proved it so: the radio (or wireless) was invented, the North Pole was discovered, the *Titanic* was sunk and the world went to its first war.

• • •

"The players are coming! The players are coming!" cried the tidy, small towns as the vaudeville troupe pulled in, hot and dusty, to "haul up the rag" and hustle the hick, to find beds for themselves and barns for their animals. Outside the tent, sharp-eyed hucksters hawked their wares and stalked their prey, selling cure-alls to suckers, "liver bags" and "electric rheumatism belts," sneaking snootfuls of "nose-paint."

Vaudeville was a paradise for quacks and the nimble-footed and light-fingered con men who slipped smoothly through the bobbing sea of straw hats called "katys," past men chafing in their "iron" shirt collars, and happily picked pockets.

Many of the performers were orphans, kids from broken homes, who came from grim, big-city tenements and slums and turned to show business as one of the few ways out. Tough-talking, fast-moving, they started as street entertainers—singing and dancing on corners and in back rooms of bars—and escaped from their neighborhoods into a troupe and a tent.

And the hotels hung up the signs warning, "No Dogs or Actors" and the "towners" locked up their daughters and hid their valuables and the rubes nailed shut their barns because these players were tricky and had sticky fingers; it was common sense and common knowledge.

If vaudeville was an escape for the performers, it was for the audience as well. Comedy was the essence of vaudeville and the tents rang with raucous laughter at jokesters, jugglers, hobos, tramps, tumblers, tank acts, midgets and magicians. "LaBelle Titcomb" sang opera arias while riding a white horse, "Monsieur Marno" played the piano standing on his head, "The Human Tank" swallowed frogs and emitted them alive. These performers took life and turned it upside down and inside out, and this, when he crawled under the tent to peek, is what Edgar Berggren saw. He saw an enchanted land where anything was possible, where people were paid to practice magic.

Edgar was the younger son, the gawky one: moody, maladroit, self-conscious and shy. The dazed dreamer. For him, sitting spellbound under the tent, vaudeville was Valhalla. At eleven, thinking he might try to make his own magic, he sent off a quarter and received *The Wizard's Manual* in the mail. It taught "Secrets of Magic, Black Art, Mind-reading, Ventriloquism and Hypnotism" (including a chapter on how to cut a man's head off and put it in a platter a yard from his body), and Edgar went right to work.

The first place he tried throwing his voice was into an apple pie his mother was taking from the stove: the pie, in a tiny, high-pitched voice, shrieked, "Help, help! Let me out! Oh, thank you, thank you." This, to a Swedish Lutheran from the Old Country, a woman with a neat blond bun and wire spectacles, in dark dresses lit by pale lace collars. A good and fastidious woman whose pies were now talking.

Soon the house, the farm were alive with voices. Nell would jump as she grabbed a babbling broom, start at disembodied chuckles, open the door at cries for help, to find no one. The house was full of phantoms; it was *enchanted,* filled with mystery and magic, as Edgar tried to read his mother's mind, make the dogs disappear, pull his father's rabbits out of hats.

Edgar was practicing, and getting pretty good, too.

John Berggren died when Edgar was sixteen, the family moved from Michigan to Illinois, and the two boys went to work, Clarence as an apprentice accountant, and Edgar in a silent-movie house where he stoked the furnace, operated the player piano and ran the projector. But Edgar's real world had become one of illusions—deceptions of hand and voice—and he would disappear for hours on end to study magic tricks and practice ventriloquism, developing his diction, projecting his voice, controlling his diaphragm and the flexibility of his lips. Creating a character.

The character he created—and the companion with whom he would spend the rest of his life—was based on a quick-witted, red-headed Irish boy, close in age to Edgar, who sold newspapers on a corner in Decatur. The boy's name was Charlie, and he was a bright and brassy kid, confident, cocksure. Edgar passed him every day and then made sketches, which he gave to a barkeeper called Mack, who was also something of a woodcarver. First working with Edgar on a clay head which would serve as a model, Mack then carved a dummy whom Edgar christened "Charlie," after his inspiration, and "McCarthy" after Mr. Mack. "Charlie McCarthy" had come alive.

The head, made of pine, was empty but for a rubber band that ran from the inside top of the skull to the back of the neck. The backbone was a broomstick, nine inches long, that terminated in a semidisc hinged to the neck. Along the hickory spine, trail cords were attached to the lower jaw. The dummy weighed forty pounds, wore a perfect size 4, and took size 2AAA shoes. A simple enough piece of construction, hardly a work of genius, and yet . . .

Soon the dummy was putting Edgar through high school, answering roll calls for missing classmates. Their first public appearance was in Chicago in an amateur tryout paying five dollars a night. Edgar was doing a ventriloquism-and-magic act; the manager said, "Berggren, you can stay if you cut the magic out." He did, at the same time neatening his name, which soon appeared in tiny print, minus an r and a g at the bottom of a second-circuit vaudeville bill. "Edgar Bergen—Voice Illusionist" was preceded by "The Great Chandor—Armenian Strongman."

Ventriloquists (also known as "belly-talkers"), strongmen, jugglers and gymnasts—hung from the lowest rung in vaudeville—were more common in carnivals and sideshows. But Charlie's fine pine hand began changing the established order of things, and soon Chandor—who lifted pianos—received less pay and less applause than this dummy, McCarthy, who also made merciless fun of him.

Reluctantly returning from his first summer on the second circuit, Edgar switched from vaudeville "vent" to freshman at Northwestern, where, to his mother's great relief, he dutifully enrolled as a premed student. But he continued giving shows with Charlie, as much for an excuse to perform as to pay his way, and soon transferred to the school of speech. In the end, lured by Charlie's growing success, moving closer to his destiny with a dummy, he left without completing his studies, dashing his mother's dreams of his becoming a doctor.

In the early twenties, recovering from the many privations of World War I, America was entering an era of great expansion: Harding's election in 1920 was less historic than the radio program announcing it, which marked the beginning of broadcasting. In the same year, the Eighteenth Amendment went into effect, prohibiting the sale of intoxicating liquors; and the Nineteenth Amendment granted women the right to vote.

Most of these events had scant effect on Edgar, too young to vote, indifferent to drink, inept with women; but throughout the twenties great developments in radio continued, and its ether waves would pull America under its spell and make Edgar Bergen one of its own.

My father—while not *himself* the perfect hero—had by now created someone who was. Awkward, silent, socially unsuccessful, Edgar created someone who caught people's fancies when he, most often, could not. Gradually he began leaving things to this dummy—so saucy, witty, self-assured—and learned to let *him* take over while behind his left shoulder, bashful, sort of beautiful, stood Edgar, as if by accident, listening in amusement while Charlie just wowed 'em. Absolutely knocked 'em dead.

For ten years, Edgar and Charlie traveled "the Sawdust Trail" by rail, moving up from the second circuit to the prized Chautauqua circuit, crisscrossing the country with troupes toppling over with trunks and teeming with animals.

Edgar and Charlie spent the twenties with trunks, their own and others'. Shoving them onto trains, tugging them up backstage stairs, wedging them into closets called dressing rooms, lugging them through snowdrifts. For ten years, the two partners lived out of a trunk, Edgar eating, often sleeping, on it, Charlie sleeping *in* it.

Naturally, not everyone had to live in and lug his own trunk; vaudeville's female legends now traveled with thirty pieces of luggage, an entourage of chauffeur, footman, perhaps two French maids, and requested that their hotel suites and dressing rooms be redecorated in time for their arrival. Sarah Bernhardt ("the Divine Sarah") lived not in a trunk but in a favorite coffin—a quite expensive one she wished to be buried in, claiming she slept inside to accustom herself to it.

Lyceum, Chautauqua, Red Path—for ten years Edgar and Charlie worked these circuits, learning on their feet (well, Edgar's feet) how to dress, move on stage, write and deliver material, shape an act, sense an audience. Become *performers*. Vaudeville artistes. This they did, and they did it quickly, having only seconds to win over what Oscar Hammerstein II called "the Big, Black Giant"— the audience that waited impatiently under the tent. Restless and ornery, steely and mean: Show me a thing or two and make it snappy, growled the many-headed monster. Miners, mill workers, farmers—they all sat, waiting to be shown a thing or two.

Charlie's name was now prominently displayed alongside that of his boss. Not that Bergen didn't tire of being part of a duo, didn't dream of working solo. He even went so far as to try his own act one afternoon show, walking bravely out on stage alone, without the comfort of his customary sidekick, and performing a mild mixture of magic and illusion and the popular tramp character, waiting, hopefully, for applause. But the Big, Black Giant wasn't buying: they chewed it up, spit it out, and Bergen was fired by the manager after the matinee.

It was Charlie or nothing, so "Bergen and McCarthy" it stayed.

Snapshots show them clowning across the country, posing proudly next to their names on circuit bills. Edgar stands stiffly before "the Big Brown Tent"—stunningly young, slender and fair. Not quite elegant, delicately handsome.

They must have been some days, those ten years of coal-crusted trains and big brown tents and tight-knit troupes, of menacing mine workers ("Here live the most dangerous people I ever met," Edgar wrote on a postcard home from a town in Kentucky) and blushing Southern belles. It was that moment in time when life is at its most lighthearted and spirits their most carefree, a moment Edgar—not a carefree man by nature—gazed back on many times later, missing the company of clowns.

Those years were finally topped in 1930 by Edgar and Charlie "playing the Palace"—the pot of gold at the end of the Sawdust Trail. Having come from big tents loudly flapping in dust storms and town halls deep in snowdrifts, they stood, speechless, before the splendor of the Palace, variety's Versailles.

Shimmering majestically on 47th and Broadway, beckoning the brightest stars, the Palace showcased some of the greatest performers of the era: Jack Benny performed there (as the violin-playing half of an act) as well as Fanny Brice, the Marx Brothers, Houdini, Al Jolson, the Barrymores, Will Rogers, Adele and Fred Astaire. "The Divine Sarah"—then well past seventy—played the Palace, established it, in fact, and thick-piled bear rugs were laid from her dressing room to the stage to muffle the sound of her wooden leg. She refused to play on the same bill with animal or blackface acts, considering them cruel and degrading, and she demanded that she be paid five hundred dollars in gold after each night's performance.

This was more like it: no sharing of dressing rooms with animal acts *here*; this was *class*. And when Edgar and Charlie stepped out onto the vast, waxed, gleaming stage, trembling more than in all their past ten years, they were blinded by the glare of footlights, lost and little in this great and gilded space. The big time was nothing like the big tent; performers who had gone before tried to tell you but there just was no preparing. Years of training and an entertainer's instincts took over while the eyes and heart adjusted and sight and sound returned.

Jesus, it was *huge* out there and packed with more people than the circuit ever saw. *This* audience sprawled in fat, soft seats upholstered in flowered cretonne, not broken chairs or splintered benches, and overhead hung crystal chandeliers that burst into light like fireworks. The hall was cooled by Siena marble, the fixtures cast from bronze trimmed in ivory.

This was the Palace and it rang with laughter, roared for more of Edgar Bergen and Charlie McCarthy, who giddily, gratefully took their bows and fairly floated into the wings.

They'd come a long way from the days when lowly "belly-talkers" were barely legible at the bottom of a bill to being the first ventriloquist act booked at the Palace; it was high praise indeed. And that was why, one time in New York when I was nine, he took me to the corner of 47th and Broadway, pointed proudly, and sighed, "Candy, *this* used to be the Palace. Your father played here years ago."

No wonder he looked like that, smiling and wistful, gazing dreamily at his past. But *I* didn't see any palace filled with magic there on that Broadway block, and I patted a policeman's horse impatiently, anxious to get to Schrafft's.

It takes time to know another's dreams, and only now do I understand why we stood there staring at that corner. It was my father's first, fine dream, and it had come true. I think he never got over that.

Edgar had realized his dream just in time. The closing of the Palace in 1932 symbolized vaudeville's death. Limping from the blow dealt by silent moving pictures, then crumpling from radio's coup de grace, vaudeville was finished; its Golden Age had passed.

But the Golden Age of radio was just beginning. Having robbed vaudeville of her brightest stars, her biggest income, radio overwhelmed America with its infinite possibilities, scope and reach. Movie stars and Broadway actors tried a turn on this newfangled, lucrative format whose sophistication and popularity grew at a dazzling pace, despite critics who claimed radio was becoming "moronic" and rendering children "psychopathic by its bedtime stories."

The early days of radio saw an awkward age of adjustment: performers panicked at the unfamiliar sight of those tall, thin things called microphones, which were sometimes disguised with lampshades to put early radio guests at ease. Vaudeville and Broadway stars not only had to accustom themselves to working with microphones but to the strangeness of performing in eerily empty studios. Not only actors were thrown off; stepping up nervously to what looked like a floor lamp and singing their hearts out, singers soon discovered that their high notes blew out the delicate tubes of the transmitters, and so the style of "crooning" was born.

Early radio listeners tuned in to soap operas, mystery shows, singing commercials, crooners, comedians, and quizzes. Under fire from the critics, networks were forced to establish specific codes of behavior, eliminating from children's programs "torture, horror, use of the supernatural or superstition likely to arouse fear" and banning profanity, vulgarity, kidnapping and "cliff-hanging." A model program: *Jack Armstrong, All-American Boy*. Of course.

It was the thirties—the Depression. In living rooms and kitchens across the country, families, often hungry, clustered around their radio receiving sets to hear Roosevelt chat by a fireside, Hitler become Chancellor of Germany, Haile Selassie plead for help for Ethiopia, and the Duke of Windsor abdicate his throne.

It was not a world that made much room for unemployed entertainers, for those refugees from vaudeville whose tents had finally folded. Some—clowns and jugglers, bareback riders, tightrope walkers—could return to the circus. But what about a ventriloquist and his dummy, too young to be washed up, and wondering what to do?

"Everybody looked down on ventriloquism. Vaudeville was dying," my father told me years later. "We thought we were through, Charlie and I. Then I decided on desperate measures. I revamped my whole act. I had a dress suit and a monocle made for Charlie, and the same for myself."

Unemployed but resplendent in white tie and tails, they slowly broke into Chicago's supper-club circuit, getting a week's tryout at the Chez Paree nightclub. Coming on stage at three o'clock in the morning for their final performance before an almost empty club, Charlie suddenly turned on his master, asking, "Who the hell ever told you you were a good ventriloquist?" Telling Edgar to go back to the farm, the dummy refused to be shushed by a blushing Bergen; Charlie was confident of getting by alone. He then spun on the stunned customers, declaring them a disgrace to civilization, rattling on as Bergen propped him on a chair and slowly backed away.

The management was catatonic, but the customers collapsed in laughter, hooting, howling, pounding the tables. Later, a serene Bergen was found backstage saying, "I simply had to get that off my chest."

Their tryout became an extended engagement during which they were seen by Elsa Maxwell, then America's social arbiter, who asked the twosome to entertain at one of her legendary parties. Noël Coward happened to be one of the guests, and after their performance demanded of Bergen, "Who wrote your material?" "I did," Bergen replied. "Well, it's damned good," Coward said, and recommended Bergen for an engagement at Manhattan's swank Rainbow Room, where they were an overnight sensation.

Their success at the Rainbow Room led them cross-country to California for a guest appearance on Rudy ("the Vagabond Lover") Vallee's radio show, which was so well received by radio listeners that their one appearance on the show was extended to three months.

Radio Review, 1936:

Standard in vaudeville and now doing his stuff in nightclubs, Edgar Bergen makes the jump into radio with nonchalant ease. He talks to himself and the replies make for amusing entertainment. His dummy bears the name of Charlie McCarthy and is a saucy little fellow. Humor is situational and character-bred rather than gaggy.

Style and delivery are natural and ingratiating. Bergen and the dummy discuss various matters in joshing idiom with vocal mannerisms thrown in. It represents the culmination of years of theater-trained work. An artiste—in the old and best meaning.

Charlie caught the country's ear, and by 1936 Edgar found himself in Hollywood with a radio show of his own, first known as *The Chase and Sanborn Hour.* The season's guest star was W. C. Fields, and much of the show's fast banter was based on a feud between Fields (who genuinely hated the dummy) and McCarthy—timidly mediated by the ever-avuncular Bergen:

FIELDS: Tell me, Charles, is it true your father was a gateleg table?
CHARLIE: Well, if it is, your father was under it.
FIELDS: Quiet, you flophouse for termites, or I'll sic a beaver on you.
BERGEN: Now, Bill . . .
CHARLIE: Mr. Fields, is that a flamethrower I see or is it your nose?
FIELDS: Why, you little blockhead, I'll whittle you down to a coat hanger. . . .

Edgar bought Bella Vista, a sprawling whitewashed Spanish house that hung high over Beverly Hills, and brought his mother west to live. Nell Berggren, who had hoped to see her younger son become a doctor, or even a dairy farmer, was still somewhat embarrassed by her son's *unusual* yet lucrative choice of vocation. In the thirties and forties America rewarded its favorite radio stars handsomely, and her son's salary—wisely invested in California land—far exceeded the earnings of the doctor she had dreamed he would become.

He was perceived as fairly eccentric by those in the Hollywood community: an odd outsider, soft-spoken, polite—certainly for a show-biz type—a scholarly man, now in his late thirties, never married, who lived quietly and cleanly with his mother and his dummy and whose idea of a perfect Saturday was to stay home alone and spend hours poring over his suitcases of old magic tricks. He tended to be taciturn, uneasy and withdrawn; in every interview, it was always Charlie who did the talking.

By 1938, Edgar and Charlie's popularity was such that they received a lion's share of the radio audience, their *Chase and Sanborn Hour* being the most widely listened-to show in the 8 to 9 P.M. time slot on Sunday evenings. To celebrate their new number one place in the ratings, Edgar and Charlie gave a costume party, instructing guests to come "as your childhood ambition." And so they did: Edgar as a seventeenth-century magician in top hat, goatee and cape, Charlie in a sultan's outfit with turban (and harem), Bob Hope as a Keystone Kop, Bette Davis as a cancan girl, Tyrone Power as a pirate, Betty Grable as a belly dancer, Roz Russell as a Gibson girl and Dick Powell as a railroad conductor.

Radio was by now so big that it set the pattern for all other fields of entertainment. Radio stars were better known than most stage and screen stars, and Hollywood was paying large sums to sign radio personalities like Bing Crosby, Bob Hope, Jack Benny, Burns and Allen, and Edgar Bergen for motion pictures.

In 1938, newsreels and front pages featured Edgar Bergen and Charlie McCarthy—or sometimes simply Charlie, neglecting to mention the man standing conscientiously, inconspicuously behind the dummy.

At Grauman's Chinese Theater in Hollywood, where celebrities are immortalized by sticking their hands and feet in wet cement, newsreels showed Edgar and Charlie, traditional in their white tie and tails, recording their hand- and footprints in the famous star-stamped court. Charlie's tiny feet firmly embedded, attendants detach his hands, holding the little extremities high for the cameras as Edgar looks on, somewhat distraught. "Hey Charlie! Over here!" yells a photographer, and a publicity man lunges to stick his hand through the dummy's backflap to turn him. "My God, is *nothing* sacred?" Charlie snaps sharply, the man jumps back and Bergen moves in, silent and steely, gently picks up his partner and obediently obliges the press, turning Charlie left and right, the two of them responding as one. "Hey, Charlie! Over here!" Edgar, Charlie—it's all the same.

As their success grew, so did the psychological speculation on the phenomenon of a ventriloquist on radio whose fame was dramatically overshadowed by that of his dummy. Newspapers and magazines tripped over one another in a frenzy to crack the case.

New York Times, 1939:

Psychologists say that Charlie differs from other dummies because he has definite spiritual qualities. His throaty, almost lecherous chuckle is a haunting thing; his whole attitude of *Weltschmerz* is astonishingly real. He says things that a human actor would never dare to say in public and gets away with them . . .

New York Herald Tribune:

On the one hand, there is a gay, irrepressible Charlie, through whom, by some strange alchemy, the shy and pallid Bergen is transformed into a brilliant comedian. On the other hand, there is an imperious and dominating Charlie, whose almost-human personality has so eclipsed his creator that Bergen cannot function as an artist

alone. "Charlie is famous," says Bergen glumly, "and I am the forgotten man. I am really jealous of the way Charlie makes friends,"
Bergen complains wistfully. "People are at ease with Charlie. He is
so uncomplicated."

For, of course, Charlie is that friendly, sociable side of Bergen
that craves companionship and affection. In real life, when people
start to respond to Bergen's friendliness, he may suddenly switch to
reserve and restraint—often bewildering and disconcerting to those
who know him.

The speculation went on, "BERGEN JEALOUS OF DUMMY . . ." and
on, "BERGEN BUILDS FRANKENSTEIN OF MIRTH AND WIT . . ." and on.

Edgar himself had little time and less patience with endless
ruminations of his exotic relationship with Charlie; he didn't—
well, he *couldn't*—hold much with motivational meanderings, with
postulations on his life profession in catchy clinical turns of phrase.
"Split personality," "inferiority complex," "alter ego," "subconscious
expression . . ." For God's sake, he'd only created Charlie as a tool in
the first place—as a simple stepping-stone to success from which
he hoped to move into musical comedy, become a young leading
man. The trouble was, the tool was too damned good; the tail was
wagging the dog.

The ventriloquist, dumbfounded by his dummy, was the out-
smarted shadow at the helm, smiling pleasantly, even paternally,
one hand discreetly hidden in the hollow of Charlie's back, the
other hand resting lightly, gracefully on the little dummy's shoulder
to steady him as he sailed ahead. Indelibly planting his impression on the country's consciousness, Charlie would sit back each
Sunday evening and in his cocky cackle vow, "I'll *mow* you *down*,
Bergen, so help me, I'll *mmooww ya down*."

Edgar tried twice more to go out on his own but admitted, "I
fell flat on my face." He created two new characters to introduce
some competition for Charlie, perhaps regain some ground: the

low-chuckling, slow-thinking Mortimer Snerd and an eager spinster called Effie Klinker. Both were substantially successful, especially the dimwitted Mortimer, but they were never comparable to Charlie, never even came close in the nation's eyes.

America had grown more sentimental than the ventriloquist about his dummy.

In 1943, when Edgar and Charlie were broadcasting from New York, Nell Berggren died; her younger son left for Los Angeles immediately, missing a show for the first time in six years on the air.

While typically tight-lipped about the loss, Edgar was deeply shaken by the death of his mother. Bella Vista was now abandoned to bachelors: Bergen, now thirty-eight and still unwed, the Swedish butler and Charlie. It occurred to some that even his single status might not be a question of free will for Bergen:

WILL CHARLIE LET BERGEN WED? IS HE A PROBLEM CHILD?

Charlie McCarthy's pappy, Edgar Bergen, is definitely the man of the moment in Hollywood and they are now inviting Charlie to the better parties so the dynamo behind the dummy will come. Being Mrs. B, I am told, is the goal among most unattached Hollywood gals today. Edgar, provided Charlie doesn't become a problem child and break up attachments, is the most attractive catch on the Hollywood horizon.

—*Los Angeles Times*

Except for a few studio-arranged dates (with Deanna Durbin and Ava Gardner), Edgar was still a loner; it was Charlie who was having all the fun—posing for fan magazines in camel's-hair coat and ascot, surrounded by shimmering starlets.

One of the shows people talked most about guest-starred Mae West. During rehearsals the week before the show, Bergen and his writers haggled with West, pleading with her to tone down the suggestiveness of her material to meet the strict FCC standards. After a standoff of sorts, a script was agreed upon for Sunday's show. But she was not, after all, Mae West for nothing. When she cooed over the air to Charlie, "Why don't you come up and see me sometime?" to which Charlie answered innocently, "And what would I do?" no one had bargained on her reading of the reply, "I'd let you play around in my woodpile." It made Monday morning's headlines:

NBC'S MAE WEST–CHARLIE MCCARTHY BROADCAST
WIDELY CONDEMNED AS OBSCENE . . . FCC SENT
STRONG LETTER TO NBC.

NBC apologized publicly, Edgar Bergen went into hiding in Palm Springs, and the show's rating went up two points.

Charlie now seemed to be everywhere at once: on the airwaves, in motion pictures with old pal W. C. Fields, in comic strips and coloring books, magazines and newsreels, on tie tacks and toys, radio sets and watches, pendants and pins. Stores sold out their Charlie McCarthy dolls and had them on back order.

One was given to a young girl of fourteen to cheer her up, keep her company while she recovered from a skull fracture suffered in an auto accident. Her name was Frances Westerman, and she was born in Birmingham, Alabama, where she had spent the happiest hours of her childhood curled snugly in her daddy's lap, or hanging on to his knee—this tall and handsome man who was her sun and moon, who smoothed her hair with long, loving hands, smiling softly at her and calling her his "little lamb."

Frances was a daddy's girl. An only child, she had a less strong bond with her mother, Lillie Mae, who was one in two sets of pale-skinned, flame-haired twin sisters.

People died of tuberculosis then, and William Westerman was

one of them, spending the last three months of his life in a sanitarium where his little daughter would come to visit, legs dangling as she perched on his bed, just her daddy and his little lamb. That was where she saw him last, pale against his pillow, as he waved to her through his open window.

And after family and friends had come and gone, leaving casseroles and condolences, as they carried his casket from the house, Frances threw herself upon it, sobbing, because inside lay the love of her life, and she was only ten.

It was the thirties: families' fortunes fizzled, the plenty of the twenties had dried up and disappeared. Lillie Mae took her daughter's hand and headed west, where poverty was more appealing, prosperity a breath away.

In Los Angeles, Lillie Mae met and married Parry Boyd (of the Boyds of Bangor, Maine), a handsome devil from a fine family who was (as Lillie Mae would say) just a *lad* short. He was a man of opinions and had a low one of work, and so was always a tad short of money as well, though he did have a job as an iceman. Lillie Mae began supporting him and Parry put down his ice and took up the flute. Soon, what William Westerman had left them was gone; and so, in short order, was Parry.

Lillie went to work, and Frances went to school, and the mother—devastated by the death of one husband and the disappearance of another—slid into silence, which her daughter faced every afternoon, the two of them spending their evenings alone together, staring soundlessly at each other across the cool white porcelain of the kitchen table in the tiny stucco cottage in the motor court on the street lined with tall palms.

Alabama accents drip with honey, and Frances, when she spoke, brought hoots to the lips of her California classmates. By the time she graduated Los Angeles High School (a peppy "pom-pom girl"), she had drained the last drop of magnolia from her voice and at least *that* possibility of embarrassment.

But Frances was beautiful. Tall and sleek, fresh and wind-swept, hers was the look American women were famous for. And that look took her racing down mirrored runways in L.A.'s I. Magnin, pirouetting in bugle beads and broad shoulders, gliding down ramps in navy gab suits and spectator shoes. Graceful and gleaming and gay.

And that is what Edgar Bergen saw when he looked out into the studio audience one night: long legs looming out of the darkness, stretching out at him endlessly from the front row. And later, he asked to meet her—for she had come as the guest of a member of his staff—because he wondered who the, ah, the one with the, ah, you know her legs were *very* long . . .

And that is how they met—this now nineteen-year-old blossom from the Deep South and this thirty-nine-year-old ventriloquist from the Midwest. He courted her for over a year—writing her, phoning her in New York, where she'd gone on to be a successful Powers model, driving past her on billboards as "the Chesterfield Girl," flipping to her in magazines as "the Ipana Girl"—a confused, confirmed bachelor scratching his head at the crossroads.

He wasn't the only one who was confused:

BERGEN WEDDING PUZZLES CHARLIE . . . HIS BOSS
IS RUMORED TO MARRY PRETTY MODEL . . . BEST MAN
CHARLIE MCCARTHY . . .
—*Los Angeles Mirror*

Then one morning in June 1945, the headlines read,

CHARLIE GETS STEPMOTHER . . . EDGAR BERGEN AND
FRANCES WESTERMAN MARRIED IN MEXICO.
—*Los Angeles Herald Examiner*

The bachelor had finally caved in.

•   •   •

In photos taken at the time of her marriage, my mother looks like a new young fawn. Hovering in a pale, fine haze like a startled creature at the edge of the forest, peering, wide-eyed, ready for flight. Long-legged, auburn-haired, bright-eyed, she is a woman whose grace and beauty catch your breath. There is a softness about her, an innocence, a willingness to please. An eagerness in her eyes.

She was twenty when she married, my father, forty. It took a lot to hold your own against celebrity like Edgar Bergen's. Frances Westerman from Birmingham found herself swept up in the rushing tide of being Mrs. Bergen and simply hung on for dear life.

The person she clung tightest to was her husband. She turned to him to teach her, looked up to him in all things. Open and innocent, worshipful and adoring, she depended on him totally—like a daughter, sort of. Depended on this forty-year-old, first-time-married "emotional hermit," as his own dummy referred to him—a man most comfortable when he did not *seem* to be speaking, or when flying alone in his plane, or when tinkering with magical, mechanical gadgetry. He was not a man comfortable with feelings, especially the kind that run strong or deep. It's not that he didn't have them; he just didn't know what to do with them except brush them aside, sweep them under a rug and edgily look the other way.

But his new bride was full of feelings. She was young and in love, brimming over with love for a middle-aged man who, one morning, woke up married.

So when on their first mornings at Bella Vista she would climb, shining, sparkling with dew, into his lap and circle him with her arms to give him all the affection, all the hope she'd held so long for someone—it was overwhelming to this shy, remote man. She offered him more than he knew how to take, and it terrified him. Here was his young bride, folded up in his arms, sighing, "Oh Edgar, I love you so much," and he would pat her quickly and say gruffly, "Now, now, we don't talk about things like that," and lower her from his lap like a long, lanky child.

The moment passed in the blink of an eye, but Frances Bergen never forgot it. Because this was not how it was supposed to happen. Not in Margaret Mitchell or the movies. This was not what newlyweds did—dismiss as inappropriate talk of love.

So Frances learned some of those lessons it takes a lifetime to unlearn again. She learned not to curl up in her husband's lap and to hang back from hugging him and to swallow "I love you"s. And that is how loneliness grows.

2

EDGAR BERGEN—FATHER OF A GIRL

Wooden-bodied Charlie McCarthy—the redwood half of the famed radio team—today had a flesh and blood rival for the affections of Edgar Bergen since the arrival of a 7 lb. 13 1/2 oz. daughter last night at Hollywood Presbyterian Hospital. Mrs. Bergen, who was married to Charlie's "stooge" last June, was reported "doing well."

—*Variety, May 10, 1946*

Doing well she was—especially when faced with the fact that Charlie's "stooge" tended to disappear at life's more intense moments, taking off in his plane and landing at some sandswept airstrip in the desert to down a beer with the locals and put up at the nearest motel. A farm boy forever, eager to establish an identity separate from his dummy, he bought up obscure patches of land and farmed them: alfalfa, dates, citrus, bell peppers. In cowboy hat, frontier pants and Western boots, he'd stalk the crops with his foremen, probing the earth with the toe of his boot, swapping theories on irrigation and cross-pollinating techniques. This walking the land and talking with "folks" was comforting, familiar, his favorite way of ducking out when life was overwhelming. In fact, that's just where he was headed as Frances arrived at the hospital already in labor: Edgar was finally found in his plane somewhere over Palm Springs; the control tower radioed him to come home.

My mother had by now adjusted to the comings and goings of the "moody Swede" she had married, accepting his absences philosophically, as essentials for the solitary soul. New to his world, she walked in it unsteadily for a time. But gradually, with ever-increasing confidence, she learned to play hostess at Bella Vista. By the time of my birth, she had brought a special grace to her husband's life, and the hermits on the hill found their closed house opened, spilling with flowers, filled with light.

My father—remote but devoted to his bride, delighted with his new daughter—found his bachelor days abruptly over and was faced with some changes himself. The house on the hill now had room for only one hermit; one of them, my parents told the press, would have to go.

"Charlie's room," with its view of the rose garden and its entrance off the patio, was redecorated and renamed "the nursery"; I moved in with my Dutch governess, Dena.

"It was a major operation when we had to take Charlie's room away from him and make it into a nursery," declared Bergen. "He had to move all his pictures of Dorothy Lamour, his West Point Cadet's hat, his Indian headdress, and all his stuff."

"Yes, it looks quite different in pink and blue and without Charlie's special, low-cut furniture. I rather miss seeing his shorts, with the initials, hanging over the chair," Frances said nostalgically.

—*Silver Screen*

My mother learned fast.

When I was born, it was only natural that I would be known in the press as "Charlie's sister." The sibling rivalry thus established was certainly unique, considering I was the only child and the sibling was, in truth, my father. Of course, even when I was very young, I knew Charlie wasn't real. Although we always called him "Charlie." And though he lived, or was kept, I should say, in a velvet-lined trunk. And though at my birth, he was simply moved to the guest room, next to the nursery, and soon everyone began again referring to "Charlie's room."

To me, Bella Vista was like a magic kingdom. Its red tile roof eased gently over the mountaintop and gave way to gardens that tumbled their way into canyons below: the rose garden, the cut-flower garden, the cactus forest, the citrus orchard, the strawberry patch. Honeysuckle ran wild and smelled sweet, mammoth magnolias shaded the croquet course on the lower lawn, and pine lined the pool. Bougainvillea burst over the roof like fireworks and camellias hung like starched organdy dresses from their bushes along the driveway. You could see the house down on Sunset, if you knew just where to look. And if the flag was flying from the flagpole or Christmas lights were twirled around the giant pine, it was a cinch to spot. "The old house on the hill," we call it now, wishing that we'd never left it.

High on a mountain, at the end of a steep, twisting road banked with toothpicked cactus clumps and towering stands of eucalyptus, Bella Vista was not readily accessible to the timid or fainthearted. Playmates had to be imported for the Bergens' daughter on Beverly Grove, transportation arranged, troop movements coordinated; cars would creep cautiously up the canyon bearing buddies. Mothers and governesses would arrive hunched over the wheel, wild-eyed and white-knuckled, deposit their cargo and brace themselves for the ride down. So most afternoons I played alone with my three dogs—a collie named Boy, a beagle named Martha, and a fox terrier called Susan: my gang.

Each afternoon when I got home from school, I'd change out of my powder-blue uniform and saddle shoes into a flannel cowboy shirt and jeans, grab my snack in a wax-paper bag and take off with my dogs, wandering the hills until it was time for dinner. Down the hill, up the treehouse, scan the canyon, then up to explore the big mountain.

On the mountain that loomed above us lay the John Barrymore estate. Katharine Hepburn lived in the old Aviary, a couple named Grimaldi in the large main house, and the conductor Lukas Foss in the guest house. My dogs and I would sneak up on the huge main house, scurrying over rocks above the waterfall that splashed into the pool, and lie in wait for the Grimaldi poodles. When caught, I was invited in for cookies and talk of the Old Country. The Grimaldis showed me sketches deftly drawn by Barrymore on closet walls, massive monastery doors shipped from France, chandeliers from Vienna, and Cyprus trees brought from Italy. Mrs. Grimaldi—round, blond, and fluffy, much like her poodles—spoke in strange cooing sounds. Mr. Grimaldi, who was a director, wore a pencil moustache and an ascot, and claimed to be the rightful heir to the throne of Monaco; he railed to me about that impostor, Prince Rainier.

Another king lived across the canyon, in a gleaming white castle enclosed by high walls. King Vidor, they called him, and though he was said to be one of Hollywood's great directors, to me he was yet another monarch. It seemed that when things went sour for royalty at home, they all came to Hollywood and became directors while they waited for things to sort themselves out.

Halfway up the mountain to the Barrymore estate, at a point that hung high over our driveway, was a natural dirt perch, a balcony, screened from view by trees. This became my hideout where I would sit for hours with my gang of dogs, eating my Fritos, guarding the house against all invaders. I was not entirely defenseless. Bobby, the Western Union deliveryman, lived down the road over the Barrymore garage, and he was my friend. Sometimes he'd take me with him on deliveries, chugging along in his beetle-green Nash, and I'd charge out proudly to present the crisp yellow envelopes to strangers framed in foyers. Bobby made me a slingshot, carved it by hand, and it never left my hip pocket. Tiptoeing stealthily through the trees like Tonto, I would stalk an enemy bush, fish out a carefully selected pebble from my shirt pocket, center it in the leather square and release the taut elastic with a snap that sent the pebble flying in a feeble arc to land a few feet from my sneakers. As darkness closed in and the coast looked clear, I'd wave my posse from the hills; untie my pony; swing my leg over the broomstick with the stuffed sock head, felt eyes, and yarn mane; pick up the plastic reins; and head happily for home.

Of course, as a cowboy, what I needed, pleaded for, dreamed of, was a horse. A *real* horse. By the time I was eight, the nursery already overflowed with toy ones: wood horses, copper horses, plastic horses, glass horses, china horses, horse books, horse paintings, horse photographs, horse clippings in horse scrapbooks. I sent for horse coupons on cereal boxes, filled out forms to win a pony; I never wanted anything as much as I wanted a horse.

My parents, wondering rightly if this was a whim, finally agreed to get me a donkey, which was not *unlike* a horse. And so, one Sunday, off I went to a burro ranch with my governess, Dee, and her boyfriend, Don, where we picked out the biggest burro I could find (more like a horse), loaded him onto the back of Don's pickup and took him home.

My mother, expecting an adorable little Sicilian donkey with a hand-painted cart, was struck dumb when we pulled up with a "moth-eaten mule." He *was,* in fact, on the aged, ratty side, but I, of course, was blinded by love. I called him Pronto, and he was *my horse*—my Trigger, my Lucky, my Champion, my Silver: we would ride the range and gallop the trails together.

It was fortunate that my imagination was active, because Pronto wasn't. Once we put him on the hill above the house, he never moved again. *Ever.* But kids are quick at compensation. Every afternoon, I'd race up the hill, slip on Pronto's bridle, leap on his back, dig my heels into his sides, and ride like the wind across the prairie, hot on the trail of outlaws and rustlers. Switching my pony with the reins for a final burst of speed, shouting, *"Hiiiyeeeaaagh! Giddap!"* I'd round up the last head of cattle, safe for the night, and keep the coyotes at bay. Then I'd loop up my lasso, take off the bridle, pat my hot, dusty horse and, spurs jingling, amble back to the ranch for some grub, my doggies at my heels. Pronto had not lifted a hoof.

In the fifties, "celebrity offspring" had carefully chronicled childhoods; many of us had been in newspapers and magazines from the day we were born, each rite of passage recorded—some even invented—on film and in stills. We were show-business families and we had a nose, an instinct for what would play and what wouldn't. Our parents were all performers, producers, directors and writers whose lives and livelihood were based on a special sixth sense of staging and timing. Their children were born into the old razzle-dazzle and we learned early how to perform—not to blink at flashbulbs, to keep our eyes open and our mouths closed. We were to the movies born and so were expected to deliver, with some poise and presence, when the cameras rolled and the flashbulbs popped and sizzled.

For many of us, "home movies" had an unusual meaning. Bella Vista was like a tiny backlot; films were shot on the grounds, edited in the workshop and screened in the Rumpus Room, a theater separate from the house, which overlooked the rose garden and the goldfish pond. Slot machines stood in the corridor that led to the theater guest room, and wine slept in a well-stocked cellar downstairs. The main room was large and spacious, brightened by a big bay window and a gleaming copper hood over the stone fireplace.

The pine floor was honey-colored, covered with a thick, fringed rug, and the sofas were deep and cushiony, the kind kids sink into and disappear. At the far end of the room rose a small stage with an upright piano, framed with curtains and a hand-painted canvas vaudeville drop of cherubs selling snake oil. A movie screen lowered from the ceiling to face the projection booth enclosed at the opposite end of the room. It was here that my father rehearsed and held weekend writers' meetings, my mother studied her singing, and my friends and I put on shows; my parents screened films for their parties and cartoons for mine.

I had seen performing transform my father from someone wary and remote into the freest, most fearless of clowns. He loved performing, and he wanted me to love it, too. I was a poised, pretty child who spoke precisely and took to the stage easily, often eagerly, even learning to "throw my voice" to an imaginary friend, "Joe," in the basement. This filled my father with pride and praise, for nothing could have pleased him more. That was the point, of course—to please my father—and so another "belly-talker" was born.

Having dealt in the finer points of voice projection, my father had no time for mumblers, and as his daughter I was expected to respond clearly and quickly to questions, enunciating and projecting properly. When I failed in that, as I often did, he turned cold and unforgiving. Not a particularly patient man, he was intolerant and short-tempered with slowness or stupidity. My father was of course famous for one-man dialogues, for snappy comebacks to his own questions: the soloist of repartee. His impatience with answers that were long in coming seemed perfectly reasonable, considering he made his living by giving his own. But when that temper turned in my direction, I froze stiff with fear, went red with shame. Not one to yell, he kept his emotions pressed and neatly hung; instead, he'd snap sharply—suddenly distant, instantly unreachable—and fix on you a stare so icy, so unfeeling that you ceased to breathe or even to exist.

For my seventh birthday, my parents gave me a supermarket. My very own market, which they had set up as a surprise in the patio. Though I didn't recall asking for a supermarket or even especially wanting one, it was a spectacular gift and I was ecstatic to have it. While it was not, naturally, as big as a *real* market, it was not much smaller, either. The custom-made, wraparound counter was waist high, built of wood and painted a bright tomato red. Behind the counter, shining red shelves soared majestically—stacked with little cans of vegetables, carrots, corn, and peas, tiny boxes of Babbo, and Betty Crocker Cake Mix. In this jewellike setting a small cash register shimmered, its drawers neatly filled with stacks of crisp Charlie McCarthy dollar bills and newly minted coins with Charlie's head on one side, Mortimer's on the other.

Quickly setting up shop in the patio, chattering happily with my first customers—Dee, the cook, the houseman—sliding cans across the counter, taking money, making change, I briskly rang up sales on my little cash register, the Merry Merchant—a symbol of supply and demand.

Suddenly my father rounded the corner, eyes bright under his peaked flying cap. Hung with light meters, lugging cameras, sound and tripod, he came to a stop at my market, heaved his equipment to the ground and began, determinedly, to try to assemble it. Finally set up, adjusting his 16 mm movie camera on its teetering tripod, swinging the bill of his cap to the back of his head, he fitted his eye to the lens, switched on the camera motor and began to film, at which point I stopped dead in my tracks.

"Action, Candy!" The scene was set, but I wasn't moving. "Come on, Candy, *hand her the peas.*" I stood, rooted, behind the counter, clutching my cash register, sullen and self-conscious. Business was booming when along comes my father. Mr. Cinéma Vérité. I lowered my eyes, answering inaudibly, behaving stiffly. Atmosphere on the supermarket set grew strained. My father grew impatient. "Speak up, Candy, and talk into the microphone," he snapped.

"And wipe that sick smile off your face." My shame increased with his annoyance until, finally, desperate and defeated, the director threw up his hands in disgust, adjusted his cap, shouldered his camera and tripod and stalked away.

I was left alone with my failure, paralyzed by the self-consciousness that would follow me later onto larger sets.

Little milestones were given majesty in Hollywood, the everyday made extraordinary. Family backyards were often studio backlots: mothers' movie sets, fathers' sound stages; and sometimes the backyards themselves were even better.

One of my playmates was Carla Kirkeby, the daughter of a hotel magnate. She lived alone with her mother in Bel Air in a small Versailles—a sugar-cube château that spread across acres. There you flipped the switch to start the electric waterfall tumbling down boulders into the pool far below, danced across gleaming parquet in the vast gilded ballroom, took the elevator, ran through the tunnel, and jumped on the trampoline on the lower lawn, then hiked up the rocks of the rumbling waterfall and raced through the French gardens to reach the garage, which was nearly as palatial as the house itself—a hotel for cars, discreet and distinguished, giving onto a cobblestone courtyard enclosed by high walls. The automobiles were sleek and shining, always in a state of readiness—a Rolls-Royce coupe, a Bentley convertible, a Jaguar roadster and a station wagon; assorted others belonged to the staff. In the very last stall shone the smallest automotive models: three miniature convertibles that were electrically powered. These were for the children, and we stampeded toward them, clambered inside and hurried down the drive. Whirring along, feet clamped down on the pedals, we whizzed by boxwood hedges and long rows of topiary trees—like two Mister Toads in mad dashes, gangsters making our getaway.

Walt Disney had a miniature train built in *his* vast backyard; a perfect knee-high working replica of a steam engine with four cars and a caboose. It puffed along narrow graveled tracks and across a tiny trestle bridge while "Uncle Walt," in engineer's cap and kerchief, sat happily astride the engine, shoveling coal and tooting the shrill steam whistle as he took us for rides.

For parents so expert at larger than life, they seemed mesmerized by the minuscule as well, fascinated with inflating the scale or reducing it. It was the life-size that failed to hold their interest.

Even in a landscape so completely at odds with it, Christmas took on fabled proportions as well. For here climate was given no quarter; here parents could create their own. You had only to dream of a white Christmas and white was what you got—boughs of massive fir trees sagging with snow. It was no accident that "sno-flocking," a costly process in which Christmas trees are sprayed with a sticky white substance flecked with silica for a realistic sparkle, found its way onto Hollywood trees—invented, perhaps, by a prop man at the request of a producer for his family's fir.

Snow fell, too, on the nighttime Christmas parade down Hollywood Boulevard, blown in swirling gusts by giant studio fans spaced along the route. This I remember particularly because as my parents, Charlie, Mortimer, and I chugged along in my father's antique Stanley Steamer—one of the many celebrity-filled convertibles—waving to the line of crowds, I got a fair dose of snow in the eyes. By then I knew that public display of tears was unacceptable so, eyes squeezed shut and furiously tearing, I kept waving and smiling crazily, like a child blind and bereft, pluckily bidding goodbye.

There were many children's parties at Christmas with assorted Santas giving gifts. One time, the man ho-hoing behind the spun-silver beard was David Niven—an elegant, urbane Father Christmas, a soigné Saint Nick. Another year, Charlton Heston played him differently—a man of unearthly substance and stature, his ho-hos booming from a great height, somewhere between Santa Claus and God; when *he* asked if you'd been good all year, it caused a real crisis of conscience.

Come December, Hollywood living rooms became Nutcracker Suites. Towering trees seemed to shed presents like pine needles, thickly covering the floor. Gifts tumbled in all directions, piling up like snowdrifts and eclipsing the carpet. The rooms were impassable before December 26th.

At Christmas, Hollywood children grew giddy and greedy, buried under offerings. It was a child's dream come true, but I wonder if we children really believed it; there was a sense, somehow, that ours were weirdly bountiful harvests, that living rooms shouldn't swell so with loot.

Like the snowfall, the number of presents varied from year to year, depending on ratings, grosses and the well-wrapped gratitude of studio heads and sponsors. These gifts of grandeur—indications of the corporate value of the receiver—were often given to the children to impress the parents on whose shelves they usually ended up: Georgian silver porringers, carved ivory animals, tiny feathered mechanical birds that, when wound, twittered in fine-ribbed gold cages. Impeccably wrapped, lavish and useless to anyone four feet high.

It was Uncle Walt Disney's gift we looked forward to most and we began to wait for it in October. A monolith in Mickey Mouse paper, instantly spotted by size and wrapping, it was the only gift bigger than the receiver, for here was a man who shared our souls. His presents stood three feet high and three feet wide and were filled with every Disney treasure: a Snow White gramophone, Tinker Bell dolls and Pixie Dust, pirate swords and porcelain Peter Pans. We were dizzy with delight to get them. But as we grew taller, the presents grew smaller, until, by adolescence, they disappeared completely—a metaphor for our early youth.

Our birthdays, too, assumed the scope and shimmer of a studio production. A treasure hunt was held for Timothy Getty's seventh birthday, and the countless children invited were asked to come as pirates and buccaneers. Golden earrings in ears and noses, sashed in satin, wearing long blue beards, the children fanned out in short, greedy squadrons assisted by butlers in breeches and big black hats adorned with skulls and crossbones. The Getty estate—now the Getty Museum—sloped almost to the sea and, as legend has it, was once the site of true pirate booty and buried doubloons. But in Timothy's time the great lawn swarmed with bands of smaller brigands feverishly in search of tiny treasure chests stuffed with chocolate gold coins.

Our parties were true extravaganzas—lavish competitions in professional skill, loving displays of parental pride. It was innocent one-upsmanship, well-intentioned, yet tough to top. Most seemed to agree that the Oscar for Best Birthday Given by a Parent went to Vincent Minnelli for Liza's sixth given at Ira Gershwin's house in Beverly Hills. That was the party parents spoke of with reverence, shaking their heads, smiling, Now *that* was a time. I don't think the children remembered but the grown-ups certainly did; my mother described it to me just recently, amazed I'd forgotten a day so splendid, so fresh was it still in her mind.

The Gershwin lawn rolled on forever, and in the center, children spun slowly on a many-colored carousel, while others clustered round the Magic Lady—a woman in a long blue gown sprinkled with stars who pulled doves from her sleeves and rabbits from hats. There were hot-dog stands and ice-cream cones and clouds of cotton candy. Clowns clowned and jugglers juggled and sleek, shining ponies circled the lawn at a tiny, clipped canter for any child who wanted a ride. It was a fairy-tale gift to a daughter from a father who was a master at making fairy tales come true.

If I don't remember her party, I do remember Liza: shy and soft-spoken, quick to smile. She peered with huge eyes through thick, long lashes, kind and gentle, generous and unspoiled. I remember always liking her for that because most of us were none of those things.

Parties, for me, were a source of terror; I was led in reluctantly, often tearfully, then hung by the edge. The day usually ended in tentative enjoyment as, party hat in hand, I curtsied goodbye at the door. Frightened and self-conscious with other, bolder children, I headed home relieved and happy, eager to hike the hills with my dogs. I remember being pleased to find Liza at these parties, often hovering at the edge as well—surprised at her shyness, grateful for her friendliness.

And I remember always asking to go to Liza's to play dress-up because in her closet hung little girls' dreams. Vincent Minnelli had seen to that, too. In her dress-up closet, on low racks at child's-eye level, glowed tiny satin ball gowns embroidered with seed pearls, wispy white tutus, flowered pink crinolines. You could choose between Vivien Leigh's riding habit from *Gone with the Wind* or Leslie Caron's ballerina costume from *An American in Paris;* my favorite was Deborah Kerr's champagne satin ball gown from *The King and I.* Each one fit as if it were made for us. And each one was. Liza's father had had the most famous leading women's costumes from MGM movies copied by the designers themselves—all scaled down to perfect six-year-old sizes.

When I turned six, in the merry month of May, I wore a party dress of yellow organdy appliquéd with French lace and stood nervously with my mother at the gate of Bella Vista, ready to receive my guests. Little girls fluttered in like pastel puffs, the palest springtime flowers, and clustered together like a bouquet. The boys stumbled in—reluctant Princes of the Blood—hair slicked fast, sheepish in their navy knee socks, squirming in their gray wool flannel shorts. Shoving each other and giggling, they kept a ritual distance from the shy smiles of the girls as if anything in organdy might contaminate their budding manhood.

Parties were held in the patio, and that year my mother had had a maypole made that streamed with brightly colored ribbons. The girls skipped in a dainty circle, weaving the ribbons into tight stripes around the pole—delicately, demurely—till the boys took a turn and it became a tug-of-war. Quickly tearing the ribbons from the pole, waving them proudly like trophies of war, they soon used them as lassoes and bridles for the girls, who were delighted with the attention. After ice-cream animals and cake, two white police dogs precisely executed their tricks in the patio; our governesses hovered nearby in crisp, crackling uniforms while our parents—the Dick Powells, Ray Millands, Jimmy Stewarts, Arthur Rubinsteins, Randolph Scotts, David Selznicks and Ronald Reagans—gathered over cocktails inside.

Then—organdy wilted, hair ribbons undone, knee socks sagging and ties askew—we raced to the Rumpus Room, wound tighter than clocks, and scrambled for a place on the sofas. I wedged myself between Jimmy Stewart's son Ronnie and Dorothy Lamour's son Ridgeley. I had crushes on both of them. The lights went out, and in the darkness, giggling and whispering, we waited for *Snow White and the Seven Dwarfs* to begin.

Here was a story about *another* princess who lived far away in *another* Magic Kingdom, in love with a prince, surrounded by odd, tiny men. At long last, her prince finds her, gathers her gently onto his horse and, with the creatures of the forest weeping and cheering, they ride together into the sunset.

The queen and the dwarfs stay home.

Our fantasy lives were shaped by movies like those of other kids of our generation, but it was our parents who *made* the fantasies, who cherished childhood more than we. Hollywood, for them, was the Sea of Dreams where they set their silver sails and filled their nets with magic. Our parents were Ivanhoe and Moses, Spartacus and Shane. They fought lions, roped stallions, slew dragons, rescued maidens; they healed the sick, sang in the rain, woke up in

Oz and got back to Kansas. Snapped their fingers—it snowed in summer. Sent a memo—it rained indoors.

And we were the children of Paradise, where nothing seemed beyond our reach. Fantasy was, for us, familiar. The extraordinary, everyday. But reality remained a stranger, and most were pleased to leave it that way.

3

My firmest early memory of my father was one afternoon when I was six. Bringing me home from watching a radio show read-through, winding up the mountain road to our house in his Chrysler Imperial, a deep emerald green, he passed the turn home and drove, instead, to a spot high on the mountain that hung out over the city and the sea.

We sat, in silence, watching the sun set; close by, the sound of chirping turned our heads to two birds perched side by side in a tree, wiry bird feet clamped fast to a branch, nuzzling and preening, smoothing and ruffling, as birds do. My father looked at me and smiled. "Look, Candy, look at the two lovebirds billing and cooing. Do you want to 'bill and coo'?"

Something told me I didn't want to look. Whatever those birds were doing, it was none of my business. I did not want to know any more about birds right then. Lovebirds in particular. I quickly looked away.

"Do you know what it means to 'bill and coo'?" my father asked me. Uh-oh. Eyes fastened on my feet dangling below me, seeing my saddle shoes for the first time, a speck of white polish on the navy blue, yet beautiful, pristine; Dee did a good job on my saddle shoes.

"Candy?" There he was again.

No, I don't. I don't know what it means to "bill and coo." But somewhere I did. Somehow, I had an idea what it meant to "bill and coo," and what's more, I was afraid I wanted to do it with my father.

" 'Bill and coo' means to hug and kiss, and that is what the love-birds do," he said.

I knew it. Tiny six-year-old heart thumping, wildly beating in my breast, a sickly smile of terror twisted on my face, intensely absorbed now in the soft folds of my socks.

Can we go home please? Can we just forget the birds? This is hard here. This is too hard for six. I am too short to understand. I am in over my head.

Dear God, how I must have loved my dad.

My sixth Christmas I made my debut as a guest on the *Edgar Bergen Show*, appearing in a skit with my father and Charlie. My father rehearsed the lines with me in his study and again in his car as we headed down Sunset to the studio for the read-through, where I proudly took my seat at the long table in the rehearsal room with my father and the writers and the other guests. "Now remember, Candy," my father warned me sternly, "wait till it's quiet to say your lines. *Don't step on the laughs.*"

The night of the show, my hair brushed and burnished, taffeta ribbons tied crisply and tight, I hovered backstage, faint, heart fluttering. It was my first time to be up there with the two of them, to make my mark, and as the program began, I waited for Charlie to give me my cue.

"And now, here are Edgar Bergen and Charlie McCarthy. . . . Our guests tonight are Mimi Benzell and *Candy Bergen*. . . ." (Applause)

EB: Ah, Charlie, my dear, sweet little Charlie, this is going to be the happiest Christmas of my life.

CHARLIE: Oh? You mean you're not giving out any presents?

EB: No, Charlie, this is an occasion for which I've waited six years, ever since my little daughter, Candy, was born.

CHARLIE: You mean you're sending her to work?

EB: No, Charlie, tonight Candy's going to be on this show and that's why I'm so happy. You know, she's the apple of my eye.

CHARLIE: Yes, of course, but don't forget, I'm the cabbage of your bankbook.

EB: Charlie, I hope you're not jealous of Candy.

CHARLIE: Oh no, Bergen, I welcome a little competition. Ha, what have I got to worry about? Let the kid have her chance.

There it was, and someone squeezed my shoulder, crumpling my puffed sleeve, and I walked out on stage to my first burst of applause, stepping up to my little low microphone alongside my father and Charlie. Reeling at the rows of faces smiling up from the darkness that spread out below us—pleased, expectant, friendly—I recited my well-learned lines with considerable poise and polish—a perfect little ham, a wind-up doll—a dummy. A daughter determined to make good.

CB: Hello, Daddy, hi, Charlie. (Applause)

CHARLIE: That's enough, folks. That's enough. Let's not let things get out of hand. Goodbye, little girl, get outta here, goodbye.

EB: Now, now, please, Charlie. Candy, my own little Candy, tonight is the happiest night of my life. Tonight, *my* little girl steps out into the footlights of life. . . .

CB: *Down*, Daddy, down. . . .

CHARLIE: Hey, this kid's getting laughs. Watch it, kid, remember—there's only *one* star on this show.

CB: Yes, Mortimer *is* clever.

CHARLIE: Well, that does it. This kid's gotta go.

CB: But I *want* to be on the show, Charlie. I want to be *just* like Daddy.

CHARLIE: Just like Daddy, huh? No ambition, eh?

CB: Now, Charlie, you don't mind my being on the show, do you?

CHARLIE: No, Candy, not at all. After all, you're growing up and it's about time you helped me support your old man.

CB: You shouldn't have said that, Charlie. Daddy resents the idea that you support him.

CHARLIE: Does he *deny* it?

CB: No, but he resents it.

CHARLIE: How do you like that? A trial-sized Lucille Ball.

My father had trained me well. Not only was I letter-perfect, I also waited for and got the laughs, commenting casually to him later, "Gee, Daddy, I had to wait a long time."

Pretty heady stuff. Some people have early success to overcome, but *six* is peaking pretty young. All that attention. All that acclaim. Appearing on stage with my father.

We were a team, my father and I, like Fred and Ginger, Irene and Vernon Castle. A dazzling duo. Didn't he declare his love for me on network radio? For all America to hear? Didn't he say it was the happiest night of his life?

Without question, it was the happiest night of mine. I would be hard-pressed to find another half so fine. I wished that *I* could be Charlie, always up there with my father. I wished I could take his place in the sun. When Charlie protested as my father put him in the trunk after each show—"Oh please, Bergen, don't lock me up! Please help me! Bergie, not the *trunk!*"—till the key clicked in the lock and the cries died out, I wondered if there was a chance my father might *leave* him in that trunk, might *forget* him or *lose* him or something. Then *I* would have to fill in. It would just be me performing for my father, making him proud.

My father might forget a great many things but he was not about to forget Charlie. None of us would ever forget Charlie.

The Christmas show was such a success that I was brought back (by popular demand) for an Easter skit, in which Charlie and

I are on an egg hunt in the Enchanted Forest when along comes my father as Prince Charming:

EB: How do you do. I'm searching for my Fairy Princess but I seem to have lost my way. Can you help me? I am Prince Charming.

CHARLIE: I know this is the Enchanted Forest, but *this* is ridiculous.

EB: No, but I *am* Prince Charming. Can't you see—I'm young, dashing and handsome?

CB: Gee, Daddy—aren't you glad we're not on *television*? (Laughter. Applause.)

CHARLIE: I'm beginning to like this girl.

I got the laughs, I read my lines, but there was more that I wanted to say. In the script I made fun of my father as Prince Charming, but that's not how I would have written it. I would have said, "You haven't lost your way—I can help you. *I'm* your Fairy Princess—it's me! I'm here!"

In the years when I was a child, my parents traveled frequently—broadcasts from the East Coast, appearances abroad—but, once home, my father saved weekends for me. Overnight bags in hand, Mom and Dee waving us off, we'd climb into his car and take off together for the tiny airport snugly nestled in the orange groves in the Valley.

In the particular romance that men have with machines, my father kept airplanes the way some men keep mistresses—never more than one at a time, changing old familiar favorites for newer, flashier models, approaching them with a titillating blend of fear, fascination and reverence, never comprehending what made them tick or their engines turn over. But he had made his peace with the Wild Blue Yonder and negotiated its skies respectfully, taking off tentatively, even tensely, giving one the sense that this particular union between man and machine was somewhat shaky—that they did not quite move as One. Not a reckless man by nature nor one to overstep his abilities, he timidly took his place in the heavens and always seemed grateful to land.

Kicking the blocks away from the wheels, the airport attendants would push the dun-colored plane from its hangar, revealing the silhouette of Charlie neatly stenciled, like a birthmark, on its side. While the mechanic made last-minute inspections, my father would circle the plane slowly, running his hand along the wings like a practiced physician, enthralled with his patient, feeling for new dings or dents, moving the wing and tail flaps, eyeing the ailerons. When the plane had passed its preflight, we hopped gingerly onto the wing and folded ourselves inside. Seat belts and earphones on, we waited as the mechanic wrenched the propeller around, cranking it till it caught, giving a thumbs-up sign to my father, who called out, "Clear props!"

"Props clear!"

"Contact!"

And he started the ignition as the prop spun furiously and the engine sputtered into life. Anxiously ticking off his checklist, he taxied away from the tiny tower, waving goodbye to the mechanics. Bringing the small radio mouthpiece to his lips, he spoke into it, "This is 6997 Charlie, request clearance for takeoff. Over."

"Roger, Edgar, we read you. 6997 Charlie, you are clear for takeoff. Over and out."

He nudged the throttle, boosting the sound of the engine; his feet moved firmly on the pedals, his hand rested lightly on the stick, and the propeller pushed us forward. We chugged down the dusty runway—faster, faster—picking up speed, suddenly lifting off and hurtling out over the tidy dark-green bunches of citrus, higher still, as row upon row became a vast, wide-wale weave— and out—soaring now to the tight, high-pitched hum of the engine that carried us up and over the spring snow of the San Bernardino Mountains and beyond.

Propped up on his briefcase and stacks of flight manuals so I could see over the nose, I listened in nervous excitement as he explained the dials and gauges to me, showed me the navigation points and said, "Okay, you take it for a while now, Monstro, head for that mountain and stay on course." And I did.

Each weekend our headings were different and our course changed. We rode donkeys down the Grand Canyon, fished for trout in Yosemite, mined ore in Nevada, and went on breakfast rides in Palm Springs.

We touched down at a dozen different runways—some of asphalt, some of dirt—taxiing down deserted airstrips with old, dog-eared windsocks, up to small-town adobe airports or log-cabin towers. Wherever we landed people greeted us gladly, recognizing either Charlie's profile on the plane or my father in it. "Well, hello, Edgar, where's Charlie?" they inevitably asked and my father answered good-naturedly, "I'm afraid Charlie couldn't come. He had to stay home—he's behind in his studies. I brought my daughter, Candy, instead."

Usually we shared a room together, and my father, as best he could, dressed me and braided my hair. On Sunday afternoons we'd arrive home, tired and dusty, my mother and Dee waiting to greet us, gasping at my lopsided braids and mismatched socks and untied sneakers.

Weekends with my father: my father who flew and was famous. Known and loved wherever we went. Known for giving life—breathing it into blocks of wood, sending blood through lifeless glass-eyed bodies. Flying and famous and giving life, making magic. Like God, sort of, or Superman, it seemed to me then.

And he'd be off on another trip—this time with the Other Woman, traveling with my mother to Europe or New York. Gamely I'd resume patrolling the hills alone with my dogs after school, having dinner with Dee. Relentlessly cheerful, infallibly good-hearted, Dee was the constant in my life, racing briskly about, blond pony-tail bobbing behind her, seeing to and looking after.

For ten years, while my parents traveled, she slept in the bed next to mine in the nursery, our days ending in darkness as eyes wide, by the glow of the radio dial, we lay facing each other, breath-lessly listening to *The Lone Ranger* and *Inner Sanctum*. Hers was the face I'd see last in the evenings, the first smile I'd see when I woke. She got me up, put me to bed, combed and washed and dried me. There was little for me she didn't do; she was so much a part of my days and nights that, on her rare evenings off, sleep would not come unless she came with it and I'd wait up to hug her good night. I loved her completely and occasionally abused her, skitter-ing around the fuzzy boundaries of the child-governess pact, chal-lenging her on the grounds of illegitimate authority. While count-ing on her complete availability, taking her constancy for granted, I depended on her totally.

On Sunday evenings at six, in my parents' absence, Dee and I would pull our chairs up to the Philco console, turn on the radio and listen to what was now *The Edgar Bergen Show—with Charlie McCarthy*, carried to millions on waves of ether. Edgar Bergen— that's my dad.

Sometimes my father would take me with him to his office on Sunset Boulevard in Hollywood. He owned a cluster of old Span-ish baroque buildings that gave onto a tiled courtyard with olive trees and elephant ears and a wishing well. His suite of offices was upstairs over the patio, and when it was still, you could hear the soft splashing of water from the moist, mossy bucket into the stone well. The inside of the old oak bucket and the bottom of the well were thickly dappled with pennies and nickels pitched there by people gambling on their future with small change. There was a restaurant in the patio, and my father and I ate at a table near the well whose wishes caught the sun in bright copper flashes.

After scaling the steep tiled steps of the office—steps that, in later years, my father would take with difficulty and some caution—a smiling secretary, efficient and overweight, would heave open the heavy oak door and cheerfully escort us inside.

It may have been called an office, but, once inside, it was more like a shrine, an anteroom for a sovereign, a high head of state—or *low* head of state, in this case, the object of worship being a dummy three and a half feet tall. A large portrait of Charlie hung in the foyer, deftly done in charcoal and pastels; neat rows of framed photographs extended from either side like wings of honor guards: Charlie shaking hands with Harry Truman, Eleanor Roosevelt, King Gustav of Sweden, Winston Churchill, Marilyn Monroe, Dwight D. Eisenhower, Mae West and W. C. Fields, and seeming easily more important than any of them.

A McCarthy family crest featuring a top hat, monocle and pine tree emblazoned on a shield was suspended over memorabilia glittering in large glass showcases: a special wooden Oscar with a movable mouth, star-shaped gold decorations on grosgrain ribbon from the King of Sweden, radio awards, a gilded, mounted microphone, endless keys to as many cities, and, shining in the center, a golden, jewel-encrusted scepter. On lower shelves, Charlie radios and Charlie watches were displayed alongside Charlie and Mortimer toy tin cars. Charlie's head grinned on enameled compacts, teaspoons, tie tacks, cuff links and comics. There were silver cigarette cases inlaid with the famous top-hatted profile, tiny gold Charlie charms with heads that swiveled over ruby boutonnieres, and crisp stacks of dollar bills with Mortimer's head on one side, Charlie's on the other, proclaiming in a federal flourish, "E PLURIBUS MOW'EM DOWN'EM." This was no ordinary office.

My father dictated letters on stationery embossed with Charlie's insignia (his profile in top hat encircled in blue), rewrote radio scripts, held meetings, and signed checks—an activity that seemed to exhaust him—in his corner office. An abstract painting of a block of wood with monocle and top hat and a radio tower sending signals in an empty landscape hung on the wall facing him, and two lamps lit the bookcase behind his desk. The lamp bases were fashioned from porcelain figurines—one of Charlie stretching a taut bow and arrow, taking aim at the figurine of Mortimer, who faced him nobly across the shelf, straw hat in hand crossed over his heart, an apple on his head. The bookshelves below were lined with volumes on vaudeville, manuals on magic, medical textbooks, investment guides, the evolution of the steam engine, the romance of the railroad, the age of aviation, the complete works of Shakespeare and biographies of Houdini and W. C. Fields.

In an adjoining empty office, I, too, dictated letters to invisible secretaries, rewrote imaginary scripts and held high-level meetings alone. I was always eager and excited to come with my father to the office, proud to be admitted to his world of dreams and doings, privileged to be made an honorary partner of the family firm—Bergen and Bergen.

Sometimes I played at Charlie's desk: a sleek, scaled-down model in pale-blond wood with his nameplate on it. What I lacked in authority as the desk's rightful owner, I gained in the assurance that he would not arrive unexpectedly. One afternoon as I fiddled happily there, giddy with a seven-year-old's delusions of grandeur, my father, finished with business, came out of his office. "Okay, Monstro, let's go home," he announced, patting me with a clean, smooth hand. My father had nice hands, elegant hands, with a platinum cat's-eye ring on the left fourth finger. He often called me "Monstro" (there was a whale of the same name in the Disney film *Pinocchio*) in that deceptively casual way that parents address their children.

Waving goodbye to the secretary and the bookkeeper, we marched down the stairs, across the courtyard, and into the long, dark tunnel that led to the garage. Doors opened off the tunnel, leading to additional, smaller offices I had never seen, one of which my father kept as a storeroom.

That day we stopped at the door in the cool, dark tunnel while my father fished for the key, explaining he'd left something inside. He unlocked the door and we walked in. The room inside was dark and airless, shapes and forms just visible in the dim gray light—a series of shapes suspended at eye level, the forms familiar like small, bulky bodies.

My father found the light and the forms took focus—becoming *bodies,* in fact—an entire row of them, clothed, in full finery, hanging, headless, from a rack. They were Charlie's bodies, I could tell that from the costumes: his traditional white tie and tails, Napoleon's full-dress uniform, Sherlock Holmes's tweed suit and cape, monogrammed pajamas and silk dressing gown, all impeccably tailored onto trim little torsos whose legs dangled limply in tiny, shiny shoes.

High on the shelf above, impaled on wooden stands, hovered the accompanying heads, anonymously hooded in brown velvet bags. They would be Charlie's heads, of course, but did he need so many? My father, seeing me staring dumbstruck at the row of heads, the rack of bodies, chuckled and gently lifted down the heads to show me.

Holding them by the short, notched wooden stalks extending like spinal cords from the neatly severed necks, he carefully slipped off the protective hoods and, one by one, Charlie's faces appeared. The first face to be revealed—the mouth slightly smiling, the upturned nose, a monocle in place over the left of the wide brown eyes, the red hair ruffled—was friendly and familiar. It was the Charlie that hung in the office foyer, shook hands in photographs, wisecracked at me across my father, who held us face-to-face, perched on opposite knees. That was a face I would never forget. But there were others materializing from the soft, smooth hoods; my father was pulling them out now like rabbits from hats. A Charlie whose face was ugly with anger, the features twisted, contorted with rage, was followed by a bleary-eyed, baldheaded Charlie—a face for whom time had not stood still. The skull was smooth, the forehead furrowed; the thick red hair had vanished, leaving only sparse gray patches that barely fringed the ears and failed to conceal the hearing aid now worn in one. The face was tired and flaccid, the expression weary—the eternal boy grown old.

Extra heads with extra faces to be inserted into waiting well-heeled bodies costumed to the nines. The possibilities were endless, the combinations infinite—this dummy had everything. Yet the eyes in all the heads stared dead and dark, the many faces lifeless. Because, after all, he needed my father for that part. Because he was nothing without my father.

When I was ten, Dee left to get married; my parents agreed I no longer needed a governess and decided on summer as the easiest time for Dena to leave. I would be away for the first time at Camp Big Bear, which would help distract me from her departure, giving me a month to adjust to her absence before I returned. In a tearful phone call Dee and I said goodbye, faced for the first time with the depth of devotion between us. But it is in reflections on the time after Dee left that my memory of my mother begins to shape and sharpen.

She was lovely to look at, uncommonly graceful, fun-loving and quick to laugh, and with these qualities, she made her way easily among strangers and new acquaintances. But the one person whose approval and acceptance she so eagerly sought, she never seemed to get: though she spent her life trying, it was always held beyond her reach. And one of the early revelations of my childhood was that however plentiful, however strong was the love that ran between us all, it was never to be spoken.

Often, before my mother came in to say good night, I'd make myself promise to tell her I loved her, but I never could. We were not in the habit. I'd decide to say it on the count of ten, but something in me always froze and then I'd be on 25, 26, 27, and she was walking across the room, 28, 29, 30, and she was walking out the door, 31, 32, 33, and her footsteps clicked softly on the marble hall, and still I hadn't been able to bring myself to say it, so terrifying was the prospect, so unfamiliar the words. It happened like that a lot. On nights like those, I was afraid I'd spend my whole life counting while everyone closed their doors and went to sleep.

My mother looked to me like a fairy princess, far too beautiful to be a mom—a fair, rare creature who lived in a magic kingdom. I always entered her dressing room as if drawn into a dream. Her domain was draped in ice-blue taffeta sprinkled with violets and sparkled with antique silver, Venetian glass, and tiny enameled boxes. Only a princess belonged here, not a six-year-old with clumsy hands. I was more at ease in the hills with my dogs.

Where I tended toward being a tomboy, my mother had grown up wrapped in cotton by her mother, Lillie Mae. My grandmother, desperately protective of her only child, ever mindful of Southern etiquette, kept her little girl high, dry and ladylike—indoors, out of harm's way. As a result, Frances was filled with fear of virtually everything. Still, she was game, a good sport.

During their courtship, when my father took her up in his airplane, she was so frightened that she threw up. Yet as a wedding gift to this passionate pilot, she mastered her fear long enough to learn how to fly. Taking lessons secretly for weeks, she completed her first solo, made a perfect landing, climbed proudly from the cockpit and fainted flat on the runway. When she presented my father with her pilot's license, he practically did the same.

She was even more terrified of water, and it was my father who taught her how to swim, pulling her up and down the length of the pool, sputtering, by a rope tied around her waist.

Determined that I not be saddled by the same fears, she saw to it that I hit the water, sat a horse, had a dog before there was time enough to think—instilling, if not a lack of fear, at least the will to overcome it. Or even, perhaps, to proceed because of it.

My mother had barely learned to be a wife before she had a daughter. In some ways, she still felt like a daughter herself. She'd had little enough fathering as a child, and unconsciously she looked now to her husband, twenty years older than she, to carry on the task.

"Your father literally raised me, Candy," my mother would often say. I suppose, in some sense, it fell to my father to raise us both. Certainly as I grew up, she seemed more like a sister than a mother to me, and in later years, we were forever compared as such.

How did she feel, having found this husband-father, at suddenly having to share him with another daughter? With a sister, perhaps, to the child in her that was still growing up? Another thing she said to me often was, "Your father always wanted a daughter, and you were the love of his life." If I was the love of my father's life, I wondered, where did that leave her?

Little girls get taller. Then someone—a Freudian fairy godmother—sits on our shoulders and whispers that fathers can't *be* Mr. Right. We keep it from ourselves, this crushing revelation, by brilliant decoys, delusions, rebellions. We're ten or eleven and life is not moving fast enough. Everything is normal, it's just that we have all this *feeling,* and it comes in strange, mythical, overblown forms. Mine was in the shape of heartbreaking crushes on horses.

By now, radio was in its decline and television ascending; my father's work was less and my parents' absences fewer. When they did travel now, more often than not they took me with them; and weekends once spent as exclusive father-daughter twosomes now became family outings with the three of us—Mom, Dad and me.

We often spent weekends and holidays at our house in Palm Springs, where my father, who first taught me how to ride, would take me, on weekends in the desert, to Shadow Mountain Stables for the Sunday morning breakfast ride. There we would join a group of eager children and a few game fathers, mount horses held by weathered wranglers and ride out into the desert, past tumbleweed and barrel cactus, through scattered spring wildflowers, down ravines and up arroyos, to arrive, an hour later, at the Chuck Wagon, sniffing the sausage, coffee and flapjacks we would eat while our horses waited in the shade.

Most mothers gladly passed up the breakfast ride, seizing the chance to sleep late, curious that anyone would choose to get up at 7:00 A.M. on a Sunday and ride for an hour on horseback to eat breakfast when you could so easily have it at home. My mother, for one, subscribed to this point of view. So it was especially hard for her to understand when her daughter fell in love with a horse.

We were introduced by a wrangler early one Sunday, assigned to each other for the morning. He was a chestnut quarter horse called (of course) King, an eight-year-old gelding that stood sixteen hands high, with powerful shoulders, a roached mane, three white socks, and a blaze down a face with fine brown eyes. I was almost eleven and stood five feet three inches, had blond hair in braids, blue eyes, and knew at once. This was it. As we started off into the desert, I hung back deliberately, riding not side by side with my father, as usual, but alone—with King.

I then asked for him—begged for him—each Sunday, began taking him on trail rides on Saturdays, wrote his name on my notebook in school, dreaming only of the weekends when we would be together again. Soon, everyone knew—King was Candy's horse, and I aimed to keep it that way: bringing him apples, sugar, carrots, earning the right to gently uncinch his saddle, easing it off his hot, steamy back, slowly slip off his bridle and fasten on his old rope halter, hugging his neck, kissing his nose, as my father told me for the fifth time that it was time to leave.

We drove home and my thoughts were only of King—my King—and Sunday afternoons, Mom, Dad and I would climb into the hot, stuffy cabin of the airplane that had been baking all weekend on the desert airstrip, strap ourselves in, taxi down the runway and take off into a slow right bank that brought us high over the stables—King's stables—and, like clockwork, sitting alone in the back, I burst into tears, stifling deep sobs, crying out in a tiny choked voice—a voice racked, ruined with emotion—"*Oh, King!*" To which my father would reply, "*Oh, Jesus!*"

That summer my parents took me, for the first time, to Europe, sailing from New York to Sweden on the SS *Gripsholm*. Then Denmark, England and finally France, where we stayed for ten days in the South on what was then called the Riviera. We stayed in swank hotels with high-ceilinged halls and walls like cold tapioca. The smells were damp and unfamiliar: Europe was Old, and that is how it smelled—old and damp and musty.

We stayed in villas that clung to rocks high over the sea and we visited others; one was called Le Roc and belonged to a man named George Schlee, on whose terrace we were to have lunch. He was awaiting the arrival of a guest—a guest whose name seemed to cause some commotion among the grown-ups assembled. A guest named Greta Garbo—though they called her by her second name. Who is that? I asked my mother, who laughed and said that she was a great actress, a great movie star, one of the greatest. And soon she arrived, by sea, in a sleek teak power boat, a white-clad sailor at the wheel. The host raced down the stone steps to greet her while the others watched from above. As she approached, the women murmured, "How beautiful . . ."

I did not understand. *This* was not a movie star. *Elizabeth Taylor* was a movie star. Susan Hayward. Lana Turner. *They* were movie stars and behaved as such. They dazed and dazzled, arrived glossed, sprayed and shaded, seductively sheathed, shimmering in sable, diamond rings and all those things—that was a movie star. Not this tall, storklike woman who caused a hush as she came and went, quietly padding on long, tanned legs and wearing baggy blue Bermudas, striped T-shirt, and dark glasses under a floppy straw hat. Folding herself into a canvas chair on the terrace, she spoke low and slow and seldom while the Côte d'Azur did its fan dance behind her. From time to time I sneaked peeks at her, hoping for a glimpse of what these grown-ups called "greatness and glamour," but she was not a *real* movie star, of that I was sure, and I felt frankly disappointed.

Our last stop was Paris, where my parents gave me the grand tour. But in the City of Light, all I saw was King. My parents, confident the affair had blown over, were shocked when, on the bridge of Alexander III, I swooned at the statues of rearing horses, stone hooves pawing the air above the Seine. In the galleries of the Louvre, standing before the portraits of kings of France, I gazed, instead, at the royal mounts, eyes wide and nostrils flaring—and in Notre Dame, bathed in a patchwork of colored light streaming from the rose window, I lit a candle for King. The candle really did it. "You and your goddamned horses!" my father said. "We show you Europe and all you see are horses! Jesus!" He had a point.

And so we left the City of Light and returned to the City of the Angels, where my parents finally caved in and bought me the horse, which they hid in a friend's stable for me to find on Christmas morning. Opening the door to the stall to find King (eating), I gasped, screamed, flung my arms around his neck and wept with joy. My King, oh, God, my King—while the horse calmly continued eating.

King was the first of many horses my parents put up with—

followed by a strawberry roan and a neurotic palomino—that found me happily spending most of my weekends grooming manes and tails, cleaning tack and mucking out stalls in the Valley.

Mine was a classic case of horse transference if ever there was one. A safe and permissible expression of romance, it was certainly simpler than the illicit love that preceded it—and infinitely easier than the ones to come.

4

Kids grew up fast in Beverly Hills, its young natives suffering from varying cases of Too Much, Too Soon. What we wanted most was to be grown up, and the sooner we got there, the better. What I wanted to be was not twelve going on thirteen but twenty-four going on twenty-five. It was hard living in Hollywood and being twelve. There was very little you could do with that. You could not be a movie star or Brenda Starr or go to premieres with Troy Donahue or drive a 190 SL. You couldn't even date. The most you could do was own your own horse, and, by thirteen, I was on my third.

I had thought things would improve at thirteen, but I found that life took on a baffling, bone-crushing intensity for me and my friends; the mere playing of our favorite song on the radio produced a sharp but exquisite sense of pain, a kind of sweet seizure that alarmed whatever adult was around as we yelped loudly, clutching our hearts with one hand and reaching frantically for the volume knob with the other, gasping as if the music we turned up were pure oxygen. "Oh, God, this song's *so neat*—" Then we sat transfixed, teary, till its end: "And so I asked the stars up above/Why must I be a teenager in love?"

To be a teen was to suffer. We were passionate about everything from movie stars to cars; all we could think of were boys, and we were never out of love.

My girlfriends, of course, were of primary importance. I was now in the Upper School of Westlake School for Girls in Holmby Hills, where I had gone since first grade. There, as young ladies in the pursuit of excellence in education, Westlake's daughters were cloistered in gracious Spanish Colonialist buildings on a wooded campus in the heart of Bel Air. Thick with banana palms, bougainvillea, magnolia, wisteria and pine, nature trails and tennis courts, it was a rare and dreamlike place, sheltered and serene, where, it was hoped, we might be shaped into upstanding young women. *Possunt Quia Videntur.* We wore uniforms with blazers bearing the school crest, regulation saddle shoes, and no makeup or jewelry "other than a simple timepiece." Uniform inspection was held in the mornings before chapel; dirty saddle shoes were a misdemeanor, and a pair of loafers could get you sent home. Smoking or drinking in uniform was usually met with expulsion, and to be reported doing either *out* of uniform meant possible probation. Teachers patrolled the halls in nylons and saddle shoes, some severe but all well-meaning, and were loved, respected and feared in turn.

Students were accepted or rejected according to whether they were or were not "Westlake material." The exact nature of the fiber required to meet the school's standards was difficult to define. It helped, certainly, if the parents were well-to-do—if only to meet the steep tuition. There were some children of "celebrities," but we were an understated, tailored bunch. The more flamboyant kids of flashier famous folks (some movie stars, singers, nightclub entertainers, even agents) went to Beverly Hills High School, where the high-gloss, well-heeled student body looked sharp and talked tough. Beverly High was Big Time, show biz, where kids who lived north of Sunset took pity on kids who lived south of Wilshire, the base poverty line. Students were snug in Jax slacks and alpaca sweaters, drove convertible T-Birds and read *Variety*. They thought Westlake girls were boring and would not put out. This was not entirely true—on either count. But, as Westlake girls, we went out with boys from Harvard, a private military school nearby—which seemed to suit everyone fine.

One of my friends at Westlake was from earliest childhood: Vicki Milland and I had danced around the maypole together at my sixth birthday party. Another friend was Lolane Garrett, who had a lush kind of beauty and was "stacked" even at thirteen—giving her an incalculable edge over the rest of us. She fell in love with darkly handsome men of twenty-three with a thrill of danger about them and rap sheets instead of diplomas. Once, during a fight with her father, an aeronautical tycoon, over just such a match, she jumped in protest, clad only in her nightgown, off the hill of their Trousdale estate, escaping with minor abrasions and front-page headlines in the *Herald Examiner*. While it couldn't be classed as a serious suicide attempt, I admired it as a romantic, reckless gesture all the same.

Pale-skinned, dark-haired, dressed head to toe in black whenever out of uniform, Liz Frank, daughter of screenwriter and director Mel Frank, was one of the few true intellectuals in the school. She shunned the sun, embracing socialism instead, and invited us over freshman year to see a film on the life of Lenin or agrarian reform in the Soviet Republic—who knew? Perched in our seats in our pastels and polka dots, listening sincerely as she explained the symbolism of the hammer and the sickle, we mistook it for a travelogue of a place we didn't want to visit.

Westlake was not anti-Semitic, at least not in so many words, but in those days you had to look closely to find many Jewish students. The year before Liz Frank joined our class, a girl named Connie Freiberg had arrived in midterm, and stood out not only as a new girl but also as our class's first Jew. And so her adjustment as a "new girl" was doubly hard. She came from Cincinnati, and her arrival was met with cool curiosity: we virtually ignored her for weeks, then, after a time, began to accuse her of attention-getting behavior. To which she replied, "Of course I'm trying to get attention! No one has *talked* to me for two months!" That changed abruptly when, in softball in spring semester, she hit a home run. Suddenly everyone wanted her on their team.

The two of us became a team of sorts, a prep school Laurel and Hardy. We had ink fights in study hall, put fetal pigs in each other's lockers, regularly disrupted and got expelled from class. Wavy-haired and wiry-bodied, Connie seemed to go in all directions at once. Her wit was fast and she soon became the court jester of the class. Because she made us laugh, she was sometimes not taken seriously. But she was also the class crusader, and no one taught me more about conscience than Connie: it was from her that I acquired even an incipient political awareness. She was concerned about blacks when all we cared about were boys, and nudged us toward more generous, democratic beliefs, urging tolerance and understanding. I looked to her on any social issue, knowing that hers would be the correct moral position.

But for most of us the burning issue was *boys*. We were on the cusp between childhood and womanhood, that period known as adolescence. Not everyone was ready for it when the time came, but most who weren't masked reluctance with bravado as we lurched into our metamorphosis. Dressed like young women, we still played hide-and-seek like little girls; but there was a sexual tension to the game now, as if our playing were a kind of training for the mating games that lay ahead. We set our hair laboriously, wore lipstick, moved out of undershirts triumphantly into padded bras, cast aside flats with socks for our first pair of heels and wobbled out on them into the world awaiting us.

And like all adolescent girls since time began, we were learning that parents—hitherto beloved, venerated parents—were a different species: at worst the enemy, often the jailor, at best an embarrassment to the uncertain new sophisticate. I was luckier than some of my classmates in the way I continued to get along with my parents; but in Edgar Bergen's household, predictably, there were new realms of embarrassment to be explored.

My first boyfriend was a Harvard School boy whose grandmother was Gloria Swanson, and one evening I was busy getting ready to go out with him to a school dance. Robe on, hair in curlers, a nervous thirteen-year-old, I jumped when the doorbell rang an hour early. My father opened it, exclaiming loudly, "Well, hellooo, Larry!" A young man's voice said, "How do you do, Mr. Bergen?" Dad asked him in, the two of them talking easily in the hall outside my room. "Candy's just getting ready," Dad said gaily. "Why don't we see how she's doing?" And I froze as he opened the door to my room, asking Larry to follow him in. Near panic in my robe and rollers, I waved frantically at my father to go back, flapping my arms furiously to stop him, hissing, "*No*, Dad! I'm not ready!" But he was coming in my room and I could hear Larry chuckling at his heels. Then my father's face flushed and he doubled over with laughter, and I knew: There was no one with him but his larynx. He had simply been throwing his voice and, well pleased with himself at having gotten me again, he smiled broadly and left the room.

In general, my parents observed my adolescence with more caution and apprehension than most. They were well aware from the first of the dangers of my growing up who I was and where I did— overprivileged and overexposed. They fought the odds against my emerging unspoiled with strictness and structure, hammering at my "sense of values." This struck me at the time as needless hardship: I was given earlier curfews, a smaller allowance, lower heels, fewer clothes and "pale pink lipstick on special occasions only."

My parents saw me getting ahead of myself, saw my looks mature before I did. At thirteen, I looked the part of a young woman and even played it convincingly too. In my spaghetti-strap Lanz dresses and my tiny new heels, I handled myself with poise and assurance with adults. I did a young girl's imitation of a grown-up that some mistook for real. But while I had the wardrobe and the looks and the attitude, I was new at this grown-up game—though I could hardly wait to play it—and had had no time to learn the ropes.

If my parents worried about my being thrust into more than I could handle, they saw that at most times I handled myself well. And, while anxious about my *looking* so sophisticated so soon, they were reassured that in most ways I was still my age. So much so, in fact, that my more mature girlfriends were always telling me, as one of the youngest in my class, "Bergen, why don't you *grow up?*"

My steady bending of school rules, clowning, wisecracking and throwing my voice in class found me frequently held after school, cleaning blackboards or confined to study hall, but I never overstepped the line into real trouble. And though I experimented secretly and unsuccessfully with smoking, my parents, who firmly forbade it, understood it as peer pressure and were confident that it would pass. My father even joked to friends that "you could smoke a ham in Candy's bathroom." If I was getting ahead of myself in some ways, I was still a kid in others.

But that began to change.

My coming of age seemed to coincide with changes in the world around me—or perhaps I perceived those changes more acutely as my eyes adjusted to the world that was suddenly available to me—and certain people in it began assuming sinister and seductive shapes.

For others, whose interest was more predatory than paternal, watched my coming of age. Not those in the traditional family circle of friends, which was close and safe and cozy, but slick newcomers to Hollywood, casual acquaintances and occasional hangers-on who clung fast to its periphery.

They were a younger, brasher bunch of show folk, failures in film, successes on television; tough-talking, hard-drinking men and women who contrasted sharply with my parents' conservative coterie of soft-spoken, meticulously mannered friends. A new generation was taking over now and they had new—or no—rules.

Every year at Christmas my parents gave a large party, the centerpiece of which was a lavish smorgasbord washed down with glasses of icy akvavit or mugs of hot, spiced glögg. The patio was tented in, a dance floor laid down, and a trio played while people toasted the holidays and the New Year.

The year I was thirteen, I remember, the smorgasbord was particularly glamorous. Old family friends were there: the Justin Darts, Jimmy Stewarts, Leonard Firestones, Freeman Gosdens, Ronald Reagans. Fred Astaire danced with my mother and Rex Harrison sang from *My Fair Lady* accompanied by Henry Mancini on the piano. Even for a child of Hollywood, it was pretty heady stuff.

That night, it was confusing. Newcomers arrived as well—strangers with familiar, famous faces, friends of friends who were welcomed in—quick to make themselves at home, slow to leave.

Jack Warner came to our house for the first time as part of a cluster of guests, wheezing in and wedging his bulk into an overstuffed chair. A plate of food was served him, but before he had a chance at it, a young woman whom I took to be an actress (she had arrived on the arm of an agent) lurched up to Warner and landed on his lap. I was watching from a sofa nearby as the old mogul tried to make out what had suddenly come between him and his food. He did not appear to know this woman—though he knew hundreds like her—and he was a man used to having women on his own terms. As she murmured small talk in his ear, he reached absentmindedly for his glass, turning in my direction to ask what was in it.

"It's glögg," I piped up a hair too eagerly, "a hot spiced wine—"

"Shut up, kid," she snapped at me and resumed with Warner's ear.

"But I was just—"

"Beat it," she snarled, and pulled his head to her mouth so ferociously that I thought she might swallow him whole, gnawing at him with sharp, capped teeth as her tight sheath rode up her thighs. (I could see the headlines, STUDIO HEAD EATEN ALIVE AT SMORGASBORD.) She was hungry for something, though I'm not sure it was him.

Maybe this was the Movie Mogul's Handshake, I thought, the Studio Head's Salute—for Warner, sprawled like a beached whale as she wriggled on his paunch, seemed indifferent to the effusive greeting from this starving stranger—more eager to get to the dish on the table in front of him than the one on his lap. And after a moment he shoved her aside, heaving himself forward in his chair and, happily seizing his plate, began popping Swedish meatballs into his mouth with his fingers, one by one.

This was my first glimpse of a Hollywood I'd never seen. A mysterious netherworld, a treacherous terrain with doomed and desperate people whom I found frightening but fascinating—the sirens on the rocks of make-believe, who soon began calling out to me. First they approached my parents with offers for me to appear in movies, on television. Offers my parents reluctantly passed on to me, trusting in my judgment even at thirteen and confident I would stay in school. I was flattered and mystified by such attention, but above all, unprepared. Thank you, no. My parents were pleased and relieved.

But then came offers that were more confusing. A few of the older cynics of this fast, flashy crowd—people I did know, but who had never been close friends of my parents—hovered over Hollywood like aging birds of prey and swooped down on our house to hunt. Bitter at being past their prime and drinking hard to forget it, they compensated by cracking loud jokes about my budding maturity, snappy one-liners on puberty and menstruation and bee-sting breasts that made me redden with self-consciousness, while my father seemed not to hear and my mother looked away in embarrassment, apologizing to me later.

They were people who made short work of others and moved

on quickly in search of fresh kill. That year it seemed to occur to a few of them that now I might be fair game, and they were suddenly attentive and alert. Men—and occasionally women as well—who had once dismissed me as a polite and pigtailed child now sized me up with narrowed eyes for reappraisal.

In the powder room of Chasen's, during a Sunday dinner with my parents, the restless wife of a famous producer took my face in her hands and brought it close to her own. "I'd like to see you," she said huskily. "Where do you live?" "With my parents," I said blithely. She recoiled in horror. "How *old* are you?" "Thirteen." "Jesus!" she gasped, and bolted out the door, like a vampire confronted by a crucifix. Men, on occasion, had had similar reactions to the same question, but I was puzzled now. When I told my parents about the strange exchange, I realized from their expressions that there was more to this woman than mere maternal interest.

Everywhere there seemed to be more to life than met the eye.

While we dated fourteen-year-old boys in white bucks and brac-es, "making out" in parking lots, angora fluff rising from our sweat-ers, we dreamed of men in movies—screen stars of the moment. Invariably, for me, it was the tall, tan, blond, blue-eyed ones—Aryan icons in khakis and crew necks, not the sensual and swarthy types worshipped by most others in the class. (George Chakiris I was willing to go halfway on but Elvis Presley was a heartthrob I never understood.) Engulfed in teenage crushes, consumed by fantasies of romance, I prepared for the time when I would find Him, plan-ning my wardrobe for the day He came to carry me away.

It happened sooner than I expected. My parents now owned a weekend house at Newport Beach, and there people made easy, unannounced visits, some by land, some by sea, sidling up to the slip in sailboats or motorboats as simply as they might park their cars at the curb. It was a close-knit coastal community, a sort of

Show Biz-by-the-Sea, and every day was a buoyant buffet, a floating cocktail hour that shuttled from ship to shore.

One afternoon, I saw a boat making for our slip below the house: a sailboat, a racer, docking under power. I ran down the gangway to meet her and help tie her off. She was edging up to the slip—a scrubbed teak deck and a pearl-gray hull—and I stood ready to catch the line. I was not ready for who was tossing it.

There, holding out the line to me and grinning as I gasped, was the heartthrob who hung on my bulletin board, the movie star I dreamed of while drifting off to sleep at night—now, just at arm's reach, arriving by sea. Friends of my parents waved gaily from the stern and we tied the boat off neatly, leaving it bobbing gently at the dock. It was *his* boat, they explained, needlessly introducing him; they had decided to drop by for a visit.

Well, *my* ship sure came in, I thought, following them along the dock. Wait till the gang hears about *this*. . . . I sat in a corner on the terrace, at a total loss for words, dumbstruck by the descent of this presence off whom I could not take my eyes for a second.

Seeing his part in my undoing, he came over and sat next to me, asking me simple questions which I answered with great difficulty. Finally, I managed one of my own. "That's a beautiful boat," I said. "Do you race her?" Oh, yes—he'd raced her south to Mexico and north up the coast; she was qualified sixth in her class. "She looks awfully fast," I said. "Sleek hull, narrow beamed. How many do you carry in crew?" Three, said he, but he could get by on two. Did I race? "Just a few times by myself but I've crewed a lot for others." Would I like to go for a sail on her now? he asked.

Sail with him? I'd seen him sailing in a movie—into the sunset, tanned hands light and steady at the helm, blond hair blowing across bright-blue eyes as he squinted far, far out to sea. I loved that movie. I loved him. "Just the two of us?" I asked, hoping. No problem, he said. He'd taken her out often alone; we wouldn't be gone long and would stay in the harbor. Just to the jetty and back.

Seeing my excitement, my parents said yes, thanking him for giving me such a treat. He backed out of the slip, I helped him haul up the sails, and soon we were flying. The afternoon wind was picking up and we shot through the water, tacking back and forth across the bay.

This is the greatest moment of my life, I thought, proudly trimming the jibsail, stealing looks at him as the sinking sun turned him copper. *Just* like he was in the movie, I thought: sailing into the sunset, blond hair whipped by the wind. Blond hair that was strangely dark at the roots, I noticed, buffeted as it was by the breeze, but I thought no more about it as he met my adoring gaze and said, smiling, "It'll be dark soon—we better go in. You're a good ship's hand; next time, I'll promote you to co-captain."

Easing alongside the slip below the house, we dropped the sails with their loud rustling, furled the main and stowed the others in their bags. I was blue from the wind and the chill but I did not want that moment to be over. Tying off the mooring lines as slowly as I could, looping layers of figure eights around the cleat, I found I could draw it out no longer. "Thank you a lot," I said, reaching out to shake his hand, "it was just great." "Anytime, sailor." He smiled and pressed a folded piece of paper into my palm. "Keep this between us." He winked. "I'd like to hear from you. Call me."

Call me, he said. I watched him take the steps in his Top-Siders easily, three at a time. Loose and lithe on long, strong legs. Call me. I quickly peeked at the paper. His telephone. Nothing more. Our secret. Call me.

Monday found me back in school, unusually distracted. *Call me.* By the end of the day, his name covered my notebooks and my name now merged with his. Pages were filled with endless scrawling to perfect my new signature plus countless designs of our mutual monogram: our initials combined in block gothic.

The piece of paper was limp from repeated folding and unfolding; from fondling. *Our secret.* I imagined him watching me and

I preened accordingly, strutting and self-aware in my movements, showing off and laughing louder; occasionally glancing over my shoulder in case he had slipped into study hall unobserved; playing volleyball with uncommon ardor on the off chance he might wander by the field.

After school, I barricaded myself in my room with supplies of milk and chocolate doughnuts, turning up the radio full blast: "White Tennis Sneakers That Are Black." Jan and Dean. My favorite. Once more, I took out the piece of paper, reaching for the aqua Princess phone I had gotten for my thirteenth birthday. *Call me.* And so I did.

He wasn't home at first; there was no answer. Heart pounding, I dialed nonstop until there was.

"Hello?"

My heart was coming to a standstill. "Hi, it's—"

"*Who?* I can't hear you. Turn the music down." I dived for the volume knob, and announced myself again.

"Well, hello there, sailor. Glad you called."

"Hi" had been a lot for me to manage; I had no idea where to go from there. He did. He was shooting, he said, just got back from the set, in fact, and was busy working late every day with a difficult co-star. How would I like him to take me for a drive one night?

How would I like him to . . . ? "Oh, sure, that would be neat," I stammered nonchalantly.

"Tomorrow night?" Tomorrow night was no good: my parents would be home. Sailing was one thing; this was another.

"What about Wednesday?" I asked. They would be away for two days.

"Okay then, Wednesday. I'll pick you up at seven-thirty; I'll be waiting in the car. Take care of yourself—"

Wednesday. He'll be waiting in the car. Take care of myself. Oh, my God.

Wednesday afternoon was spent showering and changing.

Hours of showers, frenzied setting and spraying of hair. As soon as I was ready, I began again, finally settling on the large man's shirt that billowed over blue jeans with painstakingly rolled cuffs, bobby socks and penny loafers that I always changed into after school. I didn't want to overdo it: after all, it was just a drive.

Time crept; I added a *little* more lipstick, a *touch* of eye shadow, another *dab* of perfume. I'd locked the door to my room and unhinged the screen from my window. Now I sat and watched and waited. It was seven thirty.

At a few minutes past, a pair of headlights appeared through the low fog that sometimes hugs the ground at night in Los Angeles. I wondered what kind of car he had and if I was going to faint. I wondered what would happen if my parents found out; this they would never forgive. I lowered myself out the window, down the vine and darted, crouched like a commando, from palm to palm, zigzagging across the driveway in a bid for cover.

His big black car hovered like a giant manta ray out of the circle of street lamps. As I came alongside, the door swung open: a Cadillac convertible.

Duck tail stiff with hairspray, redolent of Madame Rochas, I slid across the smooth upholstery, banging my knee on something and sending it clattering. "Oh, a phone!" I exclaimed (relieved at such a handy conversation piece). "You have a *phone* in your *car?*"

"In case the studio needs to reach me," he said, replacing the receiver in its cradle while I nodded sagely, wondering what to say next. But he was talking as he headed the car toward Sunset, climbing Coldwater Canyon, crossing Mulholland, and coasting down into the Valley below.

"How's school?" he asked. Did I have many boyfriends? Well, no, no special boyfriends, I lied; I wasn't going steady. Or anything. I bet *he* had a lot of girlfriends, though. But he laughed and said no, no girlfriends. At the moment, he had alimony payments—and his second wife was suing him for divorce. No, he laughed, no girlfriends. Lucky for me, I thought. Who would be dumb enough to divorce him? How old was he, if he didn't mind? He was staring straight ahead. Thirty-six, he said, turning off onto a dirt road that led into a citrus orchard, down through groves of orange and grape-fruit trees. *Thirty-six.*

"My farm," he said, reading the question in my expression. "I bought it as an investment last year. Land is gold, kiddo, didn't your father tell you that?"

"My father has farms too," I said proudly, "all over the place, and an office building in Hollywood and a parking lot. I think the parking lot's in Westwood."

He switched off the ignition and smiled at me. His teeth seemed to glow in the dark. It was very dark. And very still. I knew he was staring at me though my eyes were cast down; I wondered if he could hear my heart pounding. *Booming*, really. Like a gun.

Why was this moment so familiar? Why did I feel I had been here before? Face flushed with shyness and excitement, eyes locked on my loafers, the careful cuffs of my jeans, the soft rolls of my socks; heart racing with forbidden feeling, with love, with fear, with the romance of it all. Was it like the time with my father? Just the two of us in his car when I was six years old? That evening when he drove me high up over the city as the sun was setting and we watched the lovebirds nuzzling in a tree—"Do you know what it means to 'bill and coo'?" he'd asked as the blood rushed to my face. Helpless with love for him; putty in his hands. *Do you know what it means to 'bill and coo'?* I think I do, Dad. Now, I think I do.

For this man's hands were touching me now, pulling me to him, and he was kissing me—this older man who was *not* my father, this other man in whose hands I was again pure putty, this prince who had come to carry me away.

A light rain was beginning to fall, pulling the California grape-fruit off the trees to land with a soft thud on the convertible. This was well beyond "bill and coo" now, heading into deeper, darker waters, and I was trying to keep from going under. In one night, I had gone from fourteen-year-olds in white bucks and braces to thirty-six-year-old movie stars in cashmere and real estate. From guys in letter sweaters to men in divorce suits. I was in way over my head.

He got rougher and more persistent as I knocked the mobile phone from its cradle once more in a hasty retreat across the seat. My back flattened against the padded Naugahyde door; he came at me, talking softly, firmly, asking me what was the matter? What was I afraid of? Didn't I realize how many women would love to be in my place? Yes, I did, I nodded, thinking how much I wished they were.

This was no clumsy necking with boys in faculty parking lots; this was the big time, the Real Thing. There was no place here in the citrus for coy teenage crushes; he was not taking no for an answer, no longer treating me like a lovesick thirteen-year-old but like another girl in a car at night. A car pounded by grapefruit.

I became frightened as he began to lose patience, my mind searching for simpler, safer things. I had no idea where he had taken me, but, suddenly, I knew where I wanted to be: home, Auntie Em. Back in my bedroom with the horse-show ribbons and petrified prom gardenias, my sailing trophy and my stack of 45s. The sky-blue harlequin wallpaper with the apple-green butterflies, the matching Princess phone. Back in my canopy bed by the soft glow of my beloved clock radio. Home safe in my new teenager's room.

The interior of the car was hot and muggy and had turned into a subtropical zone. The windows trickled with tiny drops of water and my hair spray was coagulating, growing gummy, and my hair crackled as it stuck and matted on his face. I had persisted in playing it as a game when it had clearly never been one, and finally fed up with my "childish attitude," he soon agreed that I belonged back with my record collection, not with him.

We drove home in stony silence. I felt ashamed, relieved, apologetic. As we approached my house, all he said was, "I wouldn't mention this to your parents, okay? They might not approve." *Mention it to my parents? Might not approve? Was he insane? Was I?* I'd never had a date with a boy old enough to drive—much less telephone at the same time. I would be sent to a convent, a work camp. There was no imagining what would happen if they ever knew.

We pulled up a discreet distance from the house. He reached across me to open the door. "So long, sailor." "So long," I said, and ran up the driveway, tunneled under the ferns and hoisted myself in through the window. Changing into my nightgown, I crept out from my room to check: the housekeeper dozed in the den in front of the television. All quiet on the home front. I burrowed under the covers, snug in my bed, turning my clock radio on softly, soothed by the music, safe in its glow. My room. My radio. My, my, my. Home, sweet home.

This was the first of such encounters, but there were more where he came from—not all handsome and not all illustrious, but hardeyed and hungry and good at the game. Not yet fourteen, and life was going too fast for me. Beverly Hills was like growing up in the Garden of Eden: I was tantalized and terrified, vacillating between wanting my parents to protect me and seeing to it that my escapades went undetected. A confused and cagy criminal with a secret yearning to be caught. Restless and uneasy. I had a sudden longing to travel, to go away to school. Where did not matter—but far, far away, and *not here.*

My friend Vicki Milland was taking her sophomore year in Switzerland, as it happened; it was not too late for me to apply. I went to my parents to request a transfer overseas. They were taken aback by the idea and firmly opposed to it. My father, in particular, was adamant: I was too young to be so far from home and on my own—I would be just fourteen. Besides, I was his only child; he wanted me home.

I turned to my mother, who finally agreed to lobby on my behalf, appealing to him on the grounds of higher education, the experience of living in Europe and the opportunity to learn French. At last he conceded: one year abroad.

Switzerland was the perfect solution: cows, cuckoos, mountains, meadows—the whole country was a rest home. My parents, too, were certain I would be cloistered; perhaps they were even secretly relieved that I was going. Finally, there was only so much they could do to delay and protect me through these rites of passage, to shepherd my progress into the same world where I grew up; a world, after all, that was like no other.

5

Few schools could rival Montesano ("Healthy Mountain"), snuggled high in the Swiss Alps, for beauty or inaccessibility. Classrooms and dormitories were housed in huge old log chalets scattered across the mountaintops above the swank ski resort of Gstaad. Nestled in mountains thick with pine forests and stands of silver birch, laced by streams which fed into rivers that ran past meadows grazed by cows, it was a shrine of serenity, a picture postcard of peace and repose.

The sixty-five students ranged in age from fourteen to eighteen and came from all over Europe, the United States, Canada, South America, the Middle East and South Africa. The curriculum was standard, but emphasized French—a language we were meant to speak at all times and study two hours a day. In winter the emphasis included skiing, which we did each afternoon.

The teachers were European: faded postwar-film types. The women—pale-skinned and proper in flannel skirts and sensible shoes, hair tucked in neat chignons—resembled Deborah Kerr, at a distance; they were refined and cultivated and represented, in fact, the kind of ladies we were expected to become. The man who doubled as English and History professor reeked of Ronald Colman: neat pencil moustache, shapeless tweed jacket with patches, suede shoes. A tall, intense Italian taught languages—a dark-eyed man with a Savonarola-like zeal who was rumored to be a communist; a sober Swiss spinster taught "cuisine"; and the "maths" and science teacher radiated an abused and battered brilliance—the message that a fine mind was at work, meant for better things than dissecting field hares for sullen students.

To be a teacher in a Swiss finishing school was, I suppose, a kind of death with dignity—an Alpine end of the line. These were all decent people, kind and hardworking; and in retrospect the patience displayed by dedicated, underpaid professors with insolent young girls—some of whose allowances were equal to their salaries—seems only short of saint-like. If the language teacher hadn't arrived a communist, he certainly would have left as one.

Though Montesano was one of the most highly accredited girls' schools in Switzerland, the education offered by Swiss finishing schools was "higher education" only in the sense that it took place at 3,400 feet; it was less a course of college preparation than a crash course in how to run a château.

In educational terms, "finishing schools" were an exotic exercise in obsolescence, and they sometimes simply served as elegant warehouses for wealthy unwanted children, well-heeled refugees from unhappy households. Parents more involved with their divorce proceedings than with their kids sent them to school in Switzerland—out of sight, out of mind; to exalted day-care centers where the girls arrived accompanied by trunks of designer dresses and slick Italian ski wear, overweight and starving for affection.

Not all the students were like that, of course; many came from families like mine: parents who wanted their children to have the best education they could afford and sought it in chalets of higher learning in Switzerland. My parents sent me against *their* will, acceding to mine. But those girls whose parents considered them an inconvenience knew it, and they learned fast how to live alone.

Like street kids from the world's most fashionable neighborhoods, they became seasoned survivors, wealthy warlords to weaker students, bullying the younger kids as they had been abused at home; or trying to buy friendship with money, with favors, with promises—as they had never known it offered any other way.

These were the aristocrats of abandoned children—chic semi-orphans begging for discipline, desperate for love. Some simply never seemed to get it, though they received substitutes— parental payoffs—instead: Cartier watches, second pairs of skis, Hermès luggage, when all they wanted was a hug. Shortly it would be too late to know how to accept it when and if the time ever came. For some, it was that time already: by sixteen, certain girls were no more than the sum of their gifts. That was all they had ever been given: all they expected, all they could understand.

Chalets were known by name and reputation, assuming the colors and characteristics of their inhabitants: quaint class structures, gingerbread hothouses for budding elitists. Rivalries raged between chalets: gang warfare with bilingual leaders who, in a version of Swiss Darwinism, preyed on the young and weak. One, a six-foot French-Russian girl, would routinely pummel me, bringing her fist down square on my head, then stalk off, smiling grimly, as I lay crumpled in the hall. I took to carrying ski poles for protection.

She was a member of the "Montesano Mafia": third- and fourth-year students whose French was faultless, their skiing superb, their family connections fortuitous. These girls were considered the school's special forces, an elite task force who lived off campus in the village by the river. Theirs could have been called "Chalet Notorious," as it had the highest recorded statistics of intrigue and drama, flashy but failed suicide attempts, rumored "lesbian affairs," hushed-up pregnancies and shotgun marriages with savvy ski instructors. When we, the weak, were not being mugged by them, we worshipped them and followed their every move.

Where I was expecting Alpine Meadows, what I got was more

like *Blackboard Jungle*. If I thought life was fast at home, here it made your head spin; Beverly Hills seemed like a Mormon settlement next to Gstaad. At Westlake you could get sent home for wearing loafers instead of regulation saddle shoes; here, a model student was one who made it back to her room before breakfast after having stayed out with a ski instructor all night. Though there were ironclad curfews and strict penalties for such late-night comings and goings, they were virtually impossible to enforce. Chalets were spread across acres, and adolescent girls became escape artists when men were around; nothing could keep them in.

My chalet, "Montesano," also housed administration offices, faculty and student lounges, dining hall and kitchen. I was assigned to a large and sunny room on the third floor with French doors that opened onto a balcony with a magnificent view of the mountains. I had two older roommates: an English girl of sixteen whose father had made his fortune in textiles and a Rhodesian girl of seventeen whose father had made his in tobacco.

It was clear at once that age was a key to the caste system at Montesano, one of many ways to exclude and divide people. As one of the youngest first-year students, I was cannon fodder for the ranks. Terrified that I might be condemned as a weakling by older girls and sent into the snow to die, I faced the situation straightforwardly and lied about my age, moving it up a crucial year to fifteen and swearing Vicki Milland, who was fifteen in fact, to secrecy.

Even under my assumed age, my older, all-powerful roommates considered me more a pet than anything else: less than human, more than vermin—a cute American serf. Naturally, I did my best to prove myself and please them, rummaging in my bag of tricks like a nervous court jester, digging, digging for more.

When they got tired of my singing the whole of "Happy Birthday" in one protracted belch, I blew smoke rings. When those wore thin, I did my Flaming Mona Lisa: holding a lit cigarette between my teeth and flipping it into my mouth with my tongue, where it rested, in its crook, sometimes singeing my taste buds, while, with lips closed, I smiled serenely and smoke streamed from my nose.

A bell summoned us to meals, invariably starting a stampede of students furiously elbowing each other for first place in line. The dining-room doors opened and we inmates surged forward, shoving and shouldering our way to the tables. Permission to be seated was given by the headmistress in precise, high-pitched French that, one evening, was unusually long in coming.

Using an old sleight-of-voice trick picked up from my father, I called out in a reedy falsetto a crisp *"Asseyez-vous"* that sent every-one scrambling into her seat and falling upon her food. Everyone, that is, except the headmistress, who was left conspicuously stand-ing, shaking with rage, demanding to know who gave the order.

The combined sexual energy of sixty-five girls confined in the Alps no doubt had something to do with the ferocity with which we attacked our food. Approached from any other angle, our impa-tience to devour these meals was mystifying as—with the exception of the occasional steak and *pommes frites*, served when there were visitors to the school—it was generally agreed the food was swill.

It seems oddly fitting, then, that the only political action taken that year of 1961 by the students of a Swiss finishing school was a food strike. Barricading ourselves into the salon of Montesano on Monday morning, wearing our school ski uniforms in a show of solidarity, with only a supply of oranges, Lindt chocolates and Marlboros to sustain us, we boycotted classes, meals and Downhill Slalom until an agreement was reached to upgrade the quality of the food. By the end of the afternoon, word came through that some concessions in the cuisine would be made: the faculty—and the chef—had caved in. It was a hollow victory for girls with noth-ing else to complain about.

• • •

Itinerant Italians and Arabs migrated to Gstaad in the school season, trekking into the Bernese Oberland—the fertile crescent of finishing schools—as if to a souk where young, nubile heiresses could be had for the asking—or the taking. Some found work as waiters in the schools themselves, and some found an heiress they could call their own—a result more often of an untimely pregnancy than of true love.

Montesano was staffed with loyal retainers and had no job openings, but the men were not so easily put off. Walking back from the main chalet to their own after dinner, girls took to traveling in packs as protection against the short, wiry commandos who would spring from the bushes along the footpaths at night to try to tackle an heiress and bring her down.

Theirs was not the subtle school of courtship but a more direct approach, acrobatic rather than romantic. One night, after lights out, as we sat huddled in a second-floor bedroom smoking a butt scavenged from the balcony, we looked up to see, neatly framed in the French doors, a naked male torso hanging from the ledge above. His head was blocked by the doorsill but his body swung slowly, triumphantly, suspended like a phantom ham, before us.

When we shrieked (as much in excitement as in fear, for the Alpine nights are long), he dropped without a sound into the snowdrift below and vanished into the forest. The next day it was reported to the headmaster and we were called in to give an account. Could we give a description? Well, not a traditional one. Was he tall? Was he dark? Oh, he was dark, Monsieur, and not too tall; well-built, though, and muscular, about one hundred forty-five pounds. Did we see his face? His *face? Non,* Monsieur, we saw him clearly, but we did not see his *face.*

On weekends, we would bike to nearby villages, hike the mountains, skate on frozen ponds or take the train to Lausanne and drink. On our own and far from home for the first time, we fanned out in search of bars where age was no object and where exotic names took on new meaning: "Stingers," "Whiskey Sours," "Grass-hoppers," "Martinis," "Daiquiris," "Negronis" were often downed one on top of another.

In the afternoon, when we met at the station to go back to school, some girls would invariably be missing, so we formed and deployed search parties to find them—their hair soaked with sweat, matted to faces the same color as the floor they were lying on, usu-ally in the bathrooms of bars. Passed out after having thrown up, they lay happily on the cool, clean tile, still crisp in their no-iron knit travel suits.

Then one of us would call the house mother, announce our-selves briskly as mothers or aunts, apologize for keeping the girls too long in our suite for tea and promise to have the chauffeur put them on the next train.

In winter, Gstaad was in her glory. Glamorously swathed in snow, the village shone and glittered as people filled the once sleepy streets just to get a glimpse of her. Royalty arrived and behaved as such, gliding by in pale Pucci *après-ski* wear. The young Aga Khan seemed unpretentious, and Elizabeth Taylor and Richard Burton didn't. Jingling down the snowy street in a horse-drawn sleigh, lavishly bundled in furs, heads thrown back in throaty laughter, they gave royalty a run for their money that year and won hands down.

As soon as the snow fell, we spent each afternoon skiing under the cynical gaze of ski instructors with tanned poker faces who had seen it all. Our brother school, Le Rosey, migrated to Gstaad from Lausanne for their winter term, a move preceded by weeks of fren-zied preparations on our part: shaving of legs, washing of hair, steal-ing of clothes, skipping of meals.

There were *thés dansants* at the stately Palace Hotel, miniature hamburgers at Charlie's Tea Room, fondue dinners at the Olden, and ski parties at the Eagle Club on the summit of the Wasserngratt. On moonlit nights we would stand on our balconies and watch as a string of lights weaved its way down the pale, distant mountain from the cozy restaurant on its peak. Skiers with torches floated silently down its face, *au flambeau,* till, one by one, the lights all disappeared.

A few parents came to Gstaad to spend Christmas with their children, and fortunately, mine could be numbered among them. December found me excitedly meeting my parents at the train station, eager to show off the effects of three months in Europe, the patina of refinement I had so proudly acquired abroad.

But the first patina my mother saw was the one on my hair. "What do you have on your *hair*?" she gasped, eyeing the platinum rinse that had left it the color of old cutlery. "Moon Mist," I replied proudly, grandly squiring them to a taxi to the hotel.

"Shall we go down and have a drink in the bar?" I suggested, once they had checked in. "The Burtons are here," I rattled on, carrying the conversation so adroitly that I failed to notice as they slipped into shock, "and the Aga Khan. And I *have* to take you to the Eagle Club for lunch. . . ." Nonchalantly ordering "*un* Bloody Mary" from a waiter who smirked at my finishing-school French, I then proudly produced a pack of Salems, flipped my Zippo and expertly lit one up.

It was all *un peu de trop.* My mother looked as if she was going to faint and my father seemed frozen, turned to stone. In the fall they had left a fair fourteen-year-old; by winter, they returned to find Forever Amber. It was hardly the mastery of *these* skills that they had had in mind.

"Candy, is that *all* you've learned here in three months?" my mother asked. "Smoking and drinking and bleaching your hair?" It was, basically, all I'd learned, but I took great pride in having acquired these suave and sophisticated skills, as essential to Alpine survival as a Swiss army knife.

My parents were devastated by the pseudosophisticate they found. In only one semester away at school, I'd managed to become all they'd tried to protect me from at home. Asking me to their room the following day, they sat me down for a long and emotional talk that brought me back to my senses and my age. I was secretly relieved that they had come to rescue me, thrilled to be a child again—to stop playing Simone Signoret and go back to Sandra Dee. Sheepishly I cast Salems and stainless-steel Zippos aside, washed the platinum rinse from my hair, went on the wagon and returned to my beloved hot Ovaltine. The Prodigal Child had come home.

In fact, home was looking better and better when seen from afar. I had missed the security of my family, the familiarity of old friends. And in some ways, that Swiss Christmas, it seemed as if I'd never left it—that Hollywood that year was here.

Ardis and Bill Holden—whose eldest son, West, was my Le Rosey boyfriend—gave a lunch at their house on Lake Geneva, and friends reunited at Jördis and David Niven's chalet near Gstaad for Christmas dinner. Jamie and David Junior were there. In childhood, we had been fast friends. The first Christmas we'd spent together I was five, and my father took all of us—dressed in our "Hoppy suits"—to a broadcast of his radio show to meet Hopalong Cassidy, dressed in *his*, who was appearing as a guest.

Once impatient to get away from home, I was now impatient to return to it. The rest of the school year sped by, and finally I arrived in Beverly Hills, chic in my chignon and Italian heels, quoting French and carrying Proust (whom I hadn't yet read, only carried).

As summer at home wore on, I shed my European affectations and acquired some American ones in their place. I was learning to play parts in life with almost frightening aplomb, switching masks with alacrity; surprised and a little scared that so few seemed to notice or to challenge my assuming such sophisticated roles.

The fall of my fifteenth year, I gratefully surrendered my status as an only child. All my life I'd longed for a flesh-and-blood brother—a *real* one—wistfully watching *Ozzie and Harriet, Life with Father, Leave It to Beaver,* suburban fables that glorified the all-American home, where life is a situation comedy and brothers and sisters argue endearingly over record collections but defend each other to the death.

The only brother I'd ever fought with was Charlie—scripted bickering on the radio—and the boundaries of *that* brother-sister relationship were blurry at best, as bogus as a Charlie McCarthy dollar bill.

As an official only child, I was accorded the privilege—and it was considerable—of enjoying undivided parental attention. The downside was that I never knew attention came any other way; I'd never had to learn to share it. In the unique position of one and only child, I was, of course, the undisputed favorite, a title I clearly relished.

But I was also a lonely child, easiest with animals. I envied large, expressive families, and what I wished for most was a brother. A sister was an obvious second choice—less interesting to a tomboy like me (and also more threatening, especially a *pretty* one). No, what I wanted was a brother, someone I would fight to the death for; someone I would be willing to give my life for. And that is what I got.

If he arrived a little later than I expected, my parents hadn't planned on it at all. One day, when I was home from Switzerland for Easter vacation, my mother had sat me down nervously for a talk: "Candy, I have something to tell you and I don't know how you're going to feel about it; I'm not sure how I feel about it myself.

It was a surprise to your father and me; we hadn't planned it and we—You see, I'm going to have a baby."

It was some news. "Oh, Mom, that's wonderful," I managed, as we both swallowed hard and fought back the tears. "You mean you don't mind?" she asked. "Things will be different after all this time; I could understand if you—" No, no, I assured her. Nothing could have thrilled—or surprised—me more. But what about her? A woman of thirty-nine, how did *she* feel about her unexpected pregnancy?

There were risks, she explained, for a woman her age; the possibility the baby might not be born "healthy" terrified her and gave her trouble sleeping. There was not yet the option of amniocentesis as a means to reassure her. There was, besides, a considerable risk to herself; she had had complications in the past, a history of miscarriages.

If she was concerned for herself, she never spoke of it further. When she first told me, her concern was for me and how I would accept this sudden, significant change in all our lives. It was an important talk between mother and daughter but it was also our first intimate conversation as friends. I had never felt closer to my mother than I did that day; she had taken me into her confidence, shared her feelings and fears. She had considered me as a daughter but also as an adult. *Was* I becoming an adult? Now that a new bird was coming into the nest—did that mean it would soon be time for me to leave?

On October 12, 1961, Kris Edgar Bergen was born. After visiting my mother, who had emerged from long labor weary but well, my father and I went to inspect him. We glanced at each other apprehensively: red and wriggling behind the glass, the Bergen baby looked old and scrawny, hairless and wizened; like a boiled shrimp. We spotted others we liked better but went back to make the best of things. It would take some getting used to.

It didn't. If anyone had had reservations at first, no one remembered; Kris erased all doubt. Fair-haired, blue-eyed, he grew to be a golden boy who shone with love and spilled with laughter. Never, we thought, had there been a more beloved baby or one who brought more joy to those about him. He dazzled us all and we hovered around him like planets around the sun.

My mother radiated a new sense of serenity, and my father, at sixty, was born again with his new boy. For me, it was the beginning of a bond of such depth and intensity that I was often baffled by it, overwhelmed by the love I felt. Having waited years for my brother, I now made up for lost time, appointing myself his champion and protector. He unearthed the maternal in me: I bathed and changed him, fed and rocked him, caring for him like my own child. Impatient for him to wake, and sorry when he went to sleep, I loved him like a brother but also like a son.

Was I ever jealous? The question was beneath my dignity. A fifteen-year-old girl jealous of her long-awaited baby brother? The idea was offensive, contemptible. . . . Of course I was. What else could explain my warped behavior, slipping unnoticed into his nursery while my parents were having dinner to make the strange little choking sounds they heard coming from his room over the dining-room intercom.

After artfully interspersing tiny coughs with muttered curses in an aggravated baby voice, "Cough, cough, *goddammit,* cough, cough, oh, hell"—complaints that came straight from the crib—I returned innocently to the table. Looking up, alarmed, my mother said, "That's not funny, Candy. You really have a sick sense of humor." My father suppressed a grin. Where did she think I *got* it?

It was a testament to my love for my brother that I swallowed my jealousy. He was a child of light, and I a child of shadows. I envied his courage and confidence, his openness and freedom from fear. It was clear to me, in comparing the two of us, that my brother was by far the better deal. How did he happen, this golden child, so giving and outgoing? How did I happen, the solitary, introspective child, afraid of feelings, who preferred to play alone?

First love fell before my sixteenth year. Johnny Mathis was still holding his own; Ray Charles was big and Stevie Wonder still "Little." Movies were such melancholy, tragic romances that we weren't certain romance came any other way: *Splendor in the Grass, Strangers When We Meet, Breakfast at Tiffany's.* I sequestered myself in my room, talking on the phone, usually to Connie, and lying in bed listening to maudlin love themes on my stereo. Pounded by the thundering, twin pianos of Ferrante and Teicher, pining for my prince to come, I would drift into sleep and dreams of romance.

The last place I expected to find it was on a blind date. A girlfriend fixed me up with Terry Melcher, Doris Day's son, describing him as someone with "a beige Chrysler and a great sense of humor."

"A *beige* Chrysler?" I asked, slightly horrified. "Isn't that a little understated? What kind of shoes does he wear?"

As stated in my Shoe Code: Cordovans and wingtips could keep walking, traditional tennies would never lead you wrong, moccasins I'd follow anywhere, and Italian loafers could sweep me off my feet. Shoe fixation was but the first tiny weapon in a budding arsenal of defenses.

The first thing I saw, then, when I met my blind date was that he wore Italian loafers. Terry was twenty, had quit college, and now had a job at Columbia Records, where his mother was under contract. His resemblance to her was striking: he was tall, blond, blue-eyed and freckled, with a great infectious grin.

I liked him at once: he was special, someone whose luck would never run out. There was a touch of Tom Sawyer about him in spirit as well as in looks—a taste for tricks and trouble, an instinct for truth. He was funny and furtive, foxy and playful. There was a sweetness and innocence about our time together, a sense of safety. Our parents thought it was darling. At last I was in love.

Because of the size of my appetite and the impressive volume of my food intake, Terry took to calling me "The Sherman Tanker" ("Tanker" for short) as a term of endearment. If it wasn't what Kirk Douglas called Kim Novak, well, that was okay. And when, parked in his car in my driveway, Terry turned and whispered to me tenderly, "I love you, Tanker, honest I do," it was pure poetry to me, music to my ears.

Love was not quite like the movies—sometimes tortured, not yet tragic—but it was also full of fun: Number 11s at Hamburger Hamlet, malts at Wil Wright's, Sammy Davis at the Coconut Grove, Lake Arrowhead with Terry's parents, Newport Beach with mine, and the famous egg fights.

In time Terry got itchy. Terry's friends were older, racier members of Beverly Hills' Junior Rat Pack—Frank Sinatra's kids, Dean Martin's kids, Danny Thomas's kids. Hollywood's young elite. His life was just beginning, becoming his own. It was fast, it was free; I was not. This was no place for a high school senior in saddle shoes who was flunking Latin and getting grounded. I saw him less and less; love was getting more and more like the movies.

Soon, I began to hear that he was driving around town in his convertible with a platinum blonde named Jackie DeShannon. She was twenty-four and a rock star. She wore a hot-pink sheath with matching high heels. She had a hit single. She did not have homework.

I received a hastily written farewell citing irreconcilable age differences and hoping we'd always be friends. I thought I would die; I didn't. But under my senior yearbook picture that year (as under hundreds of others inspired by Natalie Wood's reading of it in the film) ran the quote "Though nothing can bring back the hour of splendor in the grass . . ." You know the rest.

That year, my last at Westlake, I was elected May Queen from the senior class. Since first grade I had watched wistfully as, year after year on May Day, the May Queen made her way, to the strains of "Pomp and Circumstance," down the Great Lawn. There, enthroned with her court, she received the homage of the rest of the school—maypole dances, Mexican hat dances, Philippine folk dances and modern dances in baggy leotards to the love theme from *Romeo and Juliet*. A true girls' school tableau.

Though my past was hardly heaped with laurels, May Queen was not the only honor I reaped at school. I was student body vice president, had received awards in sports and had made an occasional honors list. But *this* honor, oddly, I felt was mine to receive; the election struck my secret special self as a redundant procedure.

How was it I had come to feel so entitled?

From birth, I, my family, my life had seemed different, special. And deep down, despite all my insecurity, I was convinced, paradoxically, that I was *privileged*—as by some divine right of queens.

Mine were no run-of-the-mill delusions of grandeur; they had been reinforced at every turn, from my early appearances with my father on radio to the death of my turtle, who was buried like a head of state. Even my father's office struck me as some eccentric throne room—swelling with regal memorabilia, rhinestone-studded medallions, gilded awards and trophies that, to a child's eye, glittered like crown jewels. And the hundreds of likenesses of Charlie (a likeness of a likeness) flashed on everything from cuff links to clocks—deified, immortalized, like the head of some great if daffy dynasty.

But the May Queen was not a monarch designated by lineage; there were classmates with families more illustrious than mine. You do not get elected for being Edgar's daughter, Charlie's sister; the vote is primarily visual—an honor accorded to the fair of face. I won the throne because I looked nice on it.

This cosmetic process of selection seemed to me elitist and unfair, but even if I questioned it, on some level I was coming to expect it: since my adolescence, people had told me I was pretty. I was becoming conditioned to the privilege, flattered by being hailed the fairest, even for an afternoon. And it would be years before I would clearly perceive the price the privileged pay. Looks might enhance your sense of entitlement, but they do nothing to build your confidence in your ability to rule the realm.

My coronation was witnessed by my mother and my father, who beamed proudly from the sea of parents, as he filmed the moment with his Bolex. It was my mother's white dress I wore as I wafted up to the throne, "Pomp and Circumstance" thundering from the loudspeakers, and it was she who had helped me get ready. Kneeling on the steps of the platform, flanked by members of my court, I was crowned with spring flowers and took my rightful place on the throne.

One of life's milder moments, but did I take it lightly? No, indeed. Manifest Destiny is serious business. There were burdens that came with a birthright: royal responsibilities, awesome obligations, public protocol, my duty to the people. Uneasy lies the head that wears the crown, even one of flowers. Especially when you wear it for your father.

6

"Your college years," my father said solemnly and often, "are the best years of your life, Candy; they were for me. Now you have your happiest years before you." My father was deeply nostalgic for his cherished college days: glee clubs and football games, fraternities and fellowship. His sentimentality was contagious, and I, too, was carried away by his fond recollections of college camaraderie. Of course, underneath all of that, I sensed, was a long-held expectation that eventually I'd enter the family firm.

After a childhood under palm trees and twelve years of girls' schools, one of the things I looked for in a college was tradition: an ivy-covered campus, trees that turned to flame, wearing a striped school muffler to fall football games, and men. I had no idea yet what I wanted to study—only that I didn't want to study it in California. College should look like it did in the movies: brick bell towers and things called "quads." It should not have palm trees.

In a layout in *Holiday* magazine on Ivy League universities, I found what I was looking for. At the old and distinguished University of Pennsylvania, three-quarters of the student body were men and one-quarter were women. Students were shown picnicking in boaters and blazers on checkered tablecloths on the grassy banks of the Schuylkill; preppy young men and women in madras passed through the school quad—built of brick in the eighteenth century—and ivy was everywhere.

My college wardrobe was impeccably Ivy League: button-down shirts, Shetland crew necks, kilted skirts, pea coat, knee socks and penny loafers. A textbook preppie. In contrast, what we wore in California looked like gaudy resort wear; the telltale pink polka dots and checkered lemon-yellow stayed in the closet at home.

My first semester, I was elected Homecoming Queen (another coronation) and escorted onto the football field at halftime during the Penn-Princeton game while the band blasted out "A Pretty Girl Is Like a Melody" and someone danced around in a tiger suit. In an imitation Chanel suit sashed in red, with matching bouquet of roses, I stood, smiling vacantly, topped with a rhinestone tiara. The following day, the *Philadelphia Inquirer* ran a photograph captioned CHARLIE'S SISTER HOMECOMING QUEEN—*No Dummy She.*

In the early sixties, college campuses were not yet hotbeds of political activity but raucous last gasps of irresponsibility. Berkeley led the political pack, as always, but if the answer, my friend, was blowin' in the wind, it had bypassed Penn. It was a passive, conservative campus; the students of its famous School of Business were more concerned with *mastering* capitalism than with overthrowing it.

The closest I came to political involvement was when Susan Scranton, as president of the Young Republicans (and daughter of the governor of Pennsylvania), and I, as Miss University, were asked to escort Senator Barry Goldwater on stage for a presidential campaign speech on campus.

The sole student protest that year was against the proposed felling of a large tree to clear space for new campus construction. Along with others, I took my turn carrying a sign that read, simply, "S.O.S." (Save Open Space), marching all afternoon in a picket line around the giant elm.

• • •

As a college freshman, my thoughts inevitably turned to the future. What did I want to do with it?

As a child, what I had wanted to be was Brenda Starr—crack reporter in high-fashion clothes on dangerous assignments and on the odd jungle expedition to find her Mystery Man, Basil St. John. The elusive Basil—tall, dark and dashing, with a patch over one eye—was always disappearing somewhere up the Amazon, from where he sent a sparkly-eyed Brenda black orchids.

Brenda Starr was not on the syllabus in college. This was the East, where people read Camus, not comics. Movies were something you paid to see, not live in, and were hard besides, like homework—black-and-white and boring and in French. "Art films," they called them. New Wave, *Cinéma Vérité*. The whole point of movies, it seemed to me, was that they weren't *vérité,* but *fantaisie.* Still, try telling that to Eastern intellectuals, who thought that not only Hollywood was ridiculous, but all of California as well. It would be years before I saw another "film" in English and in color.

If, as a child in the West, I dreamed of being Brenda Starr, as a college woman in the East, I discovered Margaret Bourke-White. Photojournalism, at its peak in the forties and fifties, was still flourishing in the sixties, showcased in lush magazines like *Look* and *Life.*

I studied the work of some of its masters: Bresson, Capa, Eisenstaedt; but it was Bourke-White, then struggling with Parkinson's disease, who interested me especially—the quality of her work, her courage, her life. The only woman among *Life*'s first staff photographers, she was skilled, fearless and driven, excelling in what had been until then an exclusive male province, moving with brilliance and fierce independence alone in a man's world.

Poring over photography books in the library, I decided that that was what I wanted to do: explore other people's lives as a photojournalist. I bought an old Pentax and wandered Philadelphia, carrying it with me and shooting anything that moved.

There was a woman I passed often on campus who caught my attention as much for her striking dark looks as for the fact that she wore a Leica around her neck as constantly as other coeds wore circle pins. She was Mary Ellen Mark, then taking a graduate course in photography at Penn, and now considered by many to be this generation's Bourke-White.

She would become one of my best and oldest friends, but when we met I was awed by her single-mindedness—that she spent summers on scholarship in Turkey photographing rather than on a beach or beside a pool. She became my mentor, encouraging and supporting me and even procuring for me a key to the school's photo lab, where she taught me to process and print my own film.

Working in the silence and soft darkness, I swirled the paper in the trays of hypo, rubbing it gently with my fingers as the images gradually appeared. Printing fascinated me as much as photography; spellbound, I closeted myself dreamily in the darkroom, often emerging eight to ten hours later, shocked to find it was night.

Could I make a career as a photojournalist? Would I know how? Was that what I really wanted? Watching Mary Ellen working day and night, heart and soul—living, breathing photography—it quickly became clear to me that I did not have her courage, her commitment.

The work I did that summer did little to develop it. During the year I'd had offers to work as a model, and at the end of the spring term I went to New York and signed with Eileen Ford, who started me at the top hourly rate of sixty dollars. It was flattering to my vanity, if not constructive to my character, and I justified the frivolousness of it by the prospect of financial independence, reasoning that it would enable me to buy new cameras and equipment. The part of me that knew better kept quiet; it had not had much practice speaking up.

Many models I met that summer felt called upon to rationalize their highly profitable participation in the profession that was ultimately degrading and self-denying—in which success was achieved for all the wrong reasons: because of how you looked and in spite of who you were.

Exotic, long-limbed girls would defend their intelligence defiantly, trying desperately to climb out of the morass of "mindless models." Arriving for bookings at photographers' studios that vibrated with rock music and popped with strobes, they would produce from their bulging models' bags the entire *Alexandria Quartet,* the complete words of Dostoevski in paperback, a volume of Kierkegaard. The counters were covered with them as the models began the chilling process of transforming themselves from fresh, young, uncertain girls into sleek, shellacked creatures, dazzling birds of prey.

These tricks of the trade were acquired with time and endless self-dedication. One photographer cast down his camera and threw up his hands despairingly, declaring that unless I had my teeth filled and my eyebrows plucked, I could never hope to model. A hairdresser suggested electrolysis to improve my low hairline and a *Vogue* beauty editor complained loudly that I was "much too *healthy,*" squeezing my shoulders and arms distastefully and asking accusingly, "Are you a *swimmer*?"

I ignored the rest and went to work on the makeup; it took me time to get the hang of it. For weeks, I walked around—eyes glued half-shut with the surgical adhesive for my false lashes, cheeks black and bruised from excessive shading, mouth pale and parched with layers of lip gloss and Erace—looking not so much like a fashion model as a victim of assault and battery.

But time improved these minor skills and, in spite of a low hair-line, uneven teeth, thick eyebrows and healthy flesh, I did quite well that summer, working steadily and receiving top pay.

Back at college in the fall, ads I posed for in the summer began running in magazines, appearing on posters. It was the "Tawny" ad in particular that did me in. A Revlon campaign for a new line of cosmetics called Tawny showed me, head coyly cocked, lying on my stomach, bare-backed, hugging a leopard-skin pillow to my beaded breast, my fingers flashing false red nails.

It ran in major magazines and turned up in the window of every drugstore on campus (there were only two). Girls would smirk and snicker as they passed, "Hi, *Tawny,*" and, as fraternity-pledge pranks, boys were assigned to call me for coffee dates. I had cer-tainly asked for it.

With the tarnished Tawny money I bought two new Nikons and became photo editor of a school magazine. I chose art history, painting, journalism and creative writing as my elective courses, figuring the first two would help me with color and composition in photography and the second two with written reportage.

Joining the Penn Players in the unlikely role of Alma in Tennes-see Williams's *Summer and Smoke,* I received the school's awards for Best Actress and Most Creative Student. Still, I was ashamed of my half-baked campus notoriety and felt like a fallen woman, ridiculed and lampooned. Obviously I exaggerated much of it; nev-ertheless, I scurried along self-consciously to class—head down, shoulders hunched, eyes averted—avoiding even the most casual glance.

School grew uncomfortable, and in the spring, with my mod-eling money, I took a lease on a New York apartment and began spending more time there and less in Philadelphia. The laxness of my attitude did not go unnoticed by the faculty. One day the dean of women called me to her office to comment on my increasing absences and to caution me about my future. When she asked, "Tell me, Candice, what will you be in ten years without your BA?" it was to me the Voice of Doom. I blinked and swallowed hard, trying to contemplate life without my Bachelor of Arts degree. It was a dark and depressing thought, a doomed life sentence: branded as another pretty blonde and banished to California. Though I'd made it into a punch line by dinnertime, the question cut clean to the core.

Core? What core? The point was, I *had* no core; *that* had always come from others. From birth, I'd been suckled on the approval of others, lightheaded from the rush of fame. What would happen if I went *without*? Would I go into withdrawal? Fade into the Great Unknown? Anonymous Anonymous?

It served as the only sense of self-definition—this lifelong feedback, this indirect acclaim—for someone who hadn't had a chance yet to find out who she was. I'd come to rely on *others* to tell me.

Was the dean sounding a warning? If I continued as a "semicelebrity," what would I be like in ten years' time? Without something of substance to ground me? Why wouldn't I sacrifice life as "Charlie's sister" for the chance at a real life of *serious* pursuits? Wasn't I prepared, for once, to pursue a profession, a higher interest, in relative *obscurity*? Wasn't I even willing to try?

All around me, other women were: Mary Ellen; my roommate, Marcia Weiss, who had decided to go for her PhD in psychology; my roommate-to-be, Rusty Unger, who aspired to become a writer. Women who wanted to be architects, scientists, painters, lawyers— and *pretty* women, too, who didn't trade on their looks; women not defined by their beauty but by who they were; women who wanted to make something more of their lives.

I contrasted these young women with the woman I could so easily become: one of many movie actresses whose looks were paramount in a profession that didn't permit them to age, whose personae were invented by their publicists, and whose self-esteem depended on the size of their billing.

As my friends and I discussed our futures and I mentioned the offers I'd had over the years to test for films, my friends looked bewildered. Why, they wondered, would I want to do that? Hollywood was not real, movie stars were not serious. I had to agree. But how could I explain to them that Hollywood was also home, and that making movies had always been expected of me?

Though I did well in courses that came easily to me at Penn, classes I enjoyed—creative writing, art history, journalism—I made no effort at subjects I did not: political theory, opera, physics. I had no idea *how* to make an effort; most things had always come so easily for me that I had developed no discipline or patience for those which did not.

When I received three As in the courses in which I was able and two Fs and an Incomplete in those in which I was not, I think I was stunned that the teachers had not discreetly closed an eye to my shortcomings but had *reported* them instead. Habit had taught me to rely on the celebrity status that had always seen me through, but here it was that very "celebrity" (along with my attitude) that my professors resented, and in some cases were trying, admirably, to counteract.

I had managed to flunk two guaranteed "guts"—painting and opera—and not to finish a third. Painting, lasting two periods, was my earliest course, and inevitably I arrived late. The last class was nude drawing, and the only seat left by the time I got there was the one in back of the model's. After handing in bare-assed sketches for an entire semester, I was, understandably, given an F. I missed my opera final because of measles, but wouldn't have passed it anyway.

To my knowledge, it was the first time anyone had ever received a failing grade in music *and* painting; my schoolmates were astonished, some even impressed.

The administration wasn't. If I'd planned to turn over a new scholastic leaf in the fall, the college had other ideas. The letter read:

Dear Mr. Bergen:

The Executive Committee of the College for Women at its recent meeting reviewed the record of your daughter, Candice, and found that she had an "F" in Art 218, an "F" in Music 30, and an "Incomplete" in Art 140. The Committee therefore decided to drop Candice from the rolls at this time. In addition, Candice has not been accepted by a major department and in view of her total academic record major acceptance would be most difficult.

It is hoped that Candice will find success and happiness in some other field.

Sincerely,

What possible success and happiness could I ever hope to find now, facing an ominous future without my BA? Ashamed and miserable, I bought a stack of "Love comics" and boarded the train to New York. What was going to become of me?

Though I was indignant and flippant on the surface, the letter's impact on me was dramatic. I read my copy over and over in disbelief. Such a thing had never happened to me before—this flat statement of failure and rejection. For the first time in my life, I had not been made an *exception to the rules*. I, to whom rules did not apply. I, who casually manipulated or ignored them, counting on people's willingness to waive them in my case. My special case.

At Penn, though they gave me every encouragement, they did not have time for students who were unserious, who weren't willing to make the grade. The University did not make exceptions of pretty girls with famous fathers. And I always respected them for that.

• • •

*S*uccess *and happiness in some other field.*

As it happened, I did not have to face my academic failure for long. Sidney Lumet had contacted me before I left college. He was going to direct a film of Mary McCarthy's bestseller, *The Group.* He'd seen a photograph of me hugging a leopard-skin pillow (or a leopard), he said, and was interested in me for the part of Lakey.

We met in New York. At first I was reluctant. But he explained it was going to be a "little film," a "New York film," in black-and-white, with unknown actresses. Was I interested? Maybe life without a BA wouldn't be so bleak after all. Of course I was interested. It was only for the summer; it wasn't a *commercial* film; I could go back to photography later, I rationalized. I called my parents to tell them.

They were surprised but pleased. "What kind of part is it?" my mother asked. "The part of Lakey," I explained. "A small but *pivotal* part. She's described in the book as 'mysterious—the Mona Lisa of the Smoking Room.' She leaves early in the film and returns at the end as a lesbian."

A pause. My parents, in unison: "A *lesbian?* Candy, you're just nineteen and the first part you want to play in a film is a *lesbian?* Why can't you start by playing an ingenue? What's wrong with that?"

"This is an *art film,*" I explained patronizingly, "not a Ross Hunter production—"

"What's wrong with Ross Hunter? He's very successful. You used to *love* Sandra Dee."

"The reason I want to do *this* film," I sighed, "is because it isn't a commercial Hollywood production but a movie by *New York* filmmakers who are serious about their *art.*"

If I was following in my father's footsteps, I was certainly going to rebel a little along the way.

Under the Rainbow

7

A new nineteen and on my own—my own decisions, my own rules, my own apartment, my own income, my own agent, my own bills, my own Blue Cross. The gate to the childhood garden of innocence forever shut behind me, I entered a new and unknown world filled with dark and unseen dangers—a world where "in case of accident or disability," I would be "covered."

My first milestone was in a brownstone, a tiny apartment in the East Sixties which my mother not only found for me but helped me to furnish as well. The decor was all in white and varying shades of green—like Oz, the Emerald City—and *almost* elegantly appointed, with Macy's French reproductions. Embellished with my own girlish accents, it looked like a dorm room in Versailles. My mother was responsible for its more tasteful aspects. The giant poster proclaiming "The Great Karmi—See Him Shoot a Cracker Off a Man's Head," which showed a man in a turban aiming a shotgun at a trembling, half-clad native with a saltine on his head; the electric train set; the large antique carousel horse; the life-sized, glass-eyed, moth-eaten, sausage-shaped stuffed lion were mine. In my closets, between pea coats and jeans, hung the wrong clothes with the right labels—often worn all at once: Gucci, Pucci, Hermès, Dior. And so I lived in seedy splendor, proudly supporting myself in a style somewhere between Holly Golightly and Princess Grace.

Between modeling at the top daily rate—then over a thousand dollars—and a tidy beginner's salary for *The Group,* I eagerly paid all my expenses. And it was no small point of pride that from the age of nineteen on I never again asked my father for money.

Money had assumed murky and mysterious powers in our house, shrouded in secrecy. My father, reputed to be a man of some wealth and business sense, shrewd in his investments, trusted no one with money and had lawyers cross-checking lawyers' accounts of accountants waiting to prey on the "artistic temperament." Yet, without saying as much, and in spite of a lifestyle quite to the contrary, he had me convinced we were poor.

Money was handily made, intelligently managed, conservatively spent, but never mentioned. Except in the abstract. Somberly. With the respect accorded a wrathful god. It was a divine currency that carried high favor, the serene stamp of approval, unqualified love.

My lunging at the leash was in part a great impatience to be let loose in life. But an equal part of it was an instinctive hunch that it would please my father—a self-made man who revered achievement, had a healthy respect for money and firmly believed in earning one's own way. Early self-sufficiency was surely a flashy step in the father-daughter love dance, the eternal pas de deux of paternal approval.

Like a tango, it took two. My father was proud but uneasy over my early independence, and joked about no longer being able to threaten me with disinheritance. If from that point on I never asked him for money, he in turn never offered me any. And over the years, the duet became a duel—a monetary mano a mano where there was no winning and no giving in.

No matter how much money I made, he charged me—often rightly—with fiscal malpractice. When I turned twenty-one, he explained, in a lecture on the value of money, that because of my financial irresponsibility he had moved the age of my inheritance to twenty-five—at which point, on the same grounds, it was moved to thirty. The possibility that I might hook up with a fortune hunter or someone even more economically inept than I worried him some; but it was above all my persistent lack of interest in my financial affairs that drove him to distraction.

In principle I agreed with him completely. I had never assumed that his money was by rights mine, and I had no trouble earning money on my own. Clearly, I was not in need. Yet I sensed that if I were, a request for assistance would be resented, and that the possibility of my asking was one he dreaded.

That he withheld funds pending proof of maturity was, on his part, a wise and sensible decision. But some less lucid part in me perceived his actions differently: What it felt like was being turned down for a life loan because of inadequate assets, insufficient worth. The long-promised but constantly postponed windfall easily became confused with the approval I so craved from my father, which he seemed to dangle, like a great and gleaming carrot, always just out of reach.

If I had hoped to sneak in through destiny's back door by taking a small part in an "art film," my cover was blown from the beginning: before production had even started, *The Group* began to attract wide attention. There was great curiosity about this slightly scandalous book being brought to the screen, and controversy over who would play its many characters. As the public's interest increased so did the studio's, and the budget and scope of the film expanded. It was now to be shot in color and its unknown cast to be given a massive publicity launch.

"The Group"—Joan Hackett, Elizabeth Hartman, Shirley Knight, Mary-Robin Redd, Joanna Pettet, Jessica Walter, Kathleen Widdoes and me—was photographed individually and collectively for *Life, Look, Vogue,* and *Mademoiselle.* Presented at a press conference in the penthouse suite of the New York Hilton, we were spaced along a spiral staircase winding down to hundreds of waiting men below—a montage suggesting that we would be auctioned off, one by one, to the highest bidders. At the foot of the staircase, the impatient pack of photographers expecting cheesecake got, instead, seven serious New York actresses and one daughter of a celebrity, all tense and tight-lipped in somber high-necked dresses. It was no tabloid tableau, and they snapped disgustedly, "Come on, girls, for Christ's sake." "Let's have a smile, sweetheart, *please*." "Jesus, what deadheads." "You girls look like you're at a wake!" "Someone give the girls some lilies!"

When it came time for us to descend the stairs and take our seats in the salon for the press conference, we passed, red-faced and on the verge of tears, through the pack of disappointed males who cracked, "Look at 'em, they're terrified," and "Not an ass or tits in the group."

Having been weaned in a movie town that was like a movie, I didn't think making a film would be unfamiliar to me. I didn't know anything about acting but—like many red-blooded American girls—I *knew* I could act. Besides, having been successfully miscast in two college plays, I felt confident I knew the ropes.

My real education was about to begin.

In their work, the other girls shone, were altogether secure. They were all hardworking perfectionists, solid professionals with two Oscar nominations and countless theater awards among them. Though ranging in age from their early to late twenties, most of them were highly trained, experienced actresses respected for their work in television, theater and films. They were not movie stars. Acting was their love, their life, and their days were devoted to learning and plying its many and mysterious skills.

Rehearsals began. I was too naive to be nervous until an actress who had a minor role came up to me and said, "I hear you're playing the lesbian. Good part. You have a great chance to make a statement there. Can't generalize your emotions, but a good chance to make a statement." Maybe there was more to this than I thought.

We read through the script and Sidney sent us home to select specific "sense memories" relevant to our class and political period in the story and to start building our "character arc." It was a language I had never heard before; I had no idea what he was talking about and was too ashamed to ask. What is a "sense memory"? How do you build an *arc*? Was I going to get a failing grade in *film,* too? Would I be called before Louis B. Mayer, who would wag a cigar in my face and ask me what I would be in ten years without my character arc?

Growing up in Hollywood, where film was the major industry and export, we were conditioned differently. Stars were born and movies made and "sense memories" never mentioned. People were cast not for "character arcs" but for something called "star quality," which was locked under contract and carefully cosseted.

We grew up believing that those stars were on that screen because they were people we liked watching, who had something the rest of us wanted. They didn't *act* that way—they *were* that way, and when they got together, the last thing they talked about was "acting." What you saw was *them,* not a technique or a craft. Some were just better at being themselves than others.

In old Hollywood, what movie stars made was magic (and money); in New York, what actors made was Art. As a kid from the show-biz side of the tracks, way out West in Sodom and Gomorrah, I had a lot to learn about Art in the East—though it seemed, at times, that New York was inhabited by no one but actors all too eager to explain the difference. Sure, I had met some of these types before—intense young actors who enrolled in classes, "learned their craft," "developed their instruments." But they seemed driven, desperate, obsessed with nothing but themselves and acting. As for acting school: Who needed the humiliation of being a strip of bacon, exploring a day in the life of a tree? I was playing enough parts in real life: this seemed absurd, assaultive, terrifying. If that kind of singular focus was the price of professionalism, I was not willing to pay it.

Shooting began with The Group's graduation—Vassar, Class of '33—in which Sidney had the cast and three hundred extras solemnly sing "Three Blind Mice" until a school song could be composed and dubbed in later. The interior scenes were shot at a studio in Manhattan where we spent most of the first two weeks eating old baked Alaska at a wedding breakfast for one of The Group.

Settling into our dingy dressing rooms at the studio—girls darting to and fro, borrowing books, brewing tea, clothes strewn right and left, signs and sayings tacked on doors—the bustling corridor seemed like a slightly squalid version of Vassar's South Tower rather than dressing rooms above a sound stage—to all appearances, a normal college dorm.

And I—exhilarated to be out on my own, terrified to find myself in such serious company—I settled into the normal routine of a college girl having a summer fling. I stayed out all night dancing, coming home at dawn in time to get my wake-up call and catch a cab across town to the studio. Since I got no sleep at home, I caught up on the set: I slept in the makeup chair while they slapped a base on me; I slept on my dressing-room floor; I curled up in dark corners of the sets—on couches, in bedrooms. As cast and crew tried to shake me into consciousness to kindly appear in a shot, they came to believe that I had some severe form of narcolepsy.

It was fine, fast company I found myself in with this film. Everywhere on the set, actresses were huddled, trancelike, in corners, furiously chewing gum, quickly putting up a hand to ward off intruders before an emotional scene, explaining tersely, "I'm *preparing*." Even if I'd had a scene that required preparation, I wasn't sure how to go about it. What did they think about there in those corners, eyes squeezed shut, "Do Not Disturb" on their faces, before taking their places on the set and bursting into tears on cue? I was amazed: How do they do that? Is that what actors do?

Naturally, some of the girls resented me; certainly, in their shoes, I would have done the same. Pauline Kael, who wrote about the filming of the movie in an angry article for *Life* called "A Goddess Upstages the Girls," summed it up. Calling me a "golden lioness of a girl . . . perfectly pleasant to talk to, a nice big girl," she went on to identify problems that irked the rest of The Group. "Here she is, an intelligent young girl, beginning—despite her disclaimers—a career in the movies, and she doesn't appear interested enough even to stay awake and observe. It is as if she hasn't yet discovered what acting is all about, not even enough to pay attention to the other girls when they are doing it. And they are *good*, most of these girls; they are something to watch. Here is the odd thing about movies. These seven are all lovely girls, used to playing the beautiful young ingenue, used to being the center of attention. But Bergen is a natural goddess. And the movies, like religious myths, dote on goddesses. . . . The camera feasts on natural beauty. It seems unfair of course, but there it is—nature is unfair."

At the film's finish, ten years after the wedding, the girls reunite for the funeral of one of The Group who plunged out of a window at the Waldorf. Sidney made two master shots, then came in for close-ups on each of us; I watched as each girl deftly took her turn. Mine was last. Sidney suggested I, too, might show some emotion here; even for Lakey, a tear would not be out of line. After all, she *had* been in love with the lissome deceased, according to the accusations of the distraught husband, played by Larry Hagman.

Now it was my turn to prepare. Nervously heading for a dark corner as I had seen the others do, perching on an apple box in my veiled bowler and black satin riding habit (elegantly mannish even in mourning), I tried to remember what I'd absorbed from watching the others: find an experience or emotion in my "life file" comparable to that required for the scene, mentally reconstruct it, and reproduce it, slipping the dredged-up feelings under the dialogue, giving life to the lines. My eyes squeezed shut, I groped in my memory, searching for tragedy. The problem there, of course, was that my past was short and perfect, unblemished even by bad luck.

In the event that you're unable to locate an appropriate experience, the wisdom went, substitute actual people in your life for those in the script. Panicked now as time ran out, I piled people in pale, tufted caskets—my family, my friends, my doorman, my dog. It was no use. The more I tried, the less I felt.

Sidney came over; he'd set up the shot and was ready. "Come on, babe, work on this now."

"But, Sidney, I *am*," I insisted. A makeup man stood by with menthol crystals that could be blown in the eyes and cause tearing in case I couldn't; there was some dishonor attached to this method, and the others never used it.

As soon as I gave up trying to cry, having now failed in Feeling, Sidney began speaking to me softly, catching my concentration, focusing my fractured attention on the scene. "You can't believe it . . . best friend . . . dead. . . . Fight the antagonism with Libby, can't believe it, best friend, best friend, best. . . . Roll 'em. Action."

My throat tightened, my eyes burned; I fought back the tears and played the scene.

"Cut!" Sidney patted me on the shoulder and said it was nice work. If it was nice work, it was his.

Making a movie failed to discourage completely my fantasies of becoming a journalist, and I managed to combine the two, enthusiastically accepting a commission from *Esquire* magazine to record my experiences on the film. This I was more than thrilled to do—

photographing the girls between setups and doggedly taking notes in my dressing room—the crafty cub reporter.

Crafty, perhaps; diplomatic, hardly. Young and self-absorbed, I scarcely suffered from an excess of sensitivity. When it became known (I told anyone who would listen) that I was keeping a journal on the film for *Esquire,* it naturally touched off tempers among a few of The Group. One or two of them were especially incensed by the idea and they steadily grew suspicious. When one day my notes mysteriously disappeared from my dressing room, one of the girls came up to me and said sweetly, "So, Can', sweetheart, how's your article coming?"

"Just peachy, thanks."

"You know, you really ought to be careful with it; people will never trust you again."

"You've got a point there."

"Sure. Wait till your next picture; by then you'll be a better writer anyway. I'm only thinking of *you,* baby, *you* know."

"Uh-huh."

"Besides, honey, you know I love you like a mother but I want to tell you—if you ever, *ever* say anything bad about me, I'll *smear* you. I swear to God, I'll call the columns and have them kill you."

"I've heard they can do that."

"The second that article's out, you're dead. Got it?"

The article came out—a parody of a school essay called "What I Did Last Summer." It was a fast-paced, flippant piece, a shade self-pitying in tone, describing the girls, the days on the set, and my loss of innocence during that slow, steamy summer. It caused a stir and was well received; it did not bring instant death.

Though mine was the smallest part in *The Group,* it was fairly flashy, and, as Edgar's pretty daughter's debut made for catchy copy,

I became a natural publicity angle for the film. A cover article in *Look* with the lead line, "The Making of *The Group*—with Candy Bergen," summarized it neatly: "Snap success in New York as a model and making her first film only puzzle her; like a child with awkward birthday gifts, she seems not to know what to do with her shiny new prospects."

This was true—and there were others who were even more at a loss. I was a publicist's nightmare, and there were many who would have been thrilled never to see me or my shiny new prospects again. The more the publicity, the greater my glibness; my arrogance seemed to increase in a direct ratio with my discomfort. Perspiring publicists would interrupt me hastily, nervously explaining to an interviewer, "I think what Miss Bergen *means* is . . ."—anxious lest I offend yet another segment of the population or, worse still, his boss.

A study in graciousness I was, nary a stone left unturned as I went through late adolescence in print, taking petty potshots in the press. I sideswiped everything from where I grew up—sniping at the surrealism of my hometown, describing Beverly Hills as "a modest suburb of Bel Air with vinyl trees and artificial grass and no garbage cans on the street"—to where I went to school—lamenting "the provincialism of my college campus," and declaring that "the only good thing to come out of Philadelphia is the cream cheese"; to acting—announcing that "actress is synonymous with fool"; to God—forsaking even the Almighty by attacking the hypocrisy of the church, declaring my half-baked atheism in a cover article of a family weekly, of all places, titled "Poor Little Rich Girl," which brought a flood of letters and pamphlets saving my soul.

They weren't the only ones worried about my soul; my parents were hurt and incensed. What had gotten into me? Why was I saying such things? How could I, of all people, be so bitter? So negative? Had my childhood been *so* miserable? My parents *that* cruel? Being born in Beverly Hills *such* a burden? No, no, I would mumble, eyes downcast, head drooping in shame; I didn't know why I did it, I was sorry. It was only that all these people were suddenly *listening* to me, taking notes; my tongue took off without telling me, there seemed to be no stopping it.

It was not as if I were unused to the public eye; but this was my first exposure to the kind of lacerating publicity Pauline Kael wrote in *Life* and it was devastating, perhaps all the more so because I knew her harsh appraisal was astute. Another testy passage said, "She doesn't know how to move, she cannot say her lines so that one sounds different from the one before. As an actress, her only flair is in her nostrils." Kael was on the nose. Nevertheless, I was stunned to be punished so severely on my tentative first time out.

"The Golden Girl," "the new Grace Kelly," "Edgar's daughter," and "Charlie's sister" was "cool," "poised," "candid," and "outspoken." They seemed to have a better idea of who she was than I did, and I met their expectations with a studied indifference that must have been infuriating. It was a bad unconscious choice, a misguided attempt to try to control a destiny that was suddenly getting out of hand. I was being pulled away from myself before I had a chance to find out who that was; furious with myself for caving in so easily to something that had seemed inevitable, defeated in the desire to be someone better.

Ponderously proclaiming my interest in "the intellectual side of the camera," lamely insisting that I wanted to "succeed as a person, not as an actress," I went on, to anyone still awake, "I want to retain my curiosity about everything. Anyone who's not concerned about how they develop as a person is doomed."

Spoken like a true Calvinist. Clearly, I was not merely concerned but obsessed; wondering, perhaps, if I were not doomed already—lost in Movieland, where there were few known survivors. For not only had I made one not-so-"little" film; I'd just accepted an offer to do another. The publicity for *The Group* had caught the eye of producer-director Robert Wise, whose films included *West Side*

Story and *The Sound of Music;* he was preparing to shoot *The Sand Pebbles,* a best-selling novel about American gunboat diplomacy in China in the 1920s. It was a major and prestigious production, due to start in Taiwan in the late fall, starring Steve McQueen. Would I test for the part of the missionary to co-star opposite him?

Would I? Well, since it's only temporary . . . one more couldn't kill me. Could it? This was *Taiwan*—the mystery of the Orient. This was travel. This was Steve McQueen.

This was fate. My atheistic natterings in the press aside, I did worry about my salvation, strongly suspecting that there was no small truth in the ancient belief that the camera steals the soul. The forces pulling me into closer and closer proximity with cameras were clearly stronger than any opposing ones of my own, and still I swore I was not going to let them get me. They were not going to steal *my* soul, by God, and, like a woman with her purse in midtown, I clutched it fiercely to my chest.

"Tell me, what's it like being so beautiful? Is it hard to be so beautiful?" grins the generous, genial talk-show host. Turning to the audience, gesturing to me, "Isn't she beautiful? How did you get to be so beautiful?"

"Oh, gee, Merv, I don't know. I'm not beautiful"—flushed, self-conscious. Eyes modestly averted, demurely downcast.

"Do you ever get tired of hearing it, though? You know, the constant compliments, people always telling you how beautiful you are. . . ."

"Oh, gosh, I don't know, I don't really think about it all that much. . . ."

When my article on *The Group* ran in *Esquire,* people refused to believe I wrote it and persistently asked who the real author was. Hold it, pal, quit patronizing. There's someone *in* here, you know.

Something about the way I looked seemed to matter so much to other people; in fact, for a time, it seemed to be the *only* thing that mattered, leaving me to feel beside the point, practically an intruder on my looks.

In photos of me taken then, I see something of what made them take notice: a confused young woman, posing ridiculously, eyes heavenward, nostrils flared, already beginning to believe them. A girl growing armored and arrogant, trying too successfully to hide her terror. Trying to be whatever people expected of her, trying to take her looks as seriously as they did—and doing pretty well at it, too.

Men seemed to want me to be more than I was, and women to want me to be less. That how I looked made so much difference to people completely confounded me, and I developed a round-shouldered, head-ducked shamble to discourage attention I knew I didn't deserve.

Yet, in no time, I was hooked on the flattery habit. It was reassuring to a girl of nineteen, insecure and eager to be liked. In New York I'd quickly fallen in with a glib and glamorous crowd on whose periphery I hovered apprehensively in my Puccis, self-conscious about shaky social credentials in a tough and tony crowd. They were that cross section of jet set, haute monde, café society and art world that would come to be known in the seventies as the Beautiful People, or B.P.

My qualifications—my looks and my small portion of fame—seemed tenuous next to theirs. For this crowd was comprised of European nobility (Hohenloes, von Furstenbergs, Poniatowskis, Pignatellis) and American dynasty (Kennedys, Cushings, Vanderbilts, Fords); of Greek tycoons and Italian industrialists; of high-strung or strung-out heirs and heiresses; and of a few celebrity artists—Dalí, Capote, Mailer and Warhol.

I was dazzled dumb by all of it, flattered to run in such fast company, thrilled even to have a peek. *Here* was *acting:* if I was over my head in work that summer, unsure how to perform my part, it may have been partly because I was working so hard at the role I'd selected in real life.

When during this string of social summer nights I was introduced to a tall and elegant Austrian count, an "older man" of thirty-seven, I was riveted as much by his innate sense of superiority as by his strong resemblance to Stewart Granger. He was intelligent and refined, and my insecurity was the perfect complement to his sense of droit du seigneur. When he peered at me across a crowded dinner table and exclaimed, "Good God, what have you done to your hair? You look positively *bovine*," I blushed the color of my scampi and slid down in my chair. Who could resist such a man?

In no time I was putty in his hands—in the hands of this older, assertive man; in the hands that looked so much like my father's, I noticed at once. Even in attitude, they were much the same. Formal in manner, distant and dignified at times, affectionate and approachable at others.

He swept me off my feet, and then off to Europe. *The Group* and its nerve-racking publicity were over; *The Sand Pebbles* wasn't to begin until November. So off we went to the Continent, first for a visit to the count's ancestral home, then for the fall bird-shooting season.

This was my introduction to real aristocracy, in droves: people of title, the distinguished issue of some of Europe's oldest families. "Old" is the operative word here; one would have thought *they* had been alive for hundreds of years, rather than just their family names. Their voices were strained with chronic boredom, their features frozen with eternal fatigue.

Even their houses were remarkably, unrelievedly ancient; the very air was humid, heavy with age. Their interiors seemed to indicate that the families within them went back to before the beginning of time; for these were rooms where time had obediently stopped somewhere just before the Industrial Revolution, where high-ceilinged rooms were quiet and cryptlike, musty with the dust of ages. The heavy fringed drapes, swagged back with silken cords, shut out the present and enclosed the past, making the rooms even more oppressive—even more *impressive*—in their cool and stately gloom.

Especially impressive to one from sunny Southern California, where it was difficult to distinguish the interiors of houses from the outsides—the rooms were so bright and airy, so flooded with light, pale and pastel, open and new. There was not much in those rooms one could point to and say, "Oh, that's been in my family for years."

Being a ventriloquist's daughter from Beverly Hills didn't get you very far in this crowd. These were legitimate aristocrats, not Hollywood royalty; not imposters, like me, who had grown up under the delusion that I was a princess, who was only crowned Queen of the May. This crowd knew the difference; *these* princesses were *real*.

And these people looked sideways at show-biz folk, a colorful but shifty bunch toward whom the proper attitude was cautious curiosity. The American West was, to them, Frontierland (though they found San Francisco "charming"); a place with no past, devoid of culture, filled with movie stars and cattle rustlers. When, during dinner parties in these houses, guests were introduced—"The Prince of This," "Le Baron de That," "*Tu connais la Comtesse*," "Have you met the Princess?"—I fumbled with my French and my forks, stung with the shame of being "*Miss* Bergen from Hollywood," whose father was in the "show" business, famous for his dealings with dummies.

Then there was the especially unfortunate part of having to explain to European nobility what *my* father did, when most of theirs had never done anything except shoot animals—the sole subject for which they showed any enthusiasm.

"My father is a ventriloquist," I would begin.

"What on earth is *that?*"

Oh, God. "Well, he has these dummies—large dolls, sort of—

and he talks to them, or makes them talk; well, they talk to each other, actually—"

"Really! How amusing. And where does he do that?"

"On the radio."

"*Talks* to *dolls* on *radio*. How extraordinary."

After a while, I just said he was in real estate.

I am ashamed now of my shame then, and it never occurred to me that *my* background might be more exotic than theirs—that Bergens had McCarthys and Snerds in *their* family tree, rabbits in hats, cards up sleeves, and spoke, if not in many languages, in many voices.

And I had a tad of that talent as well. Arch and eager, unbelievably affected, I now spoke with just a trace of transatlantic lisp—in a voice that had nothing whatever to do with who I was or where I came from. I don't know where I dredged it up—it was just a ridiculous social accessory of the time. That's how *those* people talked and, having inherited a talent for mimicry, that is soon how I talked, too.

In no time at all I had mastered it. The sibilant *s*, the phlegmatic intonation, the veneer of contempt. I was very good at it, sounding as if I'd learned English from nannies at a very young age, as a second language, with hardly a *trace* of accent. Which was precisely the effect I was aiming for—except it was somewhat awkward when people asked me how it was that I spoke such excellent English and I answered, "I'm from California."

In the same spirit of adventure, I accompanied the count on the annual shoot, covering inner terror with outer composure, wondering desperately what one wore to kill birds in. Pheasant, it seemed, were found in Austria and Czechoslovakia, partridge in Spain. But *hunting* them were the rarest birds of all—aristocrats on a shoot. In the whole period over which I had observed them, it seemed the only time I saw them truly happy. Driven by a sense of God-given purpose, swelling with manliness, they were One with their guns and the world.

Here in the dark, cold, early air before dawn, waiting expectant-
ly behind their blinds for the moment when day would break and
the beaters would begin flushing the birds toward them—here the
world was as it had always been, before it careened off course. Not
a feeling easy to come by for people who still believed, in the sixties,
in the divine right of kings. And so they sat stoically in the dampness
and the chill, shotguns at their sides, and waited for the birds to fly
overhead.

As the sky began to lighten and the beaters began to move slowly
forward, I noticed a trembling in the hands of some of the hunters.
In some, it was so marked that I wondered how they managed to
take accurate aim. (In fact, they didn't always—elsewhere that year,
I'd heard, Franco's daughter-in-law was wounded in the rear end by
a shotgun that discharged by accident.) Later, someone identified
the trembling I had seen as "hunter's passion," or, I suppose, the
fever of the hunt. And it was this short, sweet rush of adrenaline for
which they really waited there in the darkness. Hunter's passion.
Hunter's rush. It all looked like killing to me.

The birds burst suddenly from the brush, whooshing overhead
in a last bid for freedom. The hunters let fly, blasting away. Pheasant fell right and left, crashing like weird, exotic aircraft, tiny planes
with tail feathers. The doomed and luckless birds bit the dust all
around us where they lay, ruffled copper breasts heaving wildly, feet
flicking in farewell.

The loaders piled the richly plumed birds into sacks, carried
them back to camp and neatly laid them out, dozens of them, row
upon row, in a kind of plumed Persian carpet. Behind them posed
the solemn hunters, shotguns crooked through elbows, in khakis
and tweeds and Tyrolean hats and custom-made boots (broken
in by valets), flanked by their loaders and beaters—taciturn local
peasants in berets and tattered turtlenecks.

Pheasant near Vienna and Prague, then on to partridge in
Madrid, where we moved in a motorcade. Here the birds were

small—soft gray mousy things that rained like hail in a steady patter on the heads of hunters below. The loaders deftly scooped up the fallen panting heaps of fluff, neatly wringing their necks and slipping their heads into the wire loops fastened to their belts in one quick, clean movement. The number of birds swinging from the loops on their waists increased as the men moved efficiently, noiselessly—but for the small clicks of tiny necks snapping—as they went about their methodical harvest.

Their spirits high, their shells and energies spent, the hunters returned to camp, where they gently cleaned their guns, lovingly oiling the slate-gray barrels (using sometimes the finer oil from the skin around their noses), sensuously caressing the cool blue steel with a tenderness absent in their relations with people.

In Madrid, the camp was an endless empty field outside the city where, in the few hours after our arrival before dawn, there miraculously materialized an enormous snow-white tent that gave shade to banquet tables set with silver salvers, gleaming tureens, flatware and crystal. Tablecloths fluttered prettily in the breeze; immaculate waiters in crisp white jackets and stiff bow ties stood sentinel at the tables, helping the guests to their seats, filling their goblets with wine and serving them delicate dishes brought in great haste from fine restaurants in Madrid. Then we would return, in caravan, to the city; nap, shop, and reconvene for dinner.

In spite of such a grueling schedule, the count and his kind all made time to chuckle about finding someone "suitable" to marry, a woman who could hope to qualify as a "country countess," their euphemism for a wife. Did I want to be a "country countess"? The proposal was obliquely put to me.

No, certainly I did not. I could see me now, sedated by the life of an ersatz noblewoman, confined to the country in cashmere sweater sets and English tweeds, doomed to roam the land alone in a subtle loden green. Drawling out to my husband through the mist, "Did you have a good *shoot,* dear?" as he trudged home, shotgun still smoking, at the end of a long day killing deer. Though I had flirted with the fantasy of me in a photo sprawled on a watered-silk sofa across the pages of *Town and Country*, "Countess Candice of Paris and New York," these were not people to spend a lifetime with. They were to be observed in the spirit of Margaret Mead in Samoa, and moved beyond. No, the answer was no.

That suited everyone just fine, in the end; especially the count's mother, a princess from a tiny principality (like me) who seemed more like the queen in *Snow White*. I was a match made in Hollywood rather than heaven for her well-born, inbred son, and I could see her dispatching her royal huntsman to bring her back my heart.

My jet set days were over.

Modeling, movies, appraising stares, seductive smiles, suspicious looks, eager men and wary women, declarations of love too soon in coming, proposals of marriage from men who wore monograms over their hearts, French chocolates, floral offerings. Once again, it was too much, too fast.

The last time I'd felt this way, I had begged to be sent to Switzerland. This time, I already had my ticket in hand.

8

I had mapped out an idiosyncratic, month-long route to the Far East: New York to Rome, Beirut, Damascus, Cairo and Calcutta before the last leg of the trip to Hong Kong and on to Taiwan. Waiting at the airport for my flight to Rome, I was struck by my overwhelming freedom: For some time now I had had no curfews, no homework, no dorm rules, no dress codes. Yet years of conditioning made me feel like I was sneaking out of school. God knows I'd been punished for lesser offenses, shorter excursions, and this time I was going around the world—at the beginning of fall semester—and I hadn't even signed out. Not only would I not be back by midnight, I would miss my midterms, finals. Alone at the airport, anxious to board, I glanced nervously over my shoulder, waiting for the World Dean of Women to swoop down upon me waving her almighty BA. Instead, the first in a long series of boarding cards crossed my palm and I was on my way.

Ancient civilizations and textbook temples once amorphous in school took sudden shape for me in those parts of the world where they began: Baalbek, Byblos, Luxor . . . In Philadelphia, the mere mention of Alexander's library had been enough to send my head crashing onto my desk; in Alexandria, I wandered for hours in the library museum, mesmerized by the achievements of an empire that only months before had induced deep sleep. Revved up from racing place to place, I arrived in Taiwan, as scheduled, in late November, excited and ready for more.

Taiwan was what they call a "rough location." In 1965, Taipei was far from the Eden of the Orient, the garden spot of the Far East. The city was famous for its spectacular National Museum and its exotic brothels (not necessarily in that order—especially for the troops sent there from Vietnam for a week of R & R). It had no discernible traffic pattern: the thousands of taxis and pedi-cabs bounced off each other routinely like fun-fair bumper cars; and municipal plumbing had not yet been introduced, so that one stepped gingerly over the gutters of human waste that crisscrossed a city that simmered in sewage and reeked of latrines.

After our arrival, cast and crew were assembled for Thanksgiving turkey in the Army PX and given a pep talk to prepare us for the long months ahead. We were granted limited passes to the Army base, where, on occasion, old John Wayne movies were shown for the military; but we were advised, for our own safety, to stay in our hotels at night. By day as well, the actors were restricted to hotel grounds and put on official "standby" because of an intricate shooting schedule that, depending on weather, river tides and currents, was hourly subject to change.

If I had my foolish heart set on exploring during this film, using Taiwan as my travel base in the Far East, it served me right to be brought up short. Not only weren't we allowed to leave the island, but we weren't allowed to leave the hotel. My detailed dreams of weekends in Hong Kong, side trips to Saigon, Angkor Wat, Manila—all dashed to smithereens.

My attitude on the film was less than professional, resenting as I did the constraints imposed on the cast—notably *me*. I was unfamiliar with such production procedures: the only location I'd ever been on was the Lower East Side—not the Far East. After waiting for hours without working on the Shanghai dock set, I would wander off at will with my cameras, certain I would never be called, to photograph funeral processions, puppet shows, temple rituals, leper colonies—anything I found of interest in the small rural villages nearby.

In the role of Shirley Eckherdt, missionary-teacher, I was the essence of earnest, the soul of selflessness staring wistfully into the waters of the Yangtze in my summer seersucker and floppy straw hat. An angel of mercy come to save my fellow man. Far from type-casting for one who hadn't lifted a finger to save her fellow pheasant—for a girl hot from a fall shoot. And during the filming, little of Shirley's selflessness rubbed off on me.

One day I disappeared from the set to photograph a Taoist religious ceremony in the middle of a rice paddy where young barefoot initiates walked, entranced, through a bed of white-hot coals, unblinking and unscathed. When I was needed for a large master shot and couldn't be found on the set, they made it without me, only to have to set it up again and reshoot it when I reappeared, moments later, nonplussed. No sooner would *I* return than Steve McQueen would take off on his motorcycle, while the insurance representative blanched, or jump onto the back of a passing water buffalo and get bucked off in the mud. And the crew would settle down to wait again.

Steve was friendly during the shooting, inviting me to dinner in the house rented for him with his wife, Neile, and kids; advising me—in a well-meant attempt to get me to "loosen up"—that what I really needed was to "get it on" with some of his buddies.

His buddies were hardly my idea of heaven: he'd arrived in Taiwan with a commando unit of six stunt men, none under six feet and all ex-Marines. They were like his personal honor guard, and when he moved, they jumped. Hard-drinking, hard-fighting—as time on the island ticked by, McQueen and his gang grew increasingly restless and often spent nights on the prowl, roaming the little city, drinking, heckling, picking fights and pummeling.

Coiled, combustible, Steve was like a caged animal. Daring, reckless, charming, compelling; it was difficult to relax around him—and probably unwise—for, like a big wildcat, he was handsome and hypnotic, powerful and unpredictable, and could turn on you in a flash.

He seemed to trust no one and tried constantly to test the loyalty of those around him, to trap them in betrayal. Yet for one so often menacing, he had a surprising, even stunning, sweetness, a winning vulnerability.

But he seemed to live by the laws of the jungle and to have contempt for those laid down by man. He reminded one of the great outlaws, a romantic renegade; an outcast uneasy in his skin who finds himself with sudden fame and fortune. One had the sense that it came too late and mattered little in the end. And that he tried to find truth and comfort in a world where he knew he didn't belong.

On one of those rare days when the cast and crew were all accounted for, the weather well-behaved, the tide up and the current steady, Wise had just called "Action" on the prow of the gunboat when in the distance what looked like a herd of seals appeared, shiny black heads bobbing, swimming slowly but surely into the background of the shot. A launch was dispatched to investigate and returned with the information that they were not, in fact, seals but Nationalist frogmen training to recapture the Chinese mainland, and so we waited forty-five minutes until they swam past and out of frame.

It was oddball incidents such as these, coupled with unruly tides and uncooperative weather, that helped lengthen our stay in Taiwan from two months to four.

Of that time I worked, at most, three weeks. Over the other thirteen I paced my Golden Dragon Suite in the Grand Hotel (once occupied by Ike and Mamie Eisenhower), read so much I thought my eyes would fall out, and ordered room service. Food assumed mythical proportions, and, by the time I left, so did I.

While eager for "exotic locations," I was innocent of their downside disadvantages. "Exotic" locations were, by definition, difficult: out of touch, hard to reach. Alien. Strange. What's "colorful" for the tourist becomes uncomfortable for the new resident, who, a few weeks after arriving, slides stonily into culture shock from so much color. So many rice paddies. So much night soil. So little plumbing. So much "Mongolian barbecue." So many water-buffalo burgers. So much Mandarin. So little English. And months of reading *Stars and Stripes*.

If my first film was all women, my second was all men: the actors played sailors by day and sailors by night—banding together, tearing up the port, drinking, carousing, "cruising for a piece of ass." I hardly regretted not having that option, but I was lonely nonetheless.

The spar I clung to in a sea of strangers was Richard Attenborough, then one of Britain's leading character actors—a terrifically bright and enthusiastic man who energized a room upon entering it. He was a veteran of long locations and knew how to cope and what to expect. He filled his free time acquiring art and informing himself on the island's politics, making underground contacts with the clandestine opposition on Taiwan.

With him, I felt instantly at ease. Over long Chinese dinners we discussed our interests. He told me that his dream was to direct a film on the life of Gandhi and asked if I would play the cameo role of Margaret Bourke-White, who had photographed Gandhi shortly before his death; he thought I resembled her. I smiled and told him she was one of my heroes; I was flattered to be asked.

He hoped to begin the project as soon as possible, he said, and was funneling all the proceeds of his acting into its development. But in spite of his passionate conviction, for the moment Hollywood wasn't buying it: the life of a little brown man spent in fasting and spinning—who would pay to see such a film?

I made other friends on Taiwan: American bureau chiefs who briefed me on the island and generously took me on tours; US military brass and eccentric Europeans living in self-imposed exile; and Taipei's diplomatic circuit, whose dinner parties I attended. But these were strangely doomed and depressing dinners, for Taiwan, at that time, was the kiss of death for a diplomat and his family—the last living post for officers of protocol, the place diplomats were sent to die. Languishing in their Taiwanese teak, comforted by crates of consular Scotch, they recalled once promising futures, brooded on their failures and ignored the steady glares of resentful wives.

I missed my home. My parents and my brother—my brother, growing bigger by the day. I missed my friends. I missed America. I even missed California: I dreamed of Disneyland and the House of Pancakes. Hamburger Hamlet. Thirty-one Flavors. I had had enough adventure. Enough exotic. I wanted to go home.

Finally, after four months, we moved on for another month's shooting in Hong Kong—the Big Apple of the Orient, Gateway to the East. Now *this* was more like it, more what I had in mind: Hong Kong was humming, and there I was happy; free, at last, to leave my room, discover, explore, make friends. Journalists and old hardcore colonialists led me through the mysterious maze of the walled city, took me sailing on sampans, on rickshaw rides around Macao, and down into dank opium dens. By the time we'd finished in Hong Kong, I'd settled in and made a fine life there; I was in love with the city and hated to leave.

• • •

We assembled again in Los Angeles for the sixth and final month of shooting at the Chinese mission reconstructed on the Fox Ranch in Malibu; I returned to a bigger, blonder brother and the comforts and coziness of home, where I celebrated my twentieth birthday. Yet no sooner had I finished the film than I was off again on another trip, a travel opportunity I couldn't resist.

My old Montesano roommate, Veronica, had written inviting me to visit her in Rhodesia that summer. ("Come on, Bergie—out of Beverly Hills and into the Bush. . . .") The idea appealed to me and I accepted at once, making such fast, last-minute arrangements that when my mother asked me if I'd be home for dinner the following night, I looked away guiltily and said, "Uh, Mom, the thing is, I'm going to Africa."

"Well, you're not going *tomorrow*, are you?"

"As a matter of fact, I am." And the next day I was off, zigzagging through Kenya, Uganda, Tanzania and Zambia on my way, winding up, weeks later, in Rhodesia, where I stayed with Veronica on her father's tobacco farm.

Reading about institutionalized racism is one thing; experiencing it is another. Blacks were casually called "bloody kaffas," considered "monkeys just down from the trees." Challenges from outsiders were deeply resented, as I fast found out; the colonialists seemed passionately united in their beliefs.

There was also the sense that, as white Rhodesians, they were living on borrowed time; black guerrillas allegedly trained in China had been reported crossing over the Rhodesian border from Bechuanaland. The farmers isolated in the countryside were edgy and nervous, running their own border patrols. They took me on weapons raids of the African compounds on the farms, confiscating wooden staves, unwieldy clubs, and crudely forged spears.

From there we would go for dinner to a neighbor's farm, where, in drill shorts and bush jackets, the men barbecued T-bones by the pool, sipping shandies and talking tobacco prices until their crisply coiffed women called them in to dinner, and life seemed to pass idyllically and very much as usual.

.Until darkness fell and it came time for guests to leave. Then the farmer and his family routinely climbed the stairs of the tall stone sleeping tower and, behind a steel door a half-foot thick, bolted themselves in for the night. In the case of a "kaffa attack," they would radio for help on the shortwave on the nightstand to the neighboring farmers, organized and trained as a posse, and stand guard with the guns kept by the bed till they arrived.

From Rhodesia I flew to South Africa, where, in an act of wishful thinking, I put "photojournalist" on my passport form; while I had had an article and photos in *Esquire,* and *Vogue* was to publish another on my trip to Africa, the form asked flatly for occupation, not "What do you want to be when you grow up?" Bobby Kennedy had just made his strong anti-apartheid speech in Johannesburg, and the Afrikaners had had enough of Americans and the press; so the "photojournalist" was asked to leave on the next available plane.

Fortunately it was a flight to Athens. In no hurry to get back to America, I became the leisured academic, the Maven of Mycenae; a regular Kenneth Clark, traipsing from temple to temple, frieze to frieze.

Though no one was asking, there was little I couldn't tell you about Greek columns: Doric or Ionic order? Fluted shaft or smooth? Muscular or elastic? Volutes? Entablatures? Anyone for architraves? In my enthusiasm I even took a side trip to Istanbul to pay homage to Hagia Sofia and its great dome.

After two weeks of peristyles and pottery, a dark, intense Greek introduced himself to me in my hotel lobby. His name was Michael Cacoyannis; he was a director whose last film, *Zorba the Greek,* had been a huge success. He was now preparing to shoot another. Peering at me closely, he asked, "Are you arrogant?"

He was looking for someone like me for his movie, cryptically called *The Day the Fish Came Out;* he had wanted Julie Christie but she had been unavailable. Would I like to spend a few months making a film in Greece? I couldn't think of a better way to spend the summer. There wouldn't be much money in it—six thousand dollars. That would be all right, I assured him, happily accepting, though my agent, when I called to tell him the good news, seemed to disagree.

The money didn't matter: there would be three months in Greece, a summer on the Aegean Sea with Michael and his tiny cast and crew, on a small eccentric film set in the future and made on a shoestring—a complete contrast to the Hollywood extravaganza I'd just finished that spring. We swam during lunch breaks, picnicked at Delphi, gathered wild basil, island-hopped in sailboats and danced outdoors until dawn.

If the film was forgettable (or perversely memorable, acquiring a small but fierce gay following), it was a small price to pay for one of the best summers of my life. Michael became a good friend, and he introduced me to his friends in Athens: writers, composers, artists, lawyers of the left. It was a welcome and essential antidote to my flirtation with the jet set in New York: late-night political discourses at cafés on Kolonakis Square that grew heated as the thick Turkish coffee turned cold, with composer Theodorakis, actress Irene Papas, lawyers Alexander Lykourezos and Stratis Stratigis; with Moshe Dayan's daughter Yael, a writer who was living in Athens and assisting Michael on the film. These new friends were a few of the many who would leave Greece a year later when the Junta took power. But they were connections that time and distance failed to diminish for me—people I would visit eight years later, when democracy had been restored and they had returned to Athens.

From Greece I went to Paris, where I met another dark, intense director, Claude Lelouch. His most recent film, *A Man and a Woman*, had been an enormous success and he was preparing his next, *Live for Life*. (Lelouch had a way with titles.) He had been speaking to Julie Christie but there had been a conflict of schedules. Was I interested? It was a small film by American standards and there wouldn't be much money in it—twelve thousand dollars. Money was immaterial, I said, again happily accepting, and again calling my agent to tell him the good news.

By now, *no* news was good news: my story was sounding too familiar. He hopped on a plane to Paris to try to talk sense to me. What *was* I—an actress or a philanthropist? My whole salary was hardly a commission. With commissions like mine, he could starve. For big money, I could be in a big film—not these artsy-fartsy things. Did I know they were making *Valley of the Dolls*? Not with me, they weren't, and, cursing his luck in clients, he flew back to New York.

I'd begun to look on locations as an opportunity to explore new lives, the way some confined actors took on new roles. I had just turned twenty and did not yet know what I wanted to do; I welcomed movies as a letter of introduction to life, a chance to forge new friends. Travel had become my priority, acting a means to that end. I was building a life, not a career.

The Lelouch film starred Yves Montand, who played a television journalist. I was his American capitalist companion, accompanying him on hot high-risk assignments while his unsuspecting wife (Annie Girardot) stayed in Paris alone. (It was a *French* film, but you'd be amazed how many American couples, when they saw it, went home without speaking to each other.)

Lelouch worked fast and furiously, with a small, efficient crew, and he traveled light. For three weeks, shooting in Africa, we were a crew of six—including Yves, me, Lelouch, two cameramen (one of whom doubled as an actor), and the producer, who took sound. It was an exhilarating, energizing way to work. The film was made in French, and Lelouch doled out each day's dialogue. To keep our reactions honest and fresh, none of the actors was given a script, and we never knew the outcome of the film until it came time to shoot the ending.

On a scale of locations, this was another Ten: France, East Africa, Amsterdam, New York. The three weeks in Africa we spent camping in the bush: rounding up rhino that rammed our Land Rover, chasing and lassoing galloping giraffes, and rescuing baby elephants to return them safely to their herd.

We went down Ngorongoro Crater, up into Aberdares, across Lake Manyara. We went up the White Nile past clumps of knobby crocs that slithered silently down muddy banks and disappeared into the milky river, past cataracts and waterfalls and herds of happy hippos. Just like the Jungle Boat ride at Disneyland, I thought excitedly; a perfect copy, croc for croc, even to the huge mechanical hippos with their tiny metallic ears.

When it came to the adventure scenes, I was eager and fairly fearless, plunging into the thick of things: hanging out of helicopters, roping rhinos from the back of fast-moving trucks. But the prospect of playing my first real love scene had me terrified, turned my nerves of steel to mush.

I had kissed Steve McQueen in *The Sand Pebbles,* but, given my role as a missionary, the love scene was chaste and Victorian, a tender but furtive peck. It was memorable only for Steve's behavior; as the camera moved in on our two heads in profile, he looked at me levelly and announced gravely, "I'm going to give you this close-up," as if it were the gift of life, then positioned me closest to the camera as we entered our embrace.

Now I was expected to thrash around on a cot in Kenya with Yves Montand while a cameraman hovered overhead. Yves Montand was an idol in France: charming, talented, debonair—and old enough to be my father. I didn't know how other actresses felt about it, but to me it sounded not dissimilar to a visit to the gynecologist—an intimate act performed on a woman by a man in impersonal, well-lit, well-attended surroundings.

Had I been truly womanly, truly worldly, one of those French actresses who did nude scenes as adroitly and as easily as they seemed to bear love children, I would face Yves on that cot wearing nothing but Yves. As it was, I was swaddled in towels, khakis and socks, dressed like an alpinist from the shoulders down.

In the end, I faced the scene forthrightly, with characteristic candor and courage—drinking so much wine at dinner that, by the time I hit the cot, I passed out. They'd set up the shot; there wasn't time, the next day, to retake it, and so, before I came to I was on. Or under. From time to time I regained consciousness to find an insulted Yves straddling me, breathing huskily, or heaving my dead weight from side to side as Lelouch circled in with his camera for close-ups. Coming around briefly as Yves kissed me under the heat of the sun gun used for nighttime illumination, I grinned sheepishly and slumped back into the safety of my stupor.

Live for Life may have been a sappy title, but for me it was not inappropriate. The more I saw and learned about other people, other places, the greater my appetite for them grew.

I was oddly euphoric on these open-ended journeys, traveling alone, at peace and at ease. I felt a total sense of freedom, which I cherished: the opportunity to pick up and run; the ability to live like a man, to do as I pleased. I held my breath for fear that I might lose it.

In strange places I felt at peace; at home I was often restless. I'd begun to adapt to new places effortlessly, to make friends or go without. But my sense of well-being evaporated as I approached home ground and my guard went up. Gone was my ease . . . my ease with people, with places, with myself; gone was the sense of what was real.

9

Coming back to America in 1967 after almost two years away, I found the country chaotic, often unrecognizable. Women loped boldly by like aggressive astronauts in space-age silver Mylar mini-skirts, flat open-toed boots, and bulbous bright earrings that looked like sonic equipment. Men in pageboy haircuts preened, ruffled and jeweled, lurching in high-heeled buckled boots, fashionably foppish, while women's heads were shorn: they wore more eyelash-es than hair, peering out from under the spiky black thatch shading each eye and trying to look like Twiggy, their patron saint.

America, they said, was a country divided: the new countercul-ture suddenly and sharply in rebellion against the old order; anar-chy versus the status quo. To choose the first, the rhetoric said, was a declaration of war on the second—who seemed not to know (or care) that there was a choice to be made at all.

At first, neither did I. That year Truman Capote gave a black-and-white masked ball for four hundred friends at the Plaza; it was the season's hottest ticket. I had just arrived back in New York and though, like so many of those attending the ball, I was not a friend of Truman Capote's, I accepted the honor of the invitation with humility and due respect.

Wandering into the ball—"blissed out," as Timothy Leary would say, by the wonder of it all—I was dressed in a white mink bunny mask with huge pink-satin-lined mink ears; Halston had loaned it to me when Amanda Burden decided not to buy it. I thought I looked sensational; it never occurred to me that I might look ridiculous.

People swayed, Peter Duchin played, and the ballroom glowed and glittered; I saw Mia and Frank Sinatra, Babe and Bill Paley, Christina and Henry Ford, and I was standing with a small group talking when a reporter approached, notebook in hand, and politely asked us if we didn't think it was a little inappropriate, this ball for four hundred people, when there was a war raging in Vietnam and people were homeless, starving and dying?

An appalled pause while people never at a loss for words were momentarily struck speechless. *Inappropriate?* Of course, it was inappropriate—it was beyond inappropriate—it was *insane.* As a reporter for *Women's Wear Daily,* she might have been a better judge of what was inappropriate than we. Yet, in the righteous wrath of people caught red-handed, we huffed and puffed her down, deflecting our guilt.

"Oh, honestly," I huffed, my bunny ears bobbing, every inch the white mink rabbit on the run.

"The *question's* inappropriate," snorted a man in a black velvet executioner's hood standing next to me.

"The *war* is inappropriate, if you're playing that game," drawled another through a black-whiskered mouse mask with a rhinestone nose and tiny stand-up ears.

"One has nothing to do with the other," snapped a princess from Paris in a towering white plumed headdress who had come, I guess, as a peacock. She lurched off regally, feathers molting, the subject clearly closed. Inappropriate, indeed.

I returned to Los Angeles to spend my twenty-first birthday with my family and friends. As the day approached, I grew hourly more

insufferable, sending out invitations bordered in black asking people to come and "mourn the passing of my youth. Shrouds not
required." And yet, while this was the official declaration of my
adulthood, my twenty-first birthday was not dissimilar to my sixth.

There were the same family friends from my parents' generation: the Justin Darts, the Freeman Gosdens, the Leonard Firestones, Rosalind Russell, the Jules Steins, the Mervyn LeRoys,
Cary Grant, the Robert Stacks, Frank McCarthy, Rupert Allen; old
school pals of mine: Connie Freiberg, Kacey Doheny, Vicki Milland; and new friends met in films: Mike Nichols, Julie Christie,
Warren Beatty and Roman Polanski. It was quite a mix.

They were served a lavish smorgasbord organized by my mother, and then I subjected them all to a screening of *Snow White*. I
remembered every frame.

The world of Disney seemed far more rational than the changed
city I'd come back to. Here, balding lawyers proclaimed themselves
local leaders in the "Youth Revolution" sweeping the country and
Realtors celebrated a Return to the Earth in their Bel Air backyards.
Hard-eyed, tight-fisted executives talked Peace, Brotherhood, and
Love the same way they spoke percentage points and distribution.
Especially love. *Lots* of love.

At lunch at the Bistro in Beverly Hills, ladies who never knew
the meaning of the word were wearing platinum and diamond LOVE
pins; dentists began draping themselves with bells and beads. Producers flashed peace signs from Mercedes to Mercedes, and all the
agents started to dress like Nehru.

LOVE, I soon learned, was the merchandising windfall of the sixties, the mother lode of marketing, the Midas of four-letter words.
There were love-ins, love beads and loveburgers. All you need is
love.

In Beverly Hills, I was taken to what was promised to be a hippie
party, given by Joan Collins and Anthony Newley in their large and
stately home. The guests were people like Raquel Welch, Sammy

Davis, Jr., Natalie Wood, Roddy McDowall, Mia Farrow and Frank Sinatra. Wait a minute, here—these people are *not* hippies. Even I knew that.

A maid in a black taffeta uniform with a stiff white organdy pinafore rustled up and hung a brass ankh on a leather thong around my neck. She was holding a basketful of party favors: ankhs, peace symbols, flowers, colored beads—like trinkets the white man traded to the Indians. Several people seemed to be in costume, wearing headbands and rawhide jackets.

Finally, I understood—they were having a *"hippie party."* And a few of the guests seemed less than enthusiastic: standing at the bar, a traditionally dressed middle-aged producer snapped impatiently at another, "Take that goddamned flower off your ear." Where were the *real* hippies?

There was another party the following night where I might find a few old friends, someone suggested. In fact, it was being given by one—not simply a friend, but my first school sweetheart, Terry Melcher. In the four years since we had last seen each other, he had become a successful record producer, moving in the music world, working with rock groups—the Byrds, among others, producing their hit single "Mr. Tambourine Man."

He lived in a house hidden high in Benedict Canyon on a tiny winding road aptly called "Cielo Drive." You could hear the music before you saw the gate to the driveway—"Strawberry Fields Forever." I arrived, alone and nervous, tripping over a water pipe, adjusting my eyes to the darkness and the sting of smoking sandalwood; squinting through the incense at strange people wedged in dim corners: the real hippies, it seemed, were here.

The women wore no makeup and their hair hung long and straight, sometimes braided with flowers or tied with bands round their foreheads; they wore jeans and fringed jackets, Indian robes looped with bells and beads, sandals and Indian moccasins. The guys were gaunt and shaggy: their hair hung long and straight, sometimes pulled into ponytails or banded at the forehead. They wore jeans and fringed jackets or Indian robes looped with bells and beads, and they padded around noiselessly in sandals and Indian moccasins. Except for their thick, drooping moustaches and long bushy beards, they looked exactly like the girls.

There were nuts and raisins and "organic" juices, and these "joints"—hideous, wet, withered things—that they kept passing like hors d'oeuvres, all of them seeming to stop in front of me as I looked frantically—like figuring out which fork—for signs of protocol. And always there was music: Beatles, Byrds, Stones, Mamas and Papas, Beach Boys, Janis Joplin, Doors—many of whom were there that night.

There were also boys who, not four years before, I'd had egg fights with: they looked like their hair had exploded and they were wearing beads and flowers and they weren't kidding. This was no dress-up—this was serious.

"Hi," I said, edgily facing a friend from high school. "I haven't seen you since you were normal, heh, heh." He smiled serenely and said what a "groovy robe" I had on; others nodded and asked if it were Indian. No, not exactly, they were lounging pajamas from Dior.

Evidently the Sweet Bird of Youth had passed me by like a Boeing and I found myself, at twenty-one, peering at the generation gap like a tourist—from the far side.

Two girls were speaking softly, their hair spun with wildflowers. "I know a man who's very rich," said one. "He had a party for three hundred people and set his house on fire so he could film the reactions of the people running out."

A guy dressed like an Indian tracker entered; someone called out, "Hi, Don."

"Hi," Don answered. "My name's Martin now, I changed it for Subid, my religion."

"Oh. Hi, Martin. Hey, could I see you Thursday?"

"Sorry, but I'm going to Venus on Thursday."

"How about Friday?"

Next to Martin, a man in an Indian chief's headdress, a fur-trimmed brocaded Edwardian jacket, a tattooed face, waxed moustache, and beard was staring at a boy with short hair, V-neck sweater and slacks, shaking his head and muttering, "What a strange guy."

And in the background, "Try to set the night on *fiiiyerr!*" Such were the love songs of the sixties; Johnny Mathis would have to sit this decade out. I felt like Alice down the Rabbit Hole—nothing was the way it was supposed to be. This was not a party. What *was* this? The rooms were dim, for one thing, lit only by candles; and there was a stillness about this house full of people sitting silently, speaking softly, moving slowly in long robes and rawhide.

I was used to parties flooded with light, people, place cards, fish forks—*normal* parties with the constant clatter of conversation, lacquered lips, Formica faces; parties where you put your mouth in gear and, from the moment you set foot inside the door until you climbed in your fur to go home, no matter what, you never stopped talking.

Here they seemed contemptuous of small talk; when you met people all they did was smile and nod. What do you say to *that?* Nobody knew I had gone to Truman Capote's party or even seemed to care about it. Nobody noticed the Cartier watch that had given my life new meaning. Nobody seemed to notice *anything,* actually, and nobody seemed or looked the same. So I hated this party where they'd changed all the rules; I was scared and uncomfortable and didn't understand. What was important here? What *mattered* now?

Suddenly, there was Terry—sort of. His hair lapped his shoulders and a moustache trailed down his chin; he wore an Indian shirt, beads and jeans. We stared at each other, at our opposite worlds—surprised and uncomfortable. "Hi, Tanker," he said softly. "It's really good to see you here." I could not manage such a simple, gracious greeting and launched instead into my snappy New York repartee, sarcastic and wired, while he watched, waiting, not much liking my new suit of armor, silently kidding me about my carefully acquired affectations. Gradually I gave up, seeing the silliness of the social game at which I had become too adept, remembering that it wasn't something to be played with Terry, who hated the hypocrisy and did not share my skills.

We went into the bedroom to talk quietly, wondering what had become of each other since Terry had been twenty and I sixteen. To look at both of us, it had been some five years; our respective transformations were striking and self-explanatory. My life was everything Terry now condemned and rejected.

"Are you happy, Tanker?" he asked rhetorically as I shifted positions, accompanied by the clatter of my pearls.

Of course I was happy, I insisted. How could anyone *not* be happy with such an exciting life?

"Don't you ever get lonely, though? You seem so old; don't you miss being a kid?"

Well, sometimes, sort of. Yes, I guess I do. And I looked at Terry, my first love but also my friend, who stared at me so honestly. And I realized that there hadn't been much honesty in my life of late.

As we talked softly into the night, I began to feel the sense of safety I'd lost when life had gotten too fast. And I sighed with relief over giving it all up for even a few hours: the armor and the artifice, the constant posing to protect myself against phantoms and age-old fears. I put away the arch grown-up that I had invented and defended to the death (against *what*, again?). When we returned to the living room, it was empty in the early morning light. I felt like a kid as I drove slowly home.

In the days before I was to return to New York, Terry and I hiked the hills where both of us had grown up, took motorcycle rides up mountain fire roads and into oak-covered canyons only California kids knew and dared to explore. We walked through fields speckled bright yellow by wild-mustard seed, went on picnics, rode horses on the beach. It was as if nothing could touch us; we were two children of Paradise who found with each other a reprieve from the adults we knew we had to be.

And so I stayed. It was an odd—and tentative—choice, unexpected and surprising even to me. Terry's life, in its way, made as little sense as the one I had just left, and I stayed at first on a day-to-day basis, simply postponing life in New York.

Bel Air yawns in the blue-white diamond dawn, stretches and rolls over into satin slumber. One of the more restricted, most expensive suburbs of Beverly Hills, it lies north of that great dividing line, Sunset Boulevard. It is referred to by those living south of Sunset as "the palatial district." It is referred to in a pamphlet issued by the Bel Air Association as "a community of splendid homes, exquisite gardens and a prestige address of premier status."

Inside the graceful grille of Bel Air's gates is a rose-covered cottage that houses the Bel Air Patrol, the community's special forces, who serve to protect its celebrity residents, among whom have been Elvis Presley, Jerry Lewis, Johnny Carson, Greer Garson, the Beatles and General Curtis LeMay.

Once inside, you are in a little kingdom of affluent insulation. A land where grass is still a lawn. It is the Happy Valley of the American Dream: people who in the space of a lifetime have come from early urban renewal to late Bel Air baroque now pass their days in frosted harmony according to God's Law or Louis B. Mayer's, pickled in brandy, preserving Protestant or Jewish mysteries as the spirit moves them.

In the sixties, however, that harmony was nowhere to be found;

the spirit went up in smoke. Bel Air found itself recoiling from an invasion of Rock People whose new "prestige address of premier status" also doubled as a crash pad for their less fortunate friends. Since their arrival the Bel Air Patrol had reported unusually high nocturnal border activity: a steady trickle of long-haired, barefooted, Indian-robed pedestrians with backpacks had been observed entering the area at nightfall and mysteriously disappearing into the interior.

Bel Air was baffled by its new land barons. The Bel Air Association sent a letter to selected suspect residents reminding them that their "Bel Air dwelling" was intended for *one family only* and asking if they could please reduce their number of house guests.

"They're quite a thorn in our sides," sighed a Bel Air Association head. "We hope no more of these Beatles and beatniks come into Bel Air. Why, we had an experience with one of the residents domiciling beatniks right here near the office. They overran the rustic places, destroyed the brush. Nitwit kids!

"The neighbors are very much frustrated by the appearance of the houses. Bel Air is a *very* fine community restricted by the covenants of deeds. *Rhonda Fleming* lives here, and Pat Boone. . . ."

The most recent arrivals included the Beach Boys' Brian Wilson and his wife and the Mamas and the Papas' John and Michelle Phillips; Terry was close friends with both couples. The Beach Boys had bought Edgar Rice Burroughs's house, a gracious Mediterranean villa, and I can't imagine what their neighbors might have objected to about its appearance—unless it was possibly that they had painted the entire house deep purple.

In the garage, when the whole Wilson family was at home, there was a Rolls-Royce Phantom—once John Lennon's—a Rolls-Royce Silver Cloud, a Mercedes, two Ferraris and a Jaguar. In the foyer of the house stood a plaster cowboy holding a birdcage, a water fountain, and a Hammond organ. In the living room was a mahogany statue of Buddha, a bronze bust of Beethoven, and a jukebox. In the den, a $7,000 concert grand piano with the legs sawed half off sat in a large sandbox, where Brian composed and sometimes spoke to the ghost of George Gershwin. There was a complete gym, a private recording studio, and a large pool that they were trying to equip to hold dolphins. Good vibrations.

John and Michelle Phillips lived in an ersatz-English elliptically topped cottage that once belonged to America's sweethearts, Jeanette MacDonald and Nelson Eddy. Directly across the street was a sugar-cube château, the brightest feather in Bel Air's cap; the Mamas and the Papas climbed their trees to see over the high stone wall of the mansion. It was the Kirkeby estate—with the elevator, electric waterfall and ballroom—where I played as a child: the symbol of the old order and the shrine of my youth. California Dreamin'.

From near and far, by sandal and sole, Bentley and Rolls, they came to the Mamas and Papas high on the hill. The house filled and swelled with people, then ebbed and emptied into the early morning mist: Zsa Zsa Gabor chatted with Janis Joplin, Art Garfunkel with Gypsy Boots, the Lovin' Spoonful with the Rolling Stones, Jim Morrison with the Beatles, when they were in town. They played billiards—more for the blur of brightly colored balls than for the game, watched Laurel and Hardy and drank tequila in the stone taproom around a heavy oak table—on which I once saw a green cake.

Mornings started in the afternoons; guests began sharing whatever was handy—swallowing Librium like Life Savers, "windowpane" acid, maybe mescaline. Then John might lead his guests outside, pick up a bow and arrow and shoot straight up into the sky, watch the arrow arc and whistle downward as his guests ran for cover, waiting to see if it landed on someone's head. This explained the avocado trees bristling with arrows and the anxious-looking gardener, who wore a red parka to announce his presence to the archers while nervously tending his wounded trees.

Well pleased with their new lifestyle, the Phillipses shared it freely. John, a Cossack hat cocked low on his forehead, would fold himself into a great Gothic chair, gently fondling the lions' heads that roared from its arms. "I think I'll buy some more land in Bel Air." He grinned slyly. "It's going to be a very groovy scene."

These people astounded and amazed me, as they say in the circus. But I was never at ease. I felt self-conscious and uncomfortable in their presence, unpleasantly aware of my pretensions, clumsy and awkward. Like a little kid who wants to play with the big guys but doesn't know how to get in the game.

"Laid back" was not yet something I had learned how to be. Besides, sitting around stoned, staring into space, could sometimes be a little boring. I wanted action, conversation. And, let's face it, with my blazer, slacks and Gucci loafers, with my transatlantic lisp, I was *beyond* straight. No number of robes and beads, no amount of dope was going to change that, though God knows I tried. While I was dazzled by these people, I was also a little afraid. They knew and I knew that I was not one of them; there was no place for me on their team.

At Terry's house on Cielo Drive I felt at home. Surrounded by tall, thick pine trees and cherry blossoms, with rose-covered rail fences and a cool mountain pool grown over with flowers, it snuggled up against a hillside—a gingerbread hideout that hung high above the city.

There were stone fireplaces, beamed ceilings, paned windows, a hayloft, an attic and four-poster beds. Built in the forties by a French film star to resemble a farmhouse in her native Normandy, it looked more Twentieth Century-Fox than French.

There was a cartoonlike perfection about it: You waited to find Bambi drinking from the pool, Thumper dozing in the flowers, to hear the dwarfs whistling home at the end of the day. It was a fairy-tale place, that house on the hill, a Never-Never Land far from the real world where nothing could go wrong.

It was the first time either of us had lived with anyone and we went about it excitedly, if a little uncertainly, like two kids dressing up and playing house. We hired a butler who cooked and served us dinner on the lawn under the trees at a table banked with flowers and lighted by flickering candelabra while we sat happily over red wine, Brie and Mallomars, watching the lights twinkle on in the city below. When the butler disappeared, a middle-aged black woman named Ruth moved in, to become more house*mother* than house-keeper; and we had a houseman named George who did odd jobs, drove Ruth to the market and fed the animals: Terry's fourteen cats, the kinkajou I had brought from Peru, and a Saint Bernard named Nana. We had a florist's bill of four hundred dollars a month. Talk about Never-Never Land.

We were younger in those days than when we first met—giddy with romance. Now, however, we had the means and freedom to act out our fantasies: with what Terry made in records and what I made in films, we were starry-eyed kids on a big budget. As Hol-lywood's children, we instinctively did things larger than life. Just like in the movies.

We were in some way like brother and sister—born blond, blue-eyed and blessed, beating a retreat from being grown-up. Whatever we did together, it was in the spirit of two kids setting out on a great adventure, exploring the stuff of dreams.

My parents had no idea I was living with Terry: I went to great lengths to ensure this. Though now a legal adult, who, through luck and pluck, had struck out successfully on her own at an early age, I could not bring myself to come clean about my actual whereabouts.

For one thing, I knew how deeply my father disapproved of Terry—his politics, his friends, his lifestyle and especially the influence they exerted on me. To my father, Terry was not simply unsuitable; he was totally unacceptable.

Deceit seemed the easiest route; I wanted to live with Terry but I wanted my father to love me, so I lied. Though Terry's house was five minutes from my parents', I cooked up elaborate charades to convince them that I was living alone in New York. (I'd kept my apartment there, but very seldom used it.) Calling my mother on one phone with the receiver of another extension rigged in front of a radio tuned to static, I created a crackling long-distance effect of which I was very proud, deftly modulating the waves of static with the volume knob. My mother and I would chat, she would ask how the weather was, I'd answer, "Hot and muggy," she'd worry that the call was costing me money, and guiltily I'd say goodbye. Then, if I went into Beverly Hills, I'd slouch down in the car to avoid being spotted.

It was a shoddy deception, but for some time it worked. I always assumed I'd return to New York, but I kept staying. After a few close calls too many—driving past my mother, for one—I pretended I'd taken an apartment in Los Angeles, so I was free to visit my parents and my brother without their suspecting where I lived.

Finally, several months later, I told my mother, ashamed of having carried it on so long. She was justifiably furious; but eventually she looked at me levelly, and, protecting us all from the certain rage she knew would follow, said, "Candy, whatever you do, don't tell your father." And I never did.

Her disapproval hadn't only to do with Terry; in 1967, a couple "living together" without the sanctity of marriage was still considered highly unconventional. Most of the girls I went to school with had by now gotten married; some already had children. If I *had* to live with somebody, my mother wanted to know, why couldn't I choose a more traditional arrangement? What was wrong with getting married?

Well, I don't know. Certainly, since I could remember, I'd dreamed of the day: being kidnapped by Robin and bundled off to Sherwood Forest where I'd cook and clean and be just plain Mrs. Hood. And, God knows, I'd always counted on my prince to come to take me away from all this, take care of me, take charge of my life—all the things that princes are famous for: thundering up on his horse, hoisting me into the saddle, and carrying me off into cartoon sunsets while the dwarfs cheered and the bunnies and deer wept with joy and the music swelled and an invisible brush painted "The End" across the screen. Ah, Walt, you have a lot to answer for.

But, to my own surprise, I wasn't much interested in marriage right then: my life was just beginning, not ending; I found I wasn't ready to "live happily ever after." Because once you find your prince, the story's over. I had a lot to do first—places to go, people to see. I was too young to be closed in the castle. When marriage begins, life ends. Everyone knew that.

Besides, Terry and I weren't meant to be married; it was even surprising that we were together, so different were we from one another. And Terry was no prince who would take charge of my life—he was still a kid just starting his own.

And I had always loved the luxury of being able to take care of myself. If this self-sufficiency was terminal, that only made me enjoy it all the more.

During the two years I spent with Terry, the three films I made (and the several I turned down) were mixed choices.

The first was *The Magus*, filmed in Majorca, starring Anthony Quinn and Michael Caine. I had loved the novel and very much wanted the part of Lily, a nymphomaniac schizophrenic (one would have thought that one of those conditions was sufficient, but by the time the screenplay was done, the pair of twins in the novel had been combined into one character). But when I got the part, though my intentions were by now more serious than they had once been, I hadn't the training or experience to back them up. My execution was inept; my looks were not enough to carry me through the complex role and convoluted script, and fear once again made me back away. I was stiff and self-conscious—sure, still, that I was in the wrong game.

One episode in particular reinforced this. The director, Guy Green, realized that they needed a close-up of an orgasm for a love scene in a dream sequence shot earlier that week. It would be just a quick shot—an insert, as it were—to be done at the end of the day. "We'll be in very tight on you. Can you just come to climax for us quickly, dear? We're racing the clock."

They had set up a makeshift bed to match the original, swathed in red satin. It was too tight a shot to include an over-the-shoulder with my partner, a German in a cat-burglar suit wearing a mask (a dream sequence, remember: by the time they were finished, no one watching it could make heads or tails of the film), and so I writhed alone. *I Writhe Alone*—it should go on my tombstone. I groaned on "Action" as the crew glanced at their watches, eager to go home. Rolling my eyes heavenward like an El Greco saint, less in an expression of passion than in supplication for help. Then, gasping, collapsing, spent, on the shiny red. "Okay, fellows! *It's a wrap!*"

It certainly is, I thought, slinking in shame to my dressing room, though, as usual, I had no grounds for complaint. It even made me grateful for love scenes with partners.

Getting Straight was the film that followed—an unpretentious, democratic production made in Oregon, whose style felt more like shooting in Europe: a minimal crew, with everyone participating and pitching in, working hard and fast. While I had grown up around glamour, studios and star systems, I was more comfortable in work situations removed from it all. I felt happier, easier, without such self-conscious encumbrances. Being waited on by wardrobe women three times my age who addressed me as "Miss Bergen" made me extremely uncomfortable; I preferred productions that reduced the distances between people rather than emphasizing them. There were inequities enough without inventing them. Here there was no competition for wall-to-wall campers because there were none. We worked as a group and as friends. There was a sense of proportion, not pretension; our energy went into our work, not our Winnebagos.

A comedy about college protests that some found unconscionable and lacking in integrity, *Getting Straight* was nevertheless a sizable success. It had humor and toughness, and a crazy, brave performance by Elliott Gould, who was as unpredictable in life as he was on screen. Once I went with him and a group of friends to a basketball game, Elliott as ever in his knitted New York Knicks cap. As we approached the entrance, we passed the many souvenir vendors who lined the sidewalk, one of whom, an older man, was selling mechanical windup dogs that whirred in circles around his shoes. Grinning, Elliott said, "Watch this," gave the man a five, stomped ferociously on one of the tiny dogs, flattening it, and ambled nonchalantly on. Others in the group laughed, but my eyes were on the old man, who bore his casualty stoically, pocketing the five and reaching to deploy a new dog.

But Elliott was a generous and good-natured co-star, easy and fun to work with, and he helped make *Getting Straight* the fun it was. For the first time I got to play a real person. A college coed instead of an Ice Queen. Someone with blood in her veins instead of mineral water. I enjoyed that especially; it felt good.

Yet I was still adept at rationalizing less discriminating, more expedient choices, and my next film was one of those. *The Adventurers* was based on a Harold Robbins novel, which the producers pretended they would turn into *War and Peace*. They were not, they insisted, setting out to make successful shlock but to transform this immensely commercial, crass novel into a film of rare sensitivity and depth. Artistry on a grand scale. By the time they were finished, you wouldn't be able to tell Harold Robbins from Leo Tolstoy. Just wait and see. A silk purse from a sow's ear, if ever I heard it.

Of course, nobody believed it. *They* didn't believe it, the studio (God knows and God help them) didn't believe it, and no one in it believed it. Least of all me. But they had such a *huge* budget—who could bear to turn down a substantial increase on a salary already well into six figures?

So we all pretended to believe that we were making honorable art: they hired obscure actors from critically acclaimed European art films; they hired the traditional stars—Olivia De Havilland, Ernest Borgnine, Rossano Brazzi; they got Renoir's grandson to photograph it and they got $10 million to make it—an enormous budget in the late sixties. And what we got was shlock. Expensive shlock. Well-shot shlock. Shlock that cost a fortune.

But we made the shlock in Rome, where we ate superbly and had a good time, and no one much mentioned the movie. We squandered our per diem on weekends in Positano and on Sardinia: we lived as well as the characters we played. For six weeks I shot in Venice, Santo Stefano and Rome, and to tell the truth, it was swell.

And then, a year later, the movie was released. *The Adventurers* was hailed as a *celebration* of shlock, a triumph of bad taste, a redefinition of trash. Almost a leader in its field.

The reviews I received were almost generous. "Miss Bergen performs as though clubbed over the head," said the *New York Times*, allowing that "the dialogue may simply have stunned her." Of the entire film, the *Times* said, "On the screen, *The Adventurers* turn out to be an even duller bunch of meatballs than they were in Harold Robbins's best-selling novel . . . most of the cast looks slightly sheepish."

Slightly? That Roman holiday haunted me for years. "Weren't you in *The Adventurers*?" an interviewer would inevitably ask accusingly, as if urging me to confess a crime. "*Was* I? Let me see. . . . Wasn't that the Harold Robbins? Oh, yes, but they *swore* it was going to be an art film, you know, and we had *no idea* . . ."

It's a wonder I didn't retire. Instead, I returned to photojournalism to soothe my pride (and hedge my bets), writing and photographing two more articles for *Esquire*: one called "Is Bel Air Burning?" about the rock invasion of Bel Air, and another on the sport of Roller Derby called "Little Women." *Cosmopolitan* assigned me a piece on the 1968 Oregon primaries and I crisscrossed the state in the candidates' press buses tagging after Eugene McCarthy, Richard Nixon and Robert Kennedy. In all these assignments I would have been an idiot not to know it was my name and not a God-given gift for journalism that got me in the door. But once inside, while I might not win any Pulitzers, I worked happily and hard with a confidence that was absent in my acting. When a twelve-page play I'd written in college was published in an anthology of short plays alongside those of William Saroyan and William Inge, netting a royalty of $6.75 when it was performed, I was thrilled. It was the smallest check I had ever received, but I was prouder of it than any other.

While I never came to feel comfortable in Terry's world, his political convictions—aided by the temper of the times, by all I saw around me—helped to forge a political conscience in me.

If you grew up a Republican in Beverly Hills, the transition to liberal was inevitably loaded with irony. I remember the day Martin Luther King was killed; our housekeeper, Ruth, tears streaming down her face, hung a transistor radio on the Electrolux and sang slow gospel songs as she moved from room to room vacuuming. The best gesture of sympathy and solidarity the rest of us could muster was to drive around Beverly Hills that day in our Mercedes with our headlights on.

Terry was incensed by the plight of the American Indian; he had spent time on reservations and would tell me of the despair and hopelessness of their lives. Soon it weighed on my conscience too, and I visited reservations, met tribal leaders and became involved in the Indian movement on my own.

Tribal traditions were sadly tattered. I had become friends with a Navajo called Chief Rolling Thunder, a great old man who was the leader of his tribe on a reservation in the Southwest.

One night I invited him for dinner. As we finished eating, he asked me if I had any fresh meat that he could have. Well, no, I said, but there were some chicken legs and ground sirloin in the freezer. No, no, it was a *whole* animal he needed. Fresh, if possible. Didn't we at least have a *whole* frozen chicken? I was sorry but we didn't and the market was closed. What did he need it for? Wouldn't ground sirloin do?

He sat silently awhile, pulling at his waist-long braid, then nodded, yes, that would have to do. He got up and pulled on his jacket; I gave him the sirloin and the chicken legs. He took them quietly, stepped out into the night and slowly climbed to the top of the mountain above the house. There he built a fire, knelt in prayer and chanted, offering up the ground sirloin and frozen chicken legs as a sacrifice. Soon rain began to pour, dousing his fire, and he returned looking defeated. It's not easy being an Indian anymore.

In the sixties, it wasn't easy being a parent, either. In six months, mine had seen me go from socialite to socialist; had listened to my sermonizing them on American militarism and materialism, the massacre of the American Indian, their destruction of the ecosystem, their invention of plastics and their introduction of pesticides and preservatives.

During my visits to my parents', my father and I would invariably get into deadlocked debates of old and new value systems. My father had no patience for, and less understanding of, the accusations and demands of the Young on the Old. What, he wanted to know, were they making such a fuss about? How in God's name could they be unhappy? What more did they want? What was their *platform?* he would snap repeatedly. "Do they have a *platform?*"

A reasonable question that left me enraged. "Their platform is not to have a platform," I would answer, exasperated. "Their platform is to rediscover the spiritual values lost for so long in this country consumed with consumerism. Their platform is a respect for the natural order of things, a return to the earth before it's too late."

And I would explain that the reason I had not touched the lamb chop on my plate was that, because of my love for animals, I had decided to become a vegetarian; that never again would I wear furs. In the same breath I urged my father to give up hunting; how could he inflict unnecessary pain on living things?

This is too much; this time I have gone too far. He loves duck shooting and is being lectured by his own daughter on the evils of the hunt two years after she herself stood under skies that rained pheasant and partridge, eating steak tartare in her tailored mink.

My mother, too, can stand no more. "What about *shoes*, then?" she wants to know, pointing to my Indian sandals, which she hates. "Aren't you being a little hypocritical—or aren't they made of leather?"

It is the opportunity I've been waiting for. "Yes!" I leap up. "They *are* made of leather, Mom, *nonviolent* leather from cows that have died a natural death—cows with good *karma*—and I've invested in a nonviolent leather company; my yoga teacher started it."

My father's hand claps his forehead, his face is flushed; my inheritance moves up from twenty-five to thirty. "You've invested your *money* in a—" The idea is unimaginable on every possible level. "Oh, Jesus," he says, disgusted and despondent, and pushes his chair from the table to stalk angrily from the room, muttering, "One week it's Indians, the next it's ducks. Now, *this*—"

Stalemated again, I would turn on my heel and head bitterly up the hill.

At Christmastime I turned elf and hung the beams with holly, trimmed the tree with gingerbread and candy canes, stuffed stockings and stoked fires. We dressed up in mufflers and overcoats, piled the old, open Rolls high with presents and chugged along under a hot sun and rustling palms to deliver gifts, pretending it was winter.

Christmas Eve, we borrowed my parents' station wagon, went around to friends' houses, loaded the wagon with turkeys, toys and clothing, and drove downtown to give them to the Salvation Army on Skid Row. We sang carols in their Christmas Eve service and sat silently during the drive home.

The closer we got to it, the greater our shame at leaving the East L.A. slums behind us and heading straight for the safety of home. We didn't know quite what to do about that part; we hated the suffering but we loved our life. So both continued, and there we stayed, guilty and grateful, and tried to figure out how we drew the longest straws.

Yet even our dreamlike life on the hill was daily growing less idyllic; dreams are, by definition, cursed with short life spans. As our differences grew more pronounced, our life turned testy and tense. It was passive versus active; Terry, older, wanted contemplation, meditation, introspection; I wanted conversation, participation, discussion. "Laid back" was boring, "be cool" was killing me. He wanted stillness; I never stopped moving. Denouncing life at a distance, an armchair social critic, he stayed aloof, while I, fired by his oratory, felt drawn into the thick of it, finding comfort in the contact, exhilaration in the connection.

He saw less and less of the world, and I missed seeing more of it. The security of our make-believe world had its limitations; Terry's life was too circumscribed and narrow, too confining for me. My professional absences were a strain on a relationship already overloaded with tensions. It was one of the reasons I worked so little, and when I did work, my independence sometimes appeared as threatening, an intrusion on our insular lifestyle; my ability to pack, pick up and leave was perceived more as abandonment than absence.

More threatening still was the nature of the work. When I went to Majorca to film *The Magus,* Terry came to visit halfway into the shooting. I had rented a tiny villa on the rocks above the sea, beautiful but isolated; I was picked up at six in the morning and returned at seven at night. During the day, Terry was marooned with nothing to do, and we saw little of each other.

One afternoon, when he came to the location to pick me up, I was inside on the set shooting, locked in a love scene with Michael Caine. I liked Michael: he was great fun to be with, wonderful in his work. But my heart was with Terry, who was, at that moment, pacing impatiently back and forth outside. All in a day's work, perhaps, but it felt like a fine line between love scenes and infidelity.

Long absences; intimate scenes with attractive actors; confusing rules of a complicated game. It bred resentment, created distance, destroyed trust. Making movies could stack an impossibly loaded deck. As if relationships weren't tough enough.

If I sometimes resented Terry's anger toward my work, Terry resented social conventions and traditions and ridiculed my meticulous observance of them, the often obsessive attention I paid them. To him, it was sheer dishonesty. To me, it was mere manners. *Manners?* In the *sixties?* Bullshit.

"Your problem is you have no soul," he said to me simply one day. "I do too," I wailed in protest, while wondering what he meant. *Soul,* I suppose, as in "I have suffered," *soul,* as in Ray Charles or Bessie Smith. Where I would have gotten such a soul was beyond me. Still, it stung—the shoe fit.

When it came to souls, Terry's was acknowledged to be spiritual, while mine—if I had one—was trapped in the physical world, shopping hungrily on the materialist plane. Disgusted by the greed and hypocrisy he saw everywhere, a disillusioned idealist, Terry sought people whose values he could respect, who lived honestly and simply by their own rules and tried to find a better way.

One night Terry went out with one of the Beach Boys and came back talking enthusiastically about the commune they'd visited: an abandoned ranch where, in the soft sunlight, a group of kids ran naked and free. They were shepherded by a man some years older than they, who took them in and cared for them. They, in turn, were devoted to him, surrounding him in sleep and clustering adoringly at his feet by day where, together, they would write and sing songs.

Terry was intrigued by this man, by his apparent spirituality and lack of materialism. He admired the naturalness of their life on the ranch, the simplicity, the closeness. He returned and recorded them singing, coming home to tell of these "soft, simple girls" sitting naked around this Christlike guy, all singing sweetly together.

I felt my eyes turn cold and squinty, my mouth pinched and tense. "Why can't they sing *dressed*?" I snapped. (I hated the sixties.) He asked politely if I would like to come out and see the ranch. It was a rhetorical question: we both knew I'd hate it and they—beatific and bare-assed and peering into the hole where my soul should have been—would hate me, so I sulked and said no thanks. Anyway, by then I'd heard enough about Charlie Manson and his minstrels.

That winter, Terry's stepfather died—the man who had legally adopted Terry and raised him strictly and lovingly for fourteen years. He had been a father to Terry and a devoted husband and producer to his wife, dedicating his life to them both. Which made it tough to write off as mere oversight the discovery that he had left his wife some twenty million dollars short.

Besides their money—forever vanished in a puff of smoke and secret Swiss bank accounts—there was the betrayal. Terry, reeling from the double shock of the death and the deceit, decided to tackle the financial fiasco himself—hoping, perhaps, to find answers and to help ease the anguish of his mother. So he disappeared into endless daily legal meetings for months on end, slowly unraveling the threads of the swindle, unable to fathom the depths of the dishonesty.

He decided abruptly to leave the house on the hill, announcing on a Monday that we were moving that Friday to his mother's weekend house at the beach. I was stunned; he gave no explanation, saying only that it was all arranged. By the end of the week, we were living in Malibu. Sharon Tate and Roman Polanski moved into the house on the hill.

For months we hardly saw each other. He was buried in financial briefs he struggled to understand, exhausted by the intricacies and the tedium, and seemed beaten by the betrayal. He never arrived at the beach before ten o'clock at night after the debilitating days of meetings and began taking sleeping pills for a few hours' unconsciousness before morning came and he got up to start again. He began to drink.

I spent my day walking with Nana, the Saint Bernard, filling the house with flowers that were never seen and making dinners that were never eaten. We saw each other less and less, until finally he confessed that he now saw me as yet another responsibility in his life, when he was collapsing under the weight of those he had just taken on. We agreed that I would soon move out.

The pills and the drinking increased, blotting out the painful confusion of a golden boy whose life had turned against him, who knew now there was no going back. That confusion ripped out the child from inside him, destroying the joy as well. The golden days were dying, the fairy tale had come to an end.

In one of our last weeks together during that slow Malibu summer, we woke to find the telescope missing from the veranda on the beach. And some days after that, a friend arrived with a message from Charlie Manson, who had been looking for Terry since we moved to Malibu.

Terry had been avoiding Manson, fed up with the Apostle of Peace and Love's constant badgering to help him cut a record and sign him to a recording contract. The Eddie Fisher of flower children. Terry had asked that no one tell Manson where we were living. Charlie, for his part, felt that Terry's behavior was less than brotherly; the essence of his message was that Terry shouldn't mess with Manson and, to prove the point, he added that if we were missing a telescope, he had borrowed it off our veranda one night last week.

A week later, Sharon Tate and three others were brutally murdered in the house on the hill. Ropes swung from beams that were once hung with hearts and holly, words were written in blood on the door.

It was hard to find anyone in the L.A. Basin who didn't boast about being invited to drop by the house that night, mystically deciding, at the last minute, not to go. Most of Southern California claimed some connection with the slaughter, marveling at their karma, shuddering at having stared death in the face.

Los Angeles was in shock. For months, no one talked of anything else. Gates and guard dogs went up everywhere overnight. Speculation spread about the mysterious murders and who the killers might be. Were they drug dealers or black militants? The righteous roared about sex and drugs and decadence and the dangers therein.

I turned on Terry, shaken and scared. "But it could have been *me*! I could have been *killed*!" He looked at me levelly and said, "But *we* could have been killed—why don't you say *we*?"

Because by that point, there was no "we" anymore. I was only thinking of myself.

Soon after, I moved out. I signed to do a film in Mexico, went to the pound and got a spindly black dog I named Leonard, and left with him a month later for three months' location. Once more on my own in the world, I felt the months of sadness and tension slowly fall away, and soon it began to look exciting. I liked it out there; I was glad to be back.

Terry and I hadn't spoken in two months when, one night in Mexico, I had the impulse to call him. I finally found him at his mother's house, where, he said, the police were waiting in the next room. They had just arrived to tell him they had found the Tate murderer: it was Charlie Manson.

Manson's arrest and the publication of his prospective "hit list" revealed the random brutality of the killings, the shocking senselessness of murders with no motive. The public's righteous posture disappeared overnight. Suddenly, no one felt safe; many lived in paranoia and fear.

Terry sold the house at the beach and rented one in town, where he lived with a pistol by his bed, a shotgun by the door, and a twenty-four-hour armed guard. No one could convince him he wasn't in some way the connection for the murders.

A year and a half later I met Vince Bugliosi, then the State's chief prosecuting attorney, at the courthouse downtown; the Manson Family trial was under way. I had been shown photos earlier in the year to see if I recognized Charles Watson, one member of the Manson Family, later convicted for the murders; the police believed he might have been at the house on the hill while I was there. I looked at the photos; I didn't think so.

When I received a subpoena to appear in court, Bugliosi arranged for me not to testify publicly, and instead sat with me in the back of the courtroom when Watson—tall, raw-boned, with sallow skin and dark, deep-set eyes—was brought out to the defense table.

Did I recognize that man? Bugliosi asked.

No, I said, I didn't.

All flower children look alike.

10

Edgar and Charlie began to work less in the sixties; much of it work for work's sake, some of it shoddy, undistinguished. Radio had died a slow and peaceful death, eclipsed by the arrival of television, and they never really found a place in this new medium. In spite of ten successful appearances in films (three with their old sparring partner, W. C. Fields) and a show of their own on television, *Do You Trust Your Wife?* (in which their role as hosts was later filled by a young comedian named Johnny Carson), the boys' real home always remained the refuge provided by radio. In an ironic way, they were all *about* radio, having taken a medium totally at odds with their act and made it theirs to keep.

There was little room in the sixties for a man and his dummy in white tie and tails. The dummy's special appeal was that he spoke the unspeakable: He said what people were thinking but were afraid to say. But in the sixties there was very little we did not say or do; sacred cows were roasted. Charlie's popularity with the public was rooted in structure, standards, manners, rituals; and in the sixties it was those things, or what they represented, that we set out to destroy.

As the decade drew to a close, Edgar and Charlie, who loved and missed performing, found themselves playing country fairs, benefits, Republican conventions, taking third position on the bill at Las Vegas, where they were excavated, like an ancient artifact, and charitably reexamined by the trades. Where the audience might look up, surprised and pleased to see them. "Oh, it's *Edgar Bergen*," they'd say, smiling, as if finding an old forgotten friend. "Whatever happened to *him*?"

While passionate about performing, my father was now less than enthusiastic about his preparation, and he rarely rehearsed routines, seldom practiced technique. He got a little lazy, using the same material he'd written in the past. Perhaps this was from fear of reentering the arena after increasing absences away; or perhaps his slow fall from favor dulled his usual sense of professionalism.

My mother, who knew all his material as well as he, urged him to write new skits; but he did not take kindly to these suggestions and often rebuffed her for making them. And so she watched her "stubborn Swede" as he went on stage to perform routines she'd heard for twenty years.

And you *could* hear it all again, because it was *good*. It was good and it was funny, and it was, in its way, magical. No matter how many times we'd seen them perform together, we still looked from one to the other when "they" spoke. Dad to Charlie to Dad—even with the old routines and rusty technique, with his lips moving for all to see (a license he'd been able to afford on radio), he—they— could still make magic on that stage.

But God, it made us sad. And him, too, though he'd never admit it—carrying his suitcases from fairs in Saint Paul to conventions in Minneapolis. A smallish, graying man lugging his dummies across the country with him; dummies that had met Roosevelt, Churchill, kings and queens; dummies that now played to empty rooms or to people eating, drinking, talking.

Impeccably dressed in the white tie and tails that he so loved to perform in, proudly erect, his little dummy in top hat and tails perched pluckily at his side, he joked that he had once been known "as the father of Charlie McCarthy," and that now he was known as "the father of Candice Bergen. No matter how hard I try, I can't seem to make it on my own."

Age and weariness pulled at my father's face, but not at the little guy's. Charlie badgered him mercilessly, never seeming to know just when to stop, letting the old man have it right and left. "So help me, Bergen, I'll kill you, I'll *mow ya down*." It was touching to see the two of them up there on stage, as if they'd traveled from another time and place—the thrill of vaudeville, swank supper clubs, the reassurance of radio. Closing his act to polite applause, Bergen would bow lightly and quickly push his dummy off the stage before the dancing girls came on.

It was like the end—and the beginning, back on the boards in vaudeville performing under the big tent. But there, an entertainer was worth something—there was a joy, an excitement, a camaraderie; that was the birth of show biz. Now, all these showgirls in sequins and feathers, German lion tamers, bad magicians . . . It was not now a world for white tie and tails, that much was sure. And I think my father felt old.

In spite of cockeyed, erratic choices, my career was in the ascendant while my father's was in sharp decline. It was probably paternal pride that made my father half joke about being known as "Candice Bergen's father"; but I knew that it hurt some, too. If it was hard on him to see his fame waning, he never actually complained about it; but it made me more uncomfortable about mine.

My success had a double edge for my mother as well. Long known as "Edgar Bergen's wife," she was now introduced as "Candice Bergen's mother"; she had serious doubts that she alone had ever existed on her own. She was an extremely beautiful woman in her own right, but people now gushed to her about *my* looks, ignoring her in the process, or believing, perhaps, that they were flattering her indirectly through me. The effect, over the years, was that she felt forgotten, invisible—passed over in favor of her husband, his dummy, her daughter, and soon, she was sure, her son, who at eight was already turning heads. In complimenting her on her children, men would shake their heads and smile at her admiringly: "My God, Frances, you should have been a *brood mare!*" That kind of talk could turn a woman's head.

People's insensitivity ceased to surprise her. Friends not heard from in years would suddenly call, make casual conversation, then announce that they were sending her a script for me. Others made no pretense at politeness, approaching her with projects for her daughter as if she were my agent instead of my mother. She had acted on television and was an accomplished singer—a woman of abilities and ambition; instead, she felt like Mildred Pierce.

At twenty-two or twenty-three, I too was insensitive to her feelings. It was a surprise to me when one day she came into the room with a telegram and said triumphantly, "This may not mean much to you but it means a lot to me. It's an invitation to play in a celebrity tennis tournament and it's addressed to '*Frances* Bergen.' Not 'Mrs. Edgar Bergen' or 'Candice's mother,' but '*Frances.*' For once, they just want *me.*"

When I perceived the depth of her resentment, I was hurt by it. But, in retrospect, I see that it was my attitude toward my success that bred the resentment rather than the success itself. If I had been able to accept the attention I received more graciously, more gratefully, instead of wisecracking constantly about it and diminishing it in public as well as in private, it might have been easier for my mother to accept—even to enjoy for my sake. She was a woman to whom manners mattered; and my father, even at the height of his career, was known for being a remarkably polite and unpretentious man. My rudeness was an embarrassment, a shame for them.

But something in me still could not resist taking compulsive cheap shots at opportunities others—including my mother—

would have been glad for. My attitude was maddening to people, to my mother especially. When the Lelouch film *Live for Life* was released, the album of the score displayed my photograph prominently on the cover and featured "Thème de Candice" on the record inside. My mother found my apparent indifference, my airy dismissal, infuriating.

"How can you be so blasé, Candy? My God, most girls would be *thrilled* to have such a thing happen. Isn't it ever enough?"

Yes, yes, it was enough. The trouble was it was too much, but I didn't know how to say that then; I barely knew how to *feel* it. What I did know instinctively, deep down, was not to take it seriously—that there would be trouble if I began to believe in the attention, if I started to care about such things. So I continued to fight a misguided battle to keep my distance, maintain my indifference; to try to stay in control. It would be years before I could handle success any differently; years before I could feel I'd earned it.

Meanwhile my mother and I fought furiously, lashing out at each other, unwilling to give way, unable to be friends. I refused to admit, even to myself, that I baited her. Wistfully I would dream of having Betty Crocker for a mother: a benign blue-haired mammal dusted with flour who would love me unconditionally, wrap me in her lap, coo to me, comfort me, "There, there, my child," give me a cookie, dry my tears with her apron and tuck me into bed.

When we fought, I felt a sense of shame and failure, guilt and anger at myself for my behavior. A terrible sense of sadness that we could not yet get it right. There was so much love between us, so much feeling—if only we could get at it. The few times when we were close left me feeling buoyant, euphoric, connected in the deepest way, as if some great cornerstone were set in place. I wanted to tell her I loved her; I wanted her to say she loved me. But neither of us yet had the courage, and the wasted caring left us both hurt and confused.

When I was a child and my father's career was at its height, my parents traveled frequently. It was a measure of my father's and my contrasting fortunes that it was now I who traveled, and he who stayed close to home. Yet I spent as much time near my family as I could, feeling still a sense of continuity there, and gratitude that they cared enough to disagree or disapprove.

My connection with my childhood was so strong that, when I finally decided to put down roots in Los Angeles instead of returning to New York, I chose to buy a house rich with childhood associations: the Aviary on the Barrymore estate where I had played often as a child. It certainly wasn't a sure nose for real estate that clinched the deal: the tiny turretlike house had no grounds and no garage and was fairly short on heating. But it was a Hollywood house, a fairy-tale house with legends and mystery and history, and it had huge charm.

And that is what the Grimaldis charged me for—the same Grimaldis on whose property I had trespassed as a child. To whom I was "the Bergens' little girl" who lived below at Bella Vista, disheveled, trailed by dogs; who would discover me roaming their property and take me on elaborate guided tours. Possibly they'd known even a six-year-old sucker when they saw one, and were softening me up for the kill they were planning years ahead. For when I returned as a prospective buyer, the milk and cookies had dried up, their largesse had disappeared. They had done their job well: I loved the romantic, impractical little house and would let nothing—not even their inflexible, outrageous asking price—stand in my way.

The Aviary was mine. Once again I prowled the property I had loved so well in my youth. While my parents no longer lived down the narrow winding road at Bella Vista, the nostalgia was overpowering, and I had the sense that I was home.

There were three houses on the Barrymore estate: the vast main house with its German rathskeller; the guesthouse with the Italian Renaissance sundial in the middle of the pool and the heated dog kennels; and the Aviary, which had also been a projection room.

Filled with fantasy and whimsy, the Aviary was the most impractical of the three, and this, of course, was the one I wanted. Katharine Hepburn had lived in the Aviary, and Marlon Brando; the little
house was heavy with Hollywood history. It was almost a ruin when
I bought it, a tiny Mediterranean tower high on the hillside, tucked
into pine and cypress trees. The little living room, the size of most
foyers, was sunken and shaped like a miniature chapel, its domed
ceiling soaring twenty-five feet into a cupola studded with stained-
glass windows of scenes from John Barrymore's films. From the
very top of the dome hung a massive iron chandelier. I filled the living room with overstuffed tapestried sofas, Persian carpets, African
chests, and a six-foot copy of a Norman Rockwell painting of Victor
Mature as Samson, the original of which hangs in the Paramount
commissary.

Up a small stair stretched a long, narrow room at the end of
which sparkled an enormous wheel of fortune I had bought at auc-
tion. Whoever sat at the head of the long plank table could, with
a flick of the wrist, send the wheel clattering and spinning red,
blue, and silver flashes behind them. There were many and sundry
clocks (none working), two phones in every room, each a different
color—one, in the dining room, under glass, like pheasant. There
were plaster cheeseburgers, toys and telescopes. Life in the Fun
House. See Candy run.

The upstairs, a huge high-ceilinged open space all skylights
and French windows, was more like a greenhouse than a bedroom.
Katharine Hepburn had used it as a studio in which to paint, choosing the smaller, darker room adjacent as a place to sleep. Barrymore
had designed the top floor originally as an aviary, covering the walls
with fairy-tale frescoes and filling the rooms with brilliant birds as
exotic as the fantasies on the walls. Until, so the story goes, he and
his wife, Dolores Costello, separated, whereupon he had the birds
killed and made into tiebacks for the draperies in the main house.
Barrymore's frescoes seemed pallid compared to his life.

The frescoes had been plastered over, and in redoing the upstairs I found a child's archaeological site—peeling away bits of plaster to find tiny mushroom houses topped with smokestacks, sultans in plumed turbans, jeweled princesses and fantastic birds trailing bright feathers.

As few fragments remained, I made my own fresco: a Stella-like rainbow splayed across the thirty-foot wall behind my bed, arcing and ending in pale pink clouds. In keeping with the huge scale of the room, the furniture was slightly oversized: at night I curled up in a brass bed of inordinate height, in a room pale with moonlight from the skylights overhead; each morning I woke early in a room the size of an airplane hangar to look out at the hills and the sea.

The Aviary had no need of all these fancy trimmings; it was magical enough on its own. In my youthful exuberance, I had turned my first house into a full-blown fantasyland. It was certainly a spectacular setting for whoever lived there—whoever *that* was. Clearly, I had no idea; I was too busy trying to invent her.

It wasn't until after the bedroom was finished that I realized just what I had wrought. The enormous pastel rainbow shimmered over my big brass bed and the great chintz-covered chairs were strewn with stuffed bears and baby pillows. At twenty-three, I'd designed a bedroom resembling nothing so much as a nursery. In its great proportions, I was suddenly small, shrinking in size as I climbed up into bed and curled into chairs: like Thumbelina. A nursery made in heaven but a nursery all the same. I'm home, Ma, I'm *home*!

Life at the Aviary was sweet. I continued to spread myself thin—photographing, writing articles, making movies; Indians, ecology and politics; but the emphasis wasn't on work. Many of my days were spent with my dog, Leonard, and a handsome horse I bought, an Arabian I named Herschel. With Leonard in the lead, we'd ride up canyons, splash through creeks and return along narrow mountain ridges, surprising quail, deer and occasional coyotes.

Living alone, owning my own house, gave me a chance to indulge my love for animals. In my twenties I was fascinated by pigs, and I collected every conceivable likeness of them. I was unprepared but delighted when, one Christmas, a friend who knew of my fetish for pigs presented me with a baby *live* one to add to my collection. I named him "Officer" (remember—it was the sixties).

The Aviary grounds were inadequate for my new arrival so I boarded the pig with my close friend and neighbor, John Calley, who also lived on the Barrymore estate, in the guesthouse. John's property included the electrically heated dog kennels built by Barrymore, and it was there that we housed Officer, who went right to work making a bed out of the bale of alfalfa that John, then a Warner Brothers executive, had requisitioned through the studio prop man.

John's housekeeper at the time was Polish, and her eyes lit up when she saw a pig. Happily chanting, "*Schwein! Schwein!*" she zealously fed him potatoes and milk in porcelain serving dishes. In no time, Officer had doubled in size. Restless now—or possibly unable to stand the stench that had settled over the kennels—he struck out on his own. Soon he could be found peacefully rooting up John's new landscaping, or terrorizing his two wolfhounds, eating their food as well, then reclining on a pad in the sun by the pool to digest and take a siesta.

Finally, John said, "Can'—the pig's gotta go." And go he did; but not to be made into bacon. He was relocated on a farm in the Valley, where he was found to be a she and renamed Rose. For years I paid twenty-five dollars a month to support her.

Nights at the Aviary were quiet when I was home, with a peaceful flow of good friends dropping by, sprawling around the Rainbow Room to watch the splashy sunset over the ocean or the lawn of lights below: Sue Mengers, who had become my agent; director

Herbert Ross and his wife, Nora; screenwriter Joel Schumacher; director Peter Hyams and his wife, George-Ann; producers Marty Elfand and Richard Roth. Hollywood is a one-company town, a close-knit community, and friendships came with particular ease to one born there: generational lines were commonly crossed; some of my friends were people whose children I'd grown up with.

While they were all people who figured prominently in the film industry, I had few close friends who were actors, perhaps because I did not feel like a bona fide actor myself, and probably also because I found most actors' conversations revolved around little other than acting, an obsession with their careers—admittedly a concern I could have used more of, but one I found tedious as an exclusive topic of conversation.

Jack Nicholson was a notable exception. Like most of my friends, he was intensely involved in his work but had an infinite curiosity about everything around him. He had a deft way with words that earned him the nickname "the Weaver," and he was never bored. With screenwriter Carol Eastman and director Henry Jaglom, we whiled away long evenings clustered around the fireplace of the Black Rabbit Inn, our favorite restaurant. I loved them for their wide frames of reference and original turns of thought, for the heated and humorous discussions that ranged from Henry Wallace's persistence to Madame Blavatsky's astral post office. With all these friends there was an easy exuberance, a sense of camaraderie; this was what I wanted life to be.

Some of my finest times were spent with my brother. Kris was a joy: on that, as on few other points, my parents and I agreed. My father, now well into his sixties, became like a child around him, chuckling and beaming, tickling and hugging; inspecting the min- iature cactus plants, checking the ant farm, the hamster run. The marble fountain in the atrium of my parents' house now crawled with tiny dinosaurs and brontosauruses, balsa B-52s and little green Marines.

I would pick him up at school, take him on hikes, horseback rides, for ice cream at 31 Flavors, tacos at the Farmers' Market, the roller coaster at Beverly Park. We were tight like spies and had special traditions of our own. One was our weekly dinner at the Luau, a restaurant on Rodeo Drive that was a cross between an opium den and Disneyland. Under fishing nets filled with conch shells, high-priced hookers worked the front bar area, while families gathered in the dining room in back, framed by fanned peacock chairs and tropical ferns.

Our ritual was to drive to the Luau, detouring past the Witches' House (a Hollywood art director's house in Beverly Hills, with elliptical roofs and crooked smokestacks) on our way; take a table near the waterfall and the miniature outrigger; and order appetizers and "Volcanos." Even the drink was like Disney: a sweet green punch in a giant coconut filled with dry ice. It billowed with smoke as it was brought to the table, alarming diners nearby and clouding egg rolls, obscuring spare ribs, and blanketing the entire tabletop in a thick fog.

When the smoke had cleared and we could find our food, we discussed witches and monsters and protective spells against them, secrets to keep them at bay. One ancient anti-witch remedy, I once told him (by now he was nervous), was to put a piece of pork-fried rice in your ear—an idea inspired by his habitual order of rice. "Really?" he asked in the little cracking voice he had then, scrutinizing my face for signs of truth. I nodded sagely, and before I could stop him, he had picked up a grain of pork-fried rice and popped it in his ear.

The following day when he complained about an earache, it was awkward explaining to my mother the probable cause. "You *what*? You told him to put a piece of pork-fried rice in his ear? Candy, what's gotten into you? If this is serious, I hope you remember whose fault it is; it might not seem so funny then." Between my brother and me, only my greater height indicated that I was the more advanced in age.

He was aware of but unfazed by my celebrity, remarking once, as we walked through Beverly Hills to get an ice cream after school, "You know, sometimes walking with you is like being with a giant banana." When I looked puzzled, perhaps a little stricken (even Pauline Kael hadn't called me *that*), he explained that he was talking about "the way some people stare." At nine, he'd neatly defined the experience of having a public face.

The problem was finding grown men whose companionship I enjoyed half as much. If evenings were idyllic, mornings found me, alone, under the rainbow, fighting a slight case of what the decade identified as "anomie." There was an emptiness in my life that slept fitfully and woke way before I did—a little furry ball of foreboding that made me vaguely afraid to face the day alone.

Mine was a solitude of my own making. It seemed to me that men came in two varieties: at best, I made safe, senseless choices, inane mismatches that posed no threat; at worst, I'd meet men who would shake awake the masochist in me, killers who thrill the victim in women lured by the gleam of vampire teeth. I went out often with men but I would date defensively, usually detached and difficult with potential suitors, as if to drive them away. Which, in most cases, I did. It took someone more skilled at the game than I to hold my interest; even better, someone who refused to play. A man who called my bluff had me in his pocket.

Not many like that came along, but when they did, an irrepressible urge to test was an indication of my interest; a pattern of gently pushing them close to the edge—hoping for someone who would push back. 1-2-3, testing . . . oops! Over he went. The chemistry of contempt: the greater my indifference, the greater their interest.

Not that it should have surprised me—it was a dynamic I knew all too well; a game that two could play.

In my search for the paternal slap on the hand, my quest for the assertive inaccessible man, I met a successful young novelist whose aloofness drew me like metal filings to a magnet, and I expressed interest by making critical observations of his work. Wasn't it a *tiny* bit bloodless? *Slightly* sterile? The endings weak and unresolved?

He was not inaccessible for nothing, and, after a few weeks with H. L. Mencken, he called to announce: "My analyst has advised me to stop seeing you; she says this relationship is destructive to my work, anxiety-provoking and counterproductive. You're disruptive to my life." Ah, well, at least he resolved *that* ending. Talk about a man who knows his own mind. And the Menace moved on. . . . Testing, testing, 1-2-3. . . .

There were others even less likely with whom I barely made it through dinner: a political satirist, a radical ecologist, a conceptual artist. Movie stars, real-estate czars and textile kings. Public figures in private planes. Eclectic tastes, but never realistic. How could they be? I was a girl who lived in an aviary under a rainbow; reality had no place with me.

One night I was expecting the arrival of a rock star who changed cars as often as he did shirts. As one expert in movie entrances, I decided that night I would make mine as Esther Williams, emerging sirenlike from the shadows, glistening with droplets after a late-night swim. Sleek and shimmering like a seal.

But rock stars know a thing or two about entrances themselves: they like to make theirs late. So I waited, shivering in the shadows, irrevocably committed to my choice of costume, jumping repeatedly in and out of the pool in order not to dry off. When the rock star finally arrived, he found me unaccountably standing outside—sneezing, dripping wet and blue with cold. An hour and a half of waiting wet in the wings had dampened, as it were, my

"Esther" effect, and I was in bed all the following week with bronchitis.

There were others, more earnest, who arrived on time. For weeks I'd been receiving letters from someone named Fletcher Jones, a wealthy businessman apparently, now divorced, with a fortune made in computers and a keen eye for pretty women and fine racehorses. Dogged in his pursuit, he was undaunted by either my silence or my curt refusals.

The letters, handwritten on stationery highly embossed with his name or racing insignia, were oddly proper, strikingly polite, and arrived not in the morning mail but in the hand of a fastidious chauffeur at the wheel of either a large maroon Rolls-Royce or a black Bentley. They were unusual in their formality and framed various requests for dinner, lunch at the track and a tour of the stables ("I know of your fondness for and appreciation of horses. . . .") along with character references from the California racing world: the Burt Bacharachs, the Mervyn LeRoys.

One morning, a letter arrived that was difficult to ignore. "Dear Candice," it began, "I am appealing to your philanthropic instincts . . . ," and went on to offer ten thousand dollars to any charity of my choice if I would kindly join him at his house for dinner. He had my philanthropic instincts in a corner; it was an offer I couldn't refuse.

Checking to make sure he existed at all and, if so, had no criminal record (I was willing to be bored for ten thousand dollars but not assaulted), I wrote him that I would be pleased to have dinner and asked that he make the checks payable to five separate organizations at two thousand dollars each: Friends of the Earth, Americans for Indian Opportunity, Save the Whales, a woman congressional candidate and East African Wildlife. A telltale compendium of causes to which he readily agreed.

One evening, a week later, he arrived as planned. He was nice-looking, I saw as we shook hands, tall, well-built, and surprisingly young, perhaps in his late thirties. His prematurely gray hair was combed in a slight pompadour that gave him a fifties look, and a cream silk collar eased out over the shoulders of his black mohair suit; he dressed expensively but without style.

There was no chauffeur that night, no Rolls or Bentley. Instead, a black Aston-Martin waited, sleekly gleaming, for him to smoothly shift and double-clutch us to the walls of his villa in Bel Air, its elegant gates mysteriously giving way as we approached.

The house was huge, a Renaissance palazzo with a replica of the Tivoli fountain sprawling along four acres. Built by one of Chiang Kai-shek's ministers after lifestyles changed on the China mainland, it now belonged to Fletcher Jones, son of a Texas dirt farmer, who had made $30 million in three years.

The entire house and most of its contents were beige—a choice he felt best displayed his paintings, and he walked me past Turner, after Manet, Picasso upon Van Gogh, rapidly rattling off data on each, comprehensively, dispassionately, like a fine arts digital readout. No wonder he's a computer king, I thought.

A butler appeared bearing long-stemmed Baccarat glasses and two white wines which Fletcher tasted, taking one for himself and nodding toward the other, a Bernkasteler Doktor. "Yes, that's fine for Madame," whom I whipped around to see. It seemed that "Madame" was me, and I took the wine that had been specially selected.

From the beige living room, we went to the beige dining room, where the butler (in a beige jacket) served us beef Wellington and asparagus hollandaise. The dinner was delicious and he was a nice man; to my surprise, I had a fine time. While Fletcher seemed heavy and humorless, his goodness was genuine and his loneliness compelling. He looked lost in this life of his, standing ruddy-faced and silver-haired in his bland sea of beige, joyless and disconnected. He talked at length about his sudden wealth, explaining plans to build a kind of Boys' Town, detailing altruistic dreams, sincere in his wish to help people. An earnest, well-intentioned man struggling against his isolation.

After coffee and cognac were served in the study (beige), he closed me in the Aston-Martin and quietly drove me home. He saw me to the door, kissed me gently on the lips, handed me an envelope from inside his breast pocket, thanked me and said good night. Inside the envelope were five checks for $2,000, neatly typed to each organization and signed by Fletcher Jones.

The next day, the chauffeur delivered a case of Bernkasteler Doktor. Surprised and pleased, I called to thank him for the dinner, the checks, the wine, and to say I had sincerely enjoyed meeting him. He asked if I would visit his Thoroughbred farm in the Santa Ynez Valley; he could fly me there in his plane, the French chef would prepare Cordon Bleu meals and, if I didn't want to stay the night, we could fly back after dinner. He was proper but persistent.

I politely refused and left, a few weeks later, to make a film in Chicago, where he called me regularly, offering me his jet to visit my family in Los Angeles for the weekend, describing the Appaloosa colt just born on the ranch that he wanted me to have, sending me a beautiful book on the Bauhaus when he learned of my interest in architecture. Gratefully I kept the book, refusing the rest.

That spring, Fletcher Jones was flying to his ranch north of Los Angeles when the twin-engine plane he was piloting mysteriously crashed into the hills. No explanation was found for the accident, in which he died alone.

For weeks afterward, guards were posted in front of the villa and the gates bore stark warnings to trespassers. It sat empty a long time, the grounds shaggy and overgrown. Eventually it was bought by Rod Stewart and ringed with barbed wire to keep out admirers. Rod Stewart, evidently, has enough people in his life; he does not live alone.

• • •

At twenty-five, after eleven films, I had still not studied acting, and it showed: a good review was a rare review, and as my awareness of my liabilities grew, so did my terror: each film was more frightening than the last. I seldom slept at night if I was shooting the next day, and yet somehow I was unaware of my fear. I concealed my anxiety, my lack of technique, by constant criticism of everything around me: the plastic flowers; the shabby script; the blatant toupees. Deflecting my terror onto my surroundings, I hid it even from myself.

But ultimately, I could never hide it from others, and it hardly made for a body of work I could be proud of. As a 1970 story in *Time* magazine put it, "Candice has been bedded by Elliott Gould in *Getting Straight*, deflowered by Bekim Fehmiu in *The Adventurers,* and raped by Oliver Reed in *The Hunting Party.*" So went my image: When I wasn't cast as the cool, rich dilettante I so resembled, I was the Snow Queen, a natural for rape scenes; the woman men love to defile.

In *The Hunting Party* alone, which opened with me being raped by my husband (Gene Hackman), I was then kidnapped by a gang of outlaws, raped in the back of a fast-moving buckboard filled with grain, raped again by the bank of a river by the leader of the gang (Oliver Reed), who subdued me in an English accent with whispers of "Whoa, little filly"; almost raped again by the first guy in the buckboard—this time in a sleepy Mexican village—then saved by Oliver, the outlaws' leader, who then gave me a slap so hard that I flew out of frame and we had to reshoot the scene. In the end, I was rescued by my sadistic husband, who then shot me in the stomach for going off with other men.

In this film, Oliver Reed (accompanied to the location in Spain by his mistress and newborn baby) stayed in character off set as well as on—brawling drunkenly, flinging plates of food after fleeing waiters and presenting me with an ultimatum that he actually delivered straight-faced: either we had a sexual relationship during the film or we had no relationship at all; direct contact would abruptly cease and we would speak no further. After I declined his courtly offer, he immediately imposed a vow of silence, speaking to me only when necessary and then through intermediaries, referring to me succinctly as "The Girl" ("Tell 'The Girl' to get off my mark").

At times like those, "The Girl" resented being one. But even my woman's rage was rarefied and my dreams of revenge were of a particularly Hollywood sort. As a result of repeated movie maulings, I fantasized a movie where the *women* do the raping and plundering for a change, and even wrote a treatment for a women's Western about a clandestine female gang that ended with the comely leader spraying the ground around the bruised and beaten bully with bullets, commanding him to "Dance!" till he begs for mercy, then scooping him onto her saddle and riding triumphantly into the sunset.

But why would I *make* such movies? Had I no sense of responsibility? No social conscience? No moral stand? Well, yes and no. I was choosing the best of what was available to me, and any qualms I had about inferior or tasteless scripts were temporarily assuaged by lucrative salaries. Feminism was only just beginning to take root and consciousness-raising was still a thing of the future; when it came to roles for women in films, there weren't many that were much better than the ones offered me. The few roles of substance and dimension were offered to actresses with "serious" reputations—Julie Christie (still), Faye Dunaway (suddenly, since *Bonnie and Clyde*), Jane Fonda (increasingly, with *They Shoot Horses, Don't They?* and *Klute*); my reputation was one of decorative appeal. But if I continued to deny being an actress, what could I expect? People took me as seriously as I took myself.

And sometimes even my physical assets were inadequate. The

woman's part in *Soldier Blue* was strong-willed and gutsy; it was for this, as well as for the film's political stance, that I wanted to play it. But the role also called for a lusty, busty lass; I, of course, was neither. The director decided that makeup should try their hand at the problem.

I was shown into the makeup room and told to undress, put on a smock and lie back in the reclining chair. A white-coated, cherub-faced man entered, explaining cheerfully that they were going to make a mold of my breasts so larger rubber breasts could be made to fit over them. They would be flesh-colored and pliant, and would stay on with surgical adhesive. The outline under my costume would look natural, and if I needed to do a nude scene, some makeup, carefully applied, would make it impossible to tell the difference.

He then asked me to open my smock: he was going to put Vaseline on my breasts, he said, so the casting clay would remove easily. To my amazement, this he did, while I stared beseechingly at the ceiling, wondering, Am I allowed to say "No" here? Am I overreacting? Behaving hysterically? Is *one* of us crazy?

He took an impression of my breasts, let the plaster harden and pried it off with neat, sucking sounds. I stared blankly at the impression of my breasts. It looked like a detail of the lunar surface. "Does anyone *see* this?" I asked. That's all I need—on the wall next to Jane Russell at the Hollywood Wax Museum, or the Universal Tour.

"Don't worry, sweetie." He patted my shoulder. "A lot of the girls do it. They glue them on and wear thin shirts and no bras and everyone thinks they're stacked. Once you put 'em on I bet you'll never want to take 'em off." He winked.

If they weren't padding me in person, they were padding me in posters. When the ad for one of my later films was submitted to the studio heads for approval, they said, "Great—just make Bergen's tits bigger and the rifles longer and you got it."

1

The morning of the turtle funeral.

2

Edgar and Charlie.

3

With Marilyn Monroe.

4

Mr. and Mrs. Edgar Bergen.

5

Candy with her parents.

A family Christmas.

6

RIGHT: Candy and Charlie.

BELOW: In "Uncle Walt's" backyard. From left: Edgar, Candy, June Allyson, Frances, Walt Disney.

The Maypole. From left: Liza Minnelli, Carla Kirkeby, Vicki Milland, Candy.

Candy face-painting with her father.

Candy with her father and Charlie.

Candy with her father.

"Mine were no run-of-the-mill delusions of grandeur."

Candy spends a day with her dog, Leonard, and her horse, Herschel.

Sex and violence, violence and sex. Thanks to the public's current preference for graphic cruelty, the threatened nude scene in *Soldier Blue* was never shot, and at the last minute I was saved from frontal nudity wearing lifelike plastic breasts. (*Would* that constitute a nude scene?)

A movie whose heart, if nothing else, was in the right place, *Soldier Blue* was based on the white man's massacre of the Indians at Sand Creek, and was one of the first films to sympathize with the Indian side of our history.

Recent market research had indicated audience preferences now favored violence over sex, and studio executives arrived on the Indian Village set in Mexico for a powwow with the director. The decision was quickly taken to emphasize the violence in the film, making the massacre scenes even more explicit.

There was a "prosthetics truck" on the set specifically for the bloody battle scenes, the inside stocked with artificial limbs and every conceivable extremity. Wooden legs swung from the top of the truck and arms were stacked along the sides. Heads stared from stands in wispy dark wigs, headbands and Indian braids, their necks severed clean, arteries dangling, ready for decapitation by the cavalry. Rubber breasts lay neatly in drawers, fitted with blood bags that would burst when lopped off by the soldiers' bayonets; and some artificial legs were wired electrically, specially rigged to simulate spasm when run over and severed by wagon wheels. Paraplegics and amputees were bused in from Mexico City for the massacre scene—men and women missing arms or legs, who were fitted with the prosthetic devices and instructed to watch in horror as the limbs were hacked from their bodies, spurting blood and twitching in the dust.

Though the violence represented was based on but a fraction of recorded history, in the end, when the film was released, it proved too much even for America's voracious appetite—and possibly for her conscience as well. The film was a success everywhere but in this country; perhaps Americans enjoy watching cruelty on the screen, but dislike being reminded of their own.

In contrast to most of the films I made, *Carnal Knowledge* was the perfect experience, one that increased my sense of self-respect instead of diminishing it. It is the film I have always been proudest to be in. Directed by Mike Nichols from a screenplay by Jules Pfeiffer and starring Jack Nicholson, Art Garfunkel, Ann-Margret and me, it was shot mostly in Vancouver and it was like working in Valhalla.

Carnal Knowledge has always been in a class by itself. From the moment it was announced, there was the sense that something special would follow, an eagerness to see what Mike Nichols (after *The Graduate* and *Catch-22*) would do next. There was some unspoken honor attached to being a part of this film, a feeling of privilege.

The film was, to simplify considerably, a tale of the wars between men and women. It was divided into two time slots, the late forties and the late sixties. The early sequences, set at Smith and Amherst Colleges, were designed as strong, spare images, with a deliberate absence of detail, as in a dream. And the entire making of *Carnal Knowledge* was dreamlike, idyllic—like working in a state of grace.

For all of us there was an effortlessness about the work, an ease to the acting that came from the precision and generosity of Mike's direction and the intelligence of the script. The difference showed especially in my work.

This was a challenge to rise to, not to avoid, and I was good in *Carnal Knowledge*; the best I'd ever been. And all it took was a great director, a great script, great actors, and a great cinematographer.

To an actor, some directors are generals and some directors are lovers. The generals are those more at home with epic spectaculars, electronic wizardry, special effects and the coordination of vast logistics than with the subtler, more intricate maneuvers of human relationships. The generals are usually too busy running the war to spend quiet time with the troops.

I was a washout with the generals. Alone, I was not one to go confidently into battle; my guard went up and I defended myself against the camera with excessive control, desperately hanging on to my dignity in a profession which I felt threatened it. In material with which I was uncomfortable, my embarrassment was especially transparent. And I was long used to provoking directors' impatience, from early appearances in my father's first home movies ("Candy, wipe that sick smile off your face") to subsequent starring roles ("Let's go again. Jesus, honey, do you have to look so *depressed*? Just relax, okay, and"—through clenched teeth—"have fun with it").

Obviously, directors often hadn't the time or the patience to cajole me out of my self-consciousness. My fears were not their problem, and I was paid to perform in the production, not to editorialize about it. Besides, directors had problems of their own. But it was undeniable that I did better work with directors of the other breed—the lovers.

Mike Nichols was a legend, not as a general among filmmakers but as an actor's ideal—a director who was attuned to the observation of behavior; who was supportive of and encouraging to actors.

He was the first director to identify the concern with control that had always impeded me and to address the fear that lay behind it. He cracked my control when a scene required him to, and capitalized on it when it was consistent with the character. In an early scene in which I met Artie at a mixer, Mike told me to try taking my skirt off for the tight two-shot and playing the scene in my slip. It produced just the right edge of discomfort, the precise note of nervousness the scene demanded.

Mike liked the cloistered atmosphere of Vancouver, which kept us a unit and focused our energies, our concentration on our work. Under normal conditions our close-knit enclave could have been a nightmare, but these were idyllic conditions; many of us had been friends before the shooting, and those who weren't became friends during it. You couldn't have asked for better company, and we rarely left each other's sight.

Jack and Artie and I shared a large house in Vancouver that came to resemble the set of the Amherst dorm. We traipsed home at the end of a day still in our forties college wardrobe of crew cuts and crew necks, pigtails and pleated skirts, white bucks, saddle shoes and bow ties, bounding in to greet the housekeeper, who cooked and cared for us like a mother as we badgered her for snacks after school.

Mike had created a tiny utopia there in Vancouver, and when, after two months, my part was done, it was terrible to have to leave. My sadness was evident to Mike, who saw to it that I had a souvenir to take home. As I opened the door to my dressing room that last day on the set, soft colors glowed in the darkness and I heard the sound of Glenn Miller's "A String of Pearls." There, waiting for me as a remembrance, was the big old Wurlitzer jukebox with revolving neon rainbow whose music we had danced to in the roadhouse scene.

I dreaded coming home to my empty house after such happy times, and I found the silence of my life deafening. I hated leaving the closeness and comfort ironically found in a company making a film about the alienation between men and women to return to my life alone: a tiny testament to the film. The Wurlitzer followed me to the Aviary, assuming a place of honor in the dining room, where it glowed with warmth like a multicolored hearth and helped me fill the empty house with soft swing sounds for quiet dinners with friends.

When I turned twenty-five, I got a new passport and wrote myself a sober warning:

"Today I got my new passport and with it an implied deadline to get my life in order. By that, I mean that if in the next five years till its expiration date, I have not yet found someone to share my life with and see no family in my future, then I will have been beaten by my own defenses, my efforts to dismantle them a failure."

As yet, my efforts had been slight. And the longer I waited, the more sophisticated my defenses became. Locked in my tower ringed with heat-seeking missiles, like Rapunzel pleading for someone to get through her radar screen, I waited wistfully under the rainbow, secured against all intruders, shouldering flamethrowers and machine guns, humming "Someday My Prince Will Come."

11

In my bedroom was a telescope with which I scanned the skies, the seas and the neighbors. There was a new flurry of activity in the house across from mine and so the focus was set on the pool area and backyard. The distance between that house and mine was small—perhaps two hundred yards—but they were separated by a narrow canyon. The telescope was almost superfluous, helping only to read lips and labels, and—if the wind was right or the conversation heated—even that became unnecessary. The dialogue drifted across the canyon and in through my windows.

I was fascinated by the new people in this house, and I watched their movements constantly—not only because the girls who sunbathed by the pool did so topless, indifferent to poolmen, gardeners or occasional cars, but because I had met and knew slightly the man who had recently moved in.

He was a film producer whose father had run one of the major studios, but he had broken with tradition to become Hollywood's first countercultural filmmaker. This he did with astounding success and bravado—actually revolutionizing film production in Hollywood, finding new formulas for making low-cost films, giving everyone on the crew participation and becoming a millionaire in his own right in the process.

His company became a Hollywood legend—the only place

where new filmmakers were welcome to work and explore. The films they made were audacious in form and content, high in quality and stunning in profit. They were young, tough, smart and totally independent of any studio structure. And he was the romantic lead of the company, its founder, its force, its fair-haired boy—a Robin Hood from New Rochelle.

In deference to his privacy, I will call him "Robin" here.

We first met at the preview of one of his films. I was moved by it and wanted to congratulate the man who produced it, and he was pointed out to me—the very tall, very thin man who slouched in deceptive shyness against the wall. I went over, introduced myself, and thanked him for the movie. He was gracious and surprisingly modest about his triumph. He introduced his wife, who stood next to him, and we all shook hands and said good night.

Months later, while doing a film in Los Angeles at Columbia, I saw him in the dining room at a table with Dennis Hopper, Peter Fonda and Jack Nicholson. Dennis in denim, ponytail and headband, Peter in fringed jacket and rawhide moccasins, Jack grizzled and grinning, and Robin, sandy hair short and tousled, boyish and well-behaved in sports shirt, loafers and slacks—his dress and demeanor almost shocking in contrast.

Around them munched the Ruling Class, the old guard studio elite, burly, graying executives who had watched him grow up—the president's prodigal son. And now he was making this *chozzerai;* turning everything upside down and inside out, and they didn't know from Dylan and marijuana, they didn't understand movies with scenes of nude actors on acid trips in cemeteries that made as much money as *Airport* and cost a fifth as much.

And this was who now had moved across from me, whose conversations I eavesdropped on so intently; snatches about "psychotropic plants," "Gurdjieffian logic," "applied Maoist theory. . . ." This was not your basic poolside banter. Especially in Beverly Hills, where it was unusual to hear exchanges more global than European grosses.

Robin and I had several friends in common, among them Jack Nicholson, Carol Eastman, Henry Jaglom and Brooke Hayward. Peering into his backyard, I remembered Brooke saying, one day, as she made me an omelette, "I think he may be the perfect man." His assets ranged from blond good looks to intelligence and perception; and "He's also happily married for fifteen years and has two children." Well, sure, I nodded, the perfect ones were always happily married, and we both sighed and swore that we would just give up looking; what we were panning was fool's gold.

The perfect man was now separated from his wife. When he called asking if we could have breakfast or coffee, I was intrigued but wary. He was insistent until I agreed, one night, to come over for coffee. "Coffee" sounded safe, short, flexible; the advantage of going to his house was that I would be free to leave when I liked. Nicely positioned for a quick getaway.

He opened the door himself: they didn't come any handsomer. Very tall, very thin, in an old sweatshirt and khakis. He didn't seem to care what he wore, beyond indifference and the awareness that on him it hardly mattered.

As we sat in the living room I stole furtive looks around the house: a rambling one-story, wood floors, zebra rug, used brick, suede sofas, pool table—pool table?—a glimpse of yellow-and-black swirly wallpaper in the bedroom. Beverly Hills Bachelor.

Seeing my smirk, he explained with a grin that he had just rented the house furnished, because he and his wife had recently agreed to separate. It was hard to see how raw the separation had left him, so deftly did he camouflage the shock.

While we talked, I was guarded and glib. I could always count on myself for that. He chose, instead, a good offense—and an excessive seductiveness as added protection. He was honest, direct, he wouldn't be drawn in, refused to fence. Calmly watching my flailing, he said softly, when I finally stopped for breath, "You know,

Bergen, underneath your bullshit, you're an incredible person. Why do you make it so difficult for people to try to get to you?"

Because no one had ever called me on it before, I guess. Because I never believed I was an incredible person. He was good at this— whatever it was.

He seemed so sure of himself—*too* sure, I thought, and I backed off and began to leave. I wasn't attracted to him, I told myself; he had no physical substance. It was like holding a cloud. He was too willowy and lanky. *I* wanted to be willowy and lanky. He was too skinny. I felt too fat.

He followed me outside, and once more, Why are you leaving? I don't know. Because it's too soon. Because you're too sure. Because I don't want to stay. And I went home and climbed into my brass bed under the rainbow and wrote in my diary, "Robin's—for coffee and confusion."

We moved on to dinners. Talking and more talking, until five in the morning. He was charming, sweet, persistent, overpowering, and smart. Extremely smart. I'd never been with anyone like him before. He listened with a ferociousness, an appreciation, an enjoy- ment; with intelligence. It made me feel more interesting, made me say words more worth hearing. I began saying how I felt, *thinking*, for the first time, about how I felt. And he pushed me to be "open" with my feelings, tried to make me secure enough to put aside my armor.

A radical in politics as well as in films, he seemed to know some- thing about everything and was always learning more, surrounded by a sea of papers and periodicals: the *New York Times*, the *Los Angeles Times*, the *Black Panther Paper*, the *New York Review of Books*, the *New Republic*, *Rolling Stone*, *Screw*, *Esquire*, *Playboy*, *Newsweek* and sheaves of political papers and pamphlets. Current events swirled furiously around him, spilling off the bed and piling up on every table, and he snacked on them any second he got.

Because of his appearance of tremendous strength and success and his very real abilities and generosity, people clung to him for support—emotional and financial. I seldom saw a situation he couldn't handle, from friends in accidents to friends in jail. They came to him and called him at all hours for help and advice of every kind and he was there in a flash, dealing adroitly, soothing, reassuring. Robin Hood saves the day.

He was all about "taking care of things"—or controlling things. He was not a crack producer for nothing, and taking care of things was what he did best. He loved it; I loved it. I would wonder later if he was capable of friendship not predicated by need. If he didn't manipulate the market a little. But I'd spent years fantasizing about a man who "took care of everything," protected his princess, carried her off. That's what I wanted; that's what I got.

Soon he began to take care of me, to make me feel that I was a vital part of his life. Too quickly, perhaps, but at the time I took no notice. I was too busy fighting to stay on my feet as day by day he kept sweeping me off them. It was tough stuff to resist: beyond his attractiveness, his energy, his competence, there was a sweetness I hadn't counted on—an incredible charm.

So I talked resistance, but in fact I was hurtling along head over heels, knowing for the first time that This Was It. Just as I was giving up, neatly tucked into my gold-and-crystal casket, surrounded by sobbing, grief-stricken dwarfs—when who should appear in a Porsche but the Prince himself. The very guy we were looking for.

Except: while suspicious by nature, for starters, I could have sworn it was all happening too fast. Too easily. I was sure it took a *little* longer to become such a fast and integral part of someone's life. Maybe it didn't always take years, but three weeks seemed strangely short. We never stopped nuzzling. And I could have sworn, every so often, that a look of concern, even skepticism, flickered for an instant in the eyes of his friends.

I could not, at the time, guess what they were thinking: that these displays of instant togetherness seemed oddly misdirected or displaced on Robin's part, that they struck the observer as slightly excessive for a man who, they knew, was deeply in love with his wife and was devastated by their separation. As were his friends. For he and his wife had always been the model marriage, the golden couple—one marriage you could put your money on. It was a marriage that mattered to people, that still held that possibility, that promise. If I couldn't interpret the worried glances of his friends, I was certainly too naive to guess at the mixture of hurt, fear and perhaps even vengeance that went into Robin's urgent courtship. He had been married for fifteen years; he had been separated barely a month. He had never lived alone. It was a wonder he was walking upright.

A few weeks into this whirlwind, Robin took me to San Francisco for the weekend, trying, unsuccessfully, to explain dialectical materialism to me during the hour's flight in first class. After checking into a suite at the Fairmont, we took a car and drove to Oakland to meet the man who was his best friend.

It was 1971, and Oakland's blacks—a large percent of the population—were angry and organized, following the politics of revolution as set down by the Black Panthers, whose battle cry and slogan was "All political power comes from the barrel of a gun."

We pulled up to an elegant building overlooking the lake: a high-rent, high-security high-rise with nattily uniformed doormen and television cameras that monitored the entrances, sending tight two-shots of visitors to the resident requested, neatly weeding out unwelcome guests. They ran a tight ship there on the lake, protecting wealthy Oakland whites from the incursion of the black population, from the barrels of their guns.

Ironically, we were waiting in the gleaming lobby for security clearance to the building's penthouse apartment, in which there lived a black man under twenty-four-hour guard against the white man's gun. His was a name that struck terror in the hearts of many whites—including those in this building. He was a target of the FBI, the local police and rival black political factions, and had just been released from prison on charges of attempted manslaughter. He was Black Panther Minister of Defense Huey P. Newton.

We were shown to the elevator, pushed "PH," and arrived at the Panther penthouse to be let in by a black man wider than the door he opened. He was introduced as "Big Man," full-time bodyguard to the Panthers' legendary leader.

Inside the apartment, someone sprang up to greet us, a beautiful man with almond-shaped eyes, a splash of a smile. Like some strong creature, muscular and fine-boned, he leaped at Robin, and they disappeared in a fierce bear hug, grabbing and slapping each other with all the passion of two men come together from opposite points on the planet.

For their own and different reasons, they loved each other deeply. Huey made Robin an "Honorary Panther," gave him a gold Panther ring, considered him his "white brother." Robin, in turn, was there for Huey in the crunches and close calls, and there were many: giving him money, finding him shelter, working with lawyers. At times, I thought he financed the Panthers single-handedly, indirectly dispatching agents of the revolution from behind his desk or beside the pool table of his Hollywood Office of Operations.

Huey gave Robin a front-row seat at the Revolution, took him away from New Rochelle, gave him, as a member of the overprivileged class, political credibility, a means to live out political fantasies. Most of all, he gave him a pass to the people; the best access, the strongest connection he would ever have. And Robin—who referred to the Panthers always as "we" (as in "We want to overthrow the white ruling class")—never let him down.

The previous year, *Life* magazine had featured me on the cover as "Activist Actress Candice Bergen." But it was a title I knew I hadn't earned: I had played it safe, made my protests tastefully and discreetly, without offending others' sensibilities. While some put public opinion, jobs, even lives, on the line, I had risked nothing for what I professed to believe in so strongly. The magazine had even praised me for this restraint—which made me feel, secretly, even guiltier.

I glanced around the Panther penthouse: wall-to-wall carpeting, black-leather sofas, teak tables, Swedish glass (*my* people), a new quadraphonic sound system. Maybe the Revolution wouldn't be so bad. In front of the sliding doors to the balcony, a telescope stood on a tripod, trained on a cell in the Oakland County Courthouse across the lake where Huey had done twelve months in solitary confinement. That was where he got the muscles, Robin told me—doing pushups in solitary. I watched them busily talking, high on each other, energized.

Huey's leg twitched nervously in well-cut slacks, his feet tapping constantly in soft black-leather boots. A knit shirt stretched over swelling arms and shoulders. I never saw him when he wasn't moving, quietly kinetic; his energy seemed endless. But what struck me was how gentle he seemed—polite, soft-spoken, in confusing contrast to the image of him from the famous photograph with Bobby Seale in their Panther berets and black-leather jackets, cradling a machine gun while sitting casually cross-legged in the large fragile fan of a peacock chair.

We spent the next day with Baba Ram Dass—or Richard Alpert, as he'd been known as a professor at Harvard before studying in India and becoming provisional head of the Spiritual Movement in America. It was Ram Dass's tapes on "nonattachment" that Robin played on long drives to Big Sur. It was Ram Dass's book *BEHERE-NOWBEHERENOWBEHERENOW*, that could always be found on Robin's and his friends' coffee tables. The Gideon of the Seventies. And it was Ram Dass who drove us, in his bright-orange Pinto, sucking serenely on a Sugar Daddy, his long beard blowing, to our hotel, where Robin, who relished the role of catalyst, had arranged for him to see Huey.

Ram Dass seemed quietly amused at the discomfort he caused in people; me especially. With his still, clear eyes like long, cool tunnels to a mind that had traveled places most men give their lives not to see, he watched the incipient hysteria in our faces, our thoughts racing like road runners, our eyes, blind with fear, flicking wildly round the room. Not seeing. Not hearing. Not being here now. And I know he knows; I am not here now. But everywhere else I can get my mind on; too frightened to stay put. Unable just to be myself for fear there's no one there.

He talked easily, with Robin's urging, of everyday events in India. Minor miracles that had become, for him, ordinary happenings but that sounded to me like loaves and fishes. And I wondered at the worlds I was missing with my darting to and fro.

When evening came and Ram Dass got up to leave, I was both sad and relieved to see him go. I picked up the clean-chewed stick of the Sugar Daddy from the ashtray and put it in my wallet, where it stayed for years in the hope that someday I could BEHERE-NOW.

That night we drove north to Joan Baez's house for dinner to discuss her Institute for the Study of Nonviolence; she wanted Robin to help her plan a fund-raiser and discuss protest strategy against the war.

It was a cozy cottage in a peaceful valley: rolling hills and farmland, horses and white fences. She came to the door, her son, Gabriel, charging past—a beautiful woman, strong and sure and smiling, standing with slender brown bare feet on hardwood floors in a simple house filled with women, all of them busy.

I liked her at once: her directness and clean intelligence, her courage and her humor. She was someone who had taken risks for what she believed in, put herself on the line, I thought, as she talked about her life with Dylan—feeding him with a spoon while he wrote because he forgot to eat or sleep, laughing and caring and seeming very much alive.

In one weekend, I'd met Huey Newton, Baba Ram Dass and Joan Baez. Arriving back at Robin's house from the airport, my mind was still on "spin cycle."

As we came in the door, we heard a low cackle and a rasping "Hiya." Alone in the living room, draped, toga-like, in a sheet, one end flung across one shoulder, sat Abbie Hoffman—a casual Caesar who had conquered Chicago.

He was not then underground but always on the run, a radical foster child in need of hideouts, handouts and hugs. Who better to come to than Robin—whose house was always open to friends in need? In return, you got a jolt of energy, manic good cheer, a kind of crazed camaraderie that concealed the anger and tough intelligence. The Boston social worker who played court jester in the Revolution, and played it brilliantly.

"Bergen has a date tonight that might interest you," Robin was telling Abbie after we'd settled down to talk.

Abbie peered through his pile of hair and flashed a crooked grin. "Oh yeah?"

Robin chuckled, moving giraffe-like around the pool table, cracking off shots. "Yeah, she's got a date with Henry. You know, Kissinger. The one with the war."

Abbie jumped up, stepping on his sheet, clutching at it, then tugging it from under his feet. His eyes were bright and beady, dancing with the fever of the hunt. "How'd you *do* it? Why didn't you *tell* me? If you'd told me sooner, if I'd known ahead—we coulda organized somethin'. We coulda put acid in his Tab, *anything*. What an opportunity—*wasted*. Shit. Can't you move it?"

I couldn't. Nor did I want to be an accomplice to sending the Secretary of State on an acid trip. I didn't much want to be going on this date at all, had in fact declined both a letter and a phone call inviting me to dinner. Though I was curious to meet Kissinger, it seemed a clear case of consorting with the enemy.

But when I'd told Robin, he'd disagreed. "It's too good to pass up, Bergen. When he calls again," he said, smiling, "and he *will*, tell him you'll go. Find out all you can about him. Confront him about the war. It's an incredible chance to have some input."

Somehow, I didn't think input, mine at least, was what he had in mind. But the next time he called, yes, I said, I'd like to have dinner.

I went home to change, checking facts, preparing questions, nervous about my mission. Henry was late, and he telephoned, explaining that the Secret Service were having trouble finding Beverly Hills.

When he finally arrived at the Aviary, loud music was coming from the poolside speakers of the house across the canyon. As I answered the doorbell, I could hear that the music was Dylan, at full volume, singing, "Something's happening and you don't know what it is, do you, Mister Jones?" In the darkness, I could just make out Robin and Abbie, stretched out on chaise longues, smiling and passing a joint.

We drove off in the simple, unmarked Secret Service car, two simple Secret Service men sitting, like twin ramrods, in the front. They put Henry on the right backseat and locked the doors. I asked if they put him on that side so the guy in front could fling his body over Henry in case of attack. It seemed only practical. They smiled thinly and stared ahead. Kissinger had two ballpoint pens clipped to his jacket pocket and seemed at once a little uneasy and solidly self-assured.

Dinner, given by old friends of my parents in honor of Kissinger's return from his first trip to China with Nixon, was an intimate, elegant affair; Frank Sinatra was among the guests who listened, rapt, to the world of Henry's Orient.

The night belonged to Kissinger. Spinning stories, weaving tales of his trip, adroitly answering careful questions, he was clearly a man at home in his glory, confidently commanding center stage. Sinatra was the first to leave.

I found myself wishing that Kissinger weren't The Enemy. He was funny and charming and all too good—too agile, too articulate, too tough to trap.

And I'm charged with "input." Oh, fine. The perfect opponent. Let's just define policy in Southeast Asia, Henry, here in the back of an unmarked car, while you take the actress back to her Aviary. How about Cambodia? Haiphong?

He was predictably polite and patient, adept with this raving dove in the backseat—perhaps accustomed, by then, to these antiwar monologues making dents in his dates. He even gave me the sense of shared secrets—probably the same set he gave every antiwar actress—which, as soon as he dropped me at home, I ran back to tell the boys.

Days passed quickly now and life had never seemed so full of force or promise. In a few intense weeks, Robin had become the main fix and focus of my life, almost to the exclusion of everything else—though I didn't go down without a fight. But my resistance was no match for Robin, who rolled over it like a Panzer division, tackling me when I retreated into safe, silent corners, coming in after me like some encounter-group commando.

In the face of my sullen silence, he would say, "Don't shut me out, Bergen. I won't let you do it. I'm going to keep coming in after you. The more you pull back. I'm not giving up on this." His lion's head loomed two inches from my face. "Talk to me. Talk to me now about what's going on. Tell me what you're feeling."

And through tightly clenched teeth, "I'm feeling claustrophobic, if you really want to know, that's all. I'm feeling like you're smothering me, sticking your head in my face and sucking up all the oxygen. I'm feeling like it would be good if you'd back off."

But it wasn't in him to back off; he would confront me until my defenses crumbled and I was thrilled to give in. Never was anyone happier to surrender and have their "no"s fall on deaf ears. This was what I had waited for: a man who wanted to take care of me; a man who wouldn't take any lip.

At his constant urging, I was at Robin's much of the time now, burrowed in among his books: Perls, Maslow, Erikson, Reich, Jung, Ram Dass, Castaneda, Watts, Lilly, Gurdjieff, Mao, Newton, Marx, Hegel. Summer reading for the New Mystical Left. The bookcase bulged with volumes on behavior modification, LSD therapy, subjugation of jealousy and maps on open marriage. I guess with so many books on the shelf, I couldn't see the writing on the wall.

Robin was up early every morning, at six thirty or seven, rattling the papers impatiently, giving his morning editorials. Then he was off to run his empire, tucking a fresh hanky in his hip pocket, a childhood anachronism that floored me, hugging, kissing me goodbye as I, the Little Woman, trailed him to the garage to see him off. We talked three or four times a day as I scampered around town, busy now buying groceries and Osterizers, candles and flowers.

And every evening at seven I waited impatiently, fluffing flowers, lighting candles, for the whine of his Porsche up the hill. I had the sauna ready and we'd take one together, have a quick swim, then read through whatever he brought home from the office and discuss the day. *His* day, mainly, since mine had become shirts and sheets, and I listened, rapt and awestruck, asking questions, making suggestions, sincerely excited by the life of this lanky man.

"You're the best, Bergen," he would say, over and over. And if he said I was "the best," that's what I pretended to be. What I wanted was for Robin to love me best, for his past to dim and disappear in my dust. What I wanted, hello, Dad, was to be the Favorite.

"I didn't fall in love with you because you were a cook, Bergen," he said one night, sawing at a steak as I sat, slumped in exhaustion from the effort. "I'm happy to eat out every night. If we want to eat home, Maya can do it." He tapped idly at the glazed carrots. It was a disguised but desperate plea.

Maya was our housekeeper. A strong, strapping young thing, sweet and soft-spoken, with long blond hair and Virgo Rising. A Viking flower child who sprinkled alfalfa sprouts like fairy dust and baked cookies called "granola bombs," tiny, rugged, rocklike things that weighed in like quasars.

She did not stop at good vibes and karmic health, but went on to saving lives and property. One weekend we came home and couldn't find Maya anywhere. Going into the backyard, I looked up and saw her, eyes closed, sitting in a half lotus high on the hill above the house. When I called to her, she opened her eyes, rose quietly and slowly clambered down.

"I had a vision last night that there would be an earthquake today and that the pool would slide down the hill. So I've been up here all day meditating to deflect the quake and I think now the danger is passed," she said, smiling serenely. Maya wanted to write screenplays.

It was a new life I was leading now: new worlds, new feelings, conversations late into the night with friends who would come over to sit around the long table in the big brick kitchen: sometimes Dennis Hopper, in from Taos, director Terry Malick, *Esquire* film critic Jake Brackman, Robin's tiny Gestalt therapist, and any radicals or political outlaws who happened to be passing through.

Robin's friends were people who followed the Spiritual Path, *exposed their feelings, showed love,* and *lived in the Now.* People who *connected* with other people who were *open.* Instead of *closed.* Like me—basically of the *closed* variety—congenitally terrified, but not without promise or potential to be loving and open. At least, that's what Robin and his friends felt. Somewhere inside me was a soul, frightened but full of feeling, longing to get out. And they tried, God, how they tried, to make me feel *loved,* to make me feel *safe.* Jewish welfare with WASPs. I was a tough nut to crack.

We traveled along the Spiritual Path in the Porsche most times, plowing along the Coast Highway to Big Sur to stay in friends' houses that hung high on the edge of cliffs where the fog would roll in, thick and pale and all around us, suddenly receding to reveal the sun and the surf below.

The "consciousness movement" was beginning to find its commercial footing then and there was a veritable smorgasbord of enlightenment techniques. Suspicious soul though I was, it was I, nonetheless, who had the first in a series of Rolfing sessions, stripping down in front of a sad-eyed poet with hands like meathooks who came recommended as "the Rolfer's Rolfer."

While I stood, nude and bemused, he took Polaroids of me before the session to compare my posture with Polaroids to be taken at the end, describing the dramatic difference I would see in the before-and-after snapshots.

In the first introductory Rolf, he began to break down the fascia connecting the muscles that held a lifetime of emotional and physical trauma. This he did by kneading his knuckles between my ribs, along the muscles of my thighs and into the soles of my feet. He did it sympathetically but with incredible pressure and force, transporting me to new frontiers of pain—much like a compassionate Inquisitor extracting a blanket confession of guilt.

I carried enough around with me at all times that I would

have confessed to anything: Yes, yes, I *did* it—just leave my fascia *alone*.

"Don't resist the pain," he said softly as I shrieked. "Try to go through the pain—out to the other side."

"Out to the other side!" I screamed, fingernails shredding the tatami, clawing my way to the door.

At the end of the session, I was grateful to be alive; he helped me to my feet and took another series of Polaroids. As I dressed, he showed them to me: the difference was not only undramatic but almost indiscernible. Still, I felt proud, buoyant, energized, and I ran outside to find Robin, who had been jealously pacing back and forth because a strange man was inside kneading my fascia.

In the evenings we'd light up, watch the sun set, the moon rise, and roll down the mountain to Nepenthe for dinner and Esalen for hot baths. Nights are cold in Big Sur and Esalen doesn't call them hot baths for nothing. They sat, steaming, by candlelight on the face of a cliff shot straight out of the sea, filled with quiet people smoking joints and watching the moon on the water.

They are not watching me; I am virtually certain of this. Yet getting undressed in the soft shadows, and the simple act of walking past them to join friends in the farthest tub is almost more than I can manage. Dropping dignity along with my clothes, I skitter past the tubs of silent, slumped bathers and hurl myself into the water for cover, gasping and close to losing consciousness in the overpowering heat.

"How-to" baths, "how-to" books, "how-to" encounter groups— that was all some people seemed to do. How-to homework. Every now and then I'd grow querulous: Whatever happened to just having fun? An old-fashioned, unconscious good time?

And yet, in spite of myself, I, too, was growing, beginning for the first time to really relax, to discover a sense of my own femininity, my own womanliness. Robin was relentless in his hammering at me to see myself, accept myself, like myself. Talking about "body image," about "coming to terms with how you look." In fact, while I'd always fought furiously to keep it, I was thrilled to see each successive piece of armor fall off.

One morning on a mountain in Big Sur, friends gathered to take a new drug, just out on the market, called MDA. Travel junkie that I was, I had taken LSD before. Having heard tales of incredible kingdoms, of talking animals and paisley-covered trees, I was curious to see them, though cautious about what it might cost. I felt like Columbus in the New World, discovering uncharted continents—a world where the ordinary became astounding. Low plaster ceilings soared like jeweled Byzantine domes over visions of people gliding softly in robes of silver thread, bishops in gold miters, women in glowing Renaissance dress. But there was a Dark Continent as well, where olive trees grabbed at me like live Van Goghs, bluejays loomed like pterodactyls. Once I saw it, I stayed home. I had seen visions enough.

But this drug, while of the psychedelic family, Harvard-born and bred, was not a hallucinogen. The characteristics of the drug, it was explained by those who knew it best, were not flashy, violent, fantastic hallucinations of many colors. This trip was quiet, slow, almost episodic, and the main properties of the drug were introspection and deep, loving feelings. The key feeling it produced, people said, was one of total openness.

I was game but scared that morning. I hardly knew these other people. I didn't know this drug at all. And it was cold outside, with a wet, white fog wrapped around the house. Everyone knew you did drugs in the sunshine, not in the fog. We all sat by the fire in the living room. There was a couple from Big Sur and two writers from New York. We talked quietly and then someone handed the capsules around and passed a glass of water.

I waited nervously, once again, for the drug to come on, for the thin snake of energy to slither up my spine and lodge in my jaw as

I tried, with yawning motions, to relax it, dispel the tension that settled there, disperse the energy. This was a drug of enlightenment, not special effects, and I worried about what the experience would be.

"Do you want to take your armor off now, Bergen?" Robin asked.

"My what?"

"You know, your big gold loops and that 'Bugs' sweater—you don't need all that."

I looked around the circle. Everyone but me looked soft, vulnerable. Soft dresses, soft shirts, soft hair and faces. And I had these flashing gold hoops and a knitted nickname. My armor, I thought, smiling, crying a little, quickly taking off my earrings and sweater. And thinking back to my man-tailored hacking jackets with shirt and tie. My armor. My tricky house with all the trimmings. My armor. My cool composure, caustic one-liners, aloof independence. My armor. Jesus, it was everywhere. In everything I said and did. And tears were streaming down my cheeks and I was laughing. And Robin was crying and laughing too.

The drug, it seemed, was on its way.

We stayed sitting, talking, crying happily. Years of feeling spilling silently, steadily down my face. And one of the girls took my hand and smiled and held it softly. I said how small and fragile hers felt, how delicate and tiny.

"Haven't you ever held a woman's hand before, Candy?"

"Well, no, not really."

"Why not?"

"I don't know. I don't really have many close women friends. And women don't, I mean, women aren't supposed to hold hands, are they?"

"Sure they are."

"Oh, they are? Well, I guess I thought it always looked . . . I always felt uncomfortable. Anyway, I never did."

"How does it feel?"

"Oh, God, it feels great. You know, it just feels great."

In truth, I didn't have many close women friends. Several times, Robin had pointed out the "significant" fact that most of my best friends were men—Mike Nichols, John Calley, Herbert Allen and Henry Jaglom. I would hold up Connie, Rusty, Mary Ellen, and my college roommate, Marcia Weiss; but Connie was by now a fixture in my life, more family than friend, and the others, Robin was quick to point out, all lived in the East and dated back to college. His implication was partly that I was threatened by friendship with women; and even if privately I thought I noted an edge of jealousy in his comments, his point was well-taken and I set out to broaden my field of female friends.

This was typical of Robin's character-renewal efforts; an abundance of criticism and a nugget of truth. And it was Robin who introduced me to my next great friend, Tessa Kennedy, who lived with Elliot Kastner, the producer of a film I worked on in London. It was love at first sight: Here was this woman who looked like one of her five children and spoke, hardly moving her mouth, in a low, deep voice that seemed to come from the soles of her feet. A talented and successful interior designer, she was one of those women— one of those Englishwomen—who did it all and made it look effortless. I felt a total sense of ease with Tessa and with her family, and over the years our friendship would only deepen. Spending time together in L.A. and in London; taking trips together—Morocco, the Middle East—we were easy and physically affectionate together, holding hands, hugging, laughing bawdily at each other's bad jokes. To this day I love Tessa and I love showing it. Women are supposed to hold hands.

Months were passing quickly for the star-crossed couple, days ripping off the calendar, scattering in the wind like a movie time dissolve: an August of Big Sur weekends had fluttered by; September, too, had passed, a shimmering ten days together in Martha's Vineyard. October was New York and November—November was Paris.

Robin had, with a partner, bought the rights worldwide to the films of Charlie Chaplin. The premiere of these was a showing of *Modern Times* in Paris. Robin was going and asked me to come. At my suggestion, we stayed at L'Hotel, a tiny, jewellike town house on the Left Bank. Romantic, exotic, quaint.

This was a considerable concession for Robin, who was not tiny and jewellike but a man six feet four who liked room to roam and space to stretch. Ducking doorways, denting his head on them, he muttered, "Quaint, my ass."

The narrow walls of the suite were upholstered in deep-green tapestried forests of fabric. The furnishings were flawless: art nouveau, leatherbound books, Chinese porcelain on the mantel over the fireplace. It looked like it had been done by a gay French hobbit.

Our second night in Paris, we met the Chaplins in their suite at the Ritz. Charlie and Oona had come from their house in Vevey, Geraldine and her husband, Carlos Saura, had arrived from Madrid, and the rest of the family would join them in time for the press conference and the premiere the following night.

The idea of meeting Chaplin was completely overwhelming, but needn't have been. Oona and Charlie seemed as uncomfortable and timid as those they met. At once courteous and shy, neither had acquired the protective finish of social shellac. Their love for each other was palpable: it was good to see them together, impossible to imagine them otherwise. Oona walked by Charlie's chair, gently smoothing his hair, and Charlie smiled wistfully, clasping her hand. "She looks just the same as the day I met her. Just as beautiful. She hasn't changed at all. Not like me."

We all went to dinner, Le Grand Charlot entering Le Grand Vefour, causing hushed but high commotion. I was seated next to Charlie, whose sight was not all it once was but surprisingly sharp when his eyes fell on pretty girls. Waiters hovered happily, reverently, and even the discreet reserve of the sleek Paris clientele was fractured by his presence.

The next night, a reception and press conference at the Ritz. Guests hung around him in busy clusters, jewels and teeth flashing, jostling for position, waiting to be received. Being eighty-three years old and on the end of a receiving line, Charlie began, after a blur of outstretched arms, to operate on conditioned reflex. His little hand rose quickly, almost mechanically, to shake hands whenever anyone approached, going out even to Oona until he saw who it was, and once to a waiter serving him a drink.

Unlike most people in that unnatural context, Chaplin never assumed an attitude of holding court. Despite his exhaustion, he was always interested, polite, almost ingenuous—far more so than the people who came to meet him, who made the Chaplins conspicuous in their simplicity, their absence of props, their lack of preoccupation with fashion.

Modern Times was a great success, but the Chaplins' visit to Paris had been exhausting, and they returned eagerly to the quiet seclusion of Vevey.

In April they were coaxed out once again—this time for a far more taxing and emotional journey, to America: to New York, to attend another screening of his films at a gala at Lincoln Center, and then on to Los Angeles, where he would be presented with a special Oscar. It would be the first time the Chaplins had returned to America since Charlie, a national hero, was driven out in 1952, a casualty of Cold War conservatism. He had not been back in twenty years and had grave doubts about returning, making up and changing his mind many times before constant urging by family and friends finally convinced him to go.

It was Robin and his partner who were largely responsible for bringing Chaplin back to America, who orchestrated events, organized the awards. And it was Robin's idea that I should be given exclusive photo rights to the Chaplins' visit to America. He presold the story to *Life,* who thought it insane not to have a backup photographer for such an event. White-faced, wild-eyed with terror at the thought of such an assignment, I was the first to agree. I knew I lacked the experience to cover that kind of story, and I felt paralyzed by the pressure.

Robin had little patience with that kind of paralysis and prodded, "In that case, Bergen, you'll have to learn fast because *Life* has agreed and the deal is made. Oona and Charlie like you and trust you; these ten days will be a tremendous strain on them and you're someone whose presence they accept."

And the Chaplins' jet was landing at a special runway at Kennedy and there I was, pushing for a place in the crazed crush of photographers and news teams stampeding through the gate. And the door of the plane swung back, and long, slow moments passed, and suddenly, there was Chaplin, shell-pink face working with emotion, tottering slightly, held fast by Oona, and the tiny pale hand went up in a tentative wave and the crowd roared and cheered and surged forward and I was crying and clicking and everyone was saying Charlie Chaplin had come home.

Life, since they had no other choice, wanted me to do a cover try on Chaplin, a portrait shot into which they would insert a photo of "The Little Tramp." As long as I was going for a *Life* cover, I wasn't wild about their adding an insert to chop it up. Since they wanted the idea of "The Little Tramp" included somehow, I suggested photographing Charlie in front of the huge banner of "The Little Tramp" that hung outside Lincoln Center.

This would have been acceptable had the weather not been cold and raw and Charlie not been obsessed with keeping warm. *Life* then arranged to borrow the twenty-foot banner, rigged it to hang in the ballroom of the Plaza and sent two photo assistants to set up umbrellas and strobe.

I was nervous, *he* was nervous; in the first few shots Charlie looked stiff and uncomfortable. He tired easily, and there was time for just a few more. I asked Oona if she wouldn't stand with him; Charlie relaxed only with her near, and for me the real story was the two of them. She disliked having her picture taken, but she loved Charlie and she stepped in smiling and gently hugged his arm. He looked at her and lit up, and that, as they say, is the shot.

Charlie boarded the plane to Los Angeles with great ambivalence. After agreeing in January to come for the Academy Awards, he felt, as the time grew closer, that he could not go through with it. The memories of what he had been put through there were too painful; the thought of returning terrified him.

During the flight, he crossed to the other side of the plane to see the Grand Canyon. His face lit up. "Oh, yes, this is the place where Doug Fairbanks did a handstand on the precipice. He told me about it." But as they got nearer Los Angeles, he grew more and more nervous, sure he shouldn't have come. He looked fearful and trapped but made a brave attempt to fight it. "Oh, well," he sighed, "it wasn't so bad. After all, I met Oona there."

We all went off to the Awards in a long line of limos, a police escort leading the way. There had been threats, talk of protests, and Robin had arranged with the Academy for a special security force. Charlie and Oona watched most of the Oscar show on TV backstage in a dressing room, pointing excitedly to friends in the huge audience. He was relieved. He had been afraid nobody would come.

Afterward, as he talked about the ceremony, his eyes were bright and childlike, wide with wonder, round with glee. "It almost made me weep—and *this* one"—he cocked his head toward a beaming Oona—"this one kept saying, 'Now don't snivel.'

"It was so *emotional,* and the audience—I felt *their* emotion. I thought some of them might hiss, but they were so sweet—all those famous people, all those artists. You know, they haven't done this to me before. It surpasses everything."

He looked around for his Oscar and did not see it. "Oh, no," he wailed, "all those sweet people and I've lost it." It was retrieved and he sat back serenely. More and more he began to look like a little English schoolboy, grinning impishly, rolling his eyes up innocently, pointing a freckled finger to himself, announcing playfully, "The little genius . . ."

Then, pulling himself to his feet, he took Oona's hand and, humming "Smile"—his theme from *Limelight*—led her gently out the door.

The excitement and force of this time could always be traced back to Robin, and more and more I deferred my life—now pallid by contrast—to his, stepping happily on his shadow, trotting eagerly at his heels.

I had little interest in doing films, and while I wrote for *Esquire*— an article on Bernie Cornfeld, and another on Oscar Levant—my work seemed frivolous, unfocused, compared to Robin's.

There seemed always to be a duality about his dealings— boosting my confidence with one hand while dismantling it with the other. Convincing me I could do anything and criticizing me constantly. Confusing. The Lord giveth and the Lord taketh away.

It was around this time that I began to understand the meaning of the word "anxiety," a word I rarely used. For one phrase I heard a lot from Robin was something he seemed to bring up more and more. I'd never heard it before, myself; the expression was "sexual non-exclusivity." Pronounced trippingly on the tongue. I didn't, at first, know what it meant. In time, it would come to mean so much. Skin rashes, mild hyperventilation, loss of appetite, chills, slight disorientation, eroded self-confidence and severe fear. Put them together and they spell symptomatic anxiety. Or sexual nonexclusivity.

"The only realistic base for any love relationship is sexual non-exclusivity," declares Robin.

"What do you mean by that exactly?"

"Where two people feel secure enough and free enough to explore sexually with other people."

"What do you mean, 'other people'? What does that mean, 'explore sexually'?"

"I'm sorry it's so threatening to you, Bergen, but you have to understand that I'm a love object for every woman who walks into my office. And so are you, only you're too insecure to see it. Start dealing with that—it's time you began growing up."

This was not the way things were supposed to go here. They were *supposed* to carry you off to the castle where you grew old together. Not theorize on sex over dinner. Wait a minute. Hello, Walt?

I lie stiff and still, in the darkness. The reflection of my house, pale and empty, hangs suspended in the mirror on the wall. During the night a heavy fog rolls in, and by dawn my house has disappeared.

12

"Tall, manly, wears long hair, mod clothing, and has outspoken nature . . . is frequently seen in company of brunette starlet . . ." Robin's FBI file read in part.

Brunette?

Starlet?

It was springtime for the starlet and the manly radical. Our birthdays came—four days apart, twenty-six and thirty-nine—and went, and this had been no ordinary year.

The war had escalated to its highest peak, and Daniel Ellsberg, for his efforts to stop it, was on trial for the theft of the Pentagon Papers. As usual, Robin was in the thick of things, participating in the Pentagon Papers Peace Project, Ellsberg's defense fund. Eventually he decided he could best serve the cause by making a film on America's involvement in the war.

At the same time, the Panthers were running Bobby Seale for mayor of Oakland. Huey—whose new title was Supreme Servant of the People, or the Servant, for short—was at the house for days at a time going over campaign strategy with Robin while I gave "Big Man," his bodyguard, chocolate chip cookies in the kitchen. In their new tactics of working for change within the system, the Panthers, Robin explained, "would hold massive rallies called Survival Conferences, where we will organize a giant giveaway of free food and shoes . . ." for which Robin footed the bill of $300,000. Which more than earned him his Panther first person plural.

The house fairly hummed with activity, and through our sauna passed some of the best and the brightest our country's Left had to offer: sitting in sweaty summits, shuffling out to cool off and continue in the pool. Pat and Dan Ellsberg came often; the trial was approaching and Nixon closing in. Together with Robin and their chief defense attorney, Leonard Weinglass, they would map out, explore defense strategies for the historic trial to come.

Pat was an intelligent and generous woman. Dan was intense, obsessive, implosive, a brilliant man with a mind that sped so far, so fast that his speech often stuttered in an attempt to catch up.

They were times of tension. People were wary, phone calls cautious. Huey would arrive unexpectedly at times, hiding from someone—rival black factions or the FBI. He would go for days without sleeping, wild-eyed, unshaven, almost incoherent. Pacing relentlessly back and forth, thrashing out some theory, dealing with some demon, knocking at three and four in the morning on the bedroom door wanting to speak to Robin, who would sit with him in the living room, where Huey would talk feverishly till dawn.

This was often more than I had signed on for and I would sit for hours as at a tennis final, head whipping back and forth from one to the other, listening, not often understanding, imagining Feds in the ferns and wondering when I would get Huey's bullet. Reality was difficult to recognize. One evening we took Dan and Pat, Huey and Big Man to a Chinese restaurant for dinner. Eyes running, gasping after the dumplings in red and spicy beef, we drank our tea and passed the fortune cookies. Mine read, "You will receive a message in the mail; destroy it at once before the FBI sees it."

Political fund-raisers were legion that year, and, with Jane Fonda, Robin decided we should give one of our own for Indochina Relief. We met at the house to plan it. Jane, bare breasted under a sheer black peasant blouse—taut, intense, stunning—was fierce in her dedication to the Revolution and spoke rapid-fire of "Stalinists and Trots" and the difficulty of resolving her own "internal contradictions."

Robin was more philosophical about his, knowing that he was equally committed politically. He did, after all, devote his considerable resources, financial and intellectual, to the cause, and passed off as humorous the contrast between his politics and his lifestyle. He even seemed to enjoy the irony, wryly cracking that with any luck the Revolution would come after his death—meanwhile allowing him to hang on to his sauna, pool and Porsche.

But what about me? Everyone, it seemed, was in jeopardy. Everyone had something to lose. Except me. She who risks nothing. It did not pass unnoticed. Where, Robin wondered, was my commitment? What had become of the plucky political animal he so admired? My zeal didn't quite match up.

My old friends, who still employed the traditional handshake in greeting instead of the Black Power salute, had already been stamped with the seal of the ruling class, condemned to wear a large letter *E* for Establishment across their chests. Robin had already reviewed and rejected them as enemies of the Revolution, irrelevant, politically unfit, and such was my strength of character that I hardly saw them anymore.

Not sufficient proof, apparently, of my commitment. Perhaps, it occurred to Robin, I wasn't all my publicity promised. Perhaps it was a simple case of mistaken identity. He had fallen in love with someone else, a psychic explorer committed to change; instead, I seemed committed to little more than preparing his dinner. What *were* my values, anyway? What did I believe in? Where was *Life*'s "Activist Actress" when the going got rough?

She was creeping along in the fast lane, trying hard to keep up, pretending to be someone she wasn't. She was missing her family, her friends, her house; she no longer laughed or had fun.

"The difference between you and me, Bergen," Robin declared

to me one day, "is that if it were the Russian Revolution you would be inside dancing with the nobility and I'd be outside with the peasants, with my face pressed against the window." Possibly. But I'd be *guilty* about dancing with the nobility, and he'd drive away from the peasants in a Porsche.

"If you're not part of the solution, you're part of the problem," he would now announce pointedly. Clearly I was part of the problem. He was right. It was true—I was not doing my share. I sat up, started listening, went to more slide shows on Indochina, spoke at rallies, attended meetings, and marched in Washington. Political homework.

In Washington, protesters were tripping over each other in their efforts to make themselves heard—group after group, day after day; at times the city seemed too small to contain its country's grievances. In an effort to show the sweeping spectrum of Americans in opposition to the war, a group called REDRESS organized its second demonstration of civil disobedience by successful, proven members of the country's Establishment. The strategy was to create media impact through the mass arrests of short-haired, tied-and-suited, middle-aged solid citizens—among them Joe Papp, George Plimpton, Dr. Spock, Robin and me—to broaden the image of the antiwar base largely known as acid freaks in gas masks.

At a press conference in the Senate Building, Ted Kennedy, Mike Gravel and Dr. Robert Lifton of Yale spoke, and I was asked to read the Redress portion of the Constitution. We then walked to the doors of the Senate chambers where George Plimpton—sheepishly explaining he couldn't stay for the arrest because he had to be back in New York to accept a Good Citizenship Award—read the petition. We promptly lay down—one hundred and fifty well-heeled, wall-to-wall citizens carpeting the Senate corridor—and waited to be arrested.

Several Senators stepped angrily over and on us on their way to work. (It was hard enough making Senate sessions on time but some days made you wonder if the job was really worth it.) Barry Goldwater, gingerly picking his way over us, tripped on my leg. Gee, it was the first time I'd seen him since, as Miss University, my freshman year in college, I'd escorted him around the campus. And here he was again, larger than life, stepping over me on his way to work. It truly *is* a global village.

We lay there quietly waiting for the police. A woman near us began to cry; Robin took her hand and stroked it. Some of us were scared, most of us were nervous; the excitement of the morning had grown anxious as we lay on the cool marble floor, holding hands, waiting silently, politely. This group had manners.

A half hour elapsed, and then we heard them coming, rounding the corner at the end of the hall—a line of police, each one taking one of our group by the arm and leading them out of the building to waiting paddy wagons.

The paddy wagons were segregated, men and women in separate ones—about eight people in each. I looked around me at these pleasant-faced women, most in their forties and fifties, many of them housewives—well-meaning, well educated, sincere in their caring, firm in their position against the war, committed to taking a stand. They were Betty Crocker, Julia Child—mothers, doctors, lawyers, writers; one took snapshots of her new friends in the paddy wagon with her Instamatic and later sent us all souvenir prints.

Inside the police station, we were fingerprinted and lined up for mug shots. Just like in the movies. The police pocketed extras of mine and quietly asked me to sign them. We were put in a holding tank, six to a cell, then taken to tough-jawed policewomen who booked us and took information for our records.

Even under rarefied conditions—a few short hours, a frozen baloney sandwich—we all wanted out of that jail. Glad that we'd had a glimpse of one, guilty that it was on our own terms, we were released late that afternoon, free to return to the comforts of privilege and position. As if we'd ever left them.

The next morning there were headlines around the country and, while you could hardly call us marked men, there were one hundred and fifty new names on the nation's police records . . . "arrested for obstructing a corridor by lying down."

My parents were horrified by my arrest—but then, horror was almost a constant when they contemplated my life these days. Our political battles had only gotten worse over the years: while I kept company (more than my parents knew) with the likes of Huey Newton and Abbie Hoffman, my father was, as always, a staunch member of L.A.'s renowned Republican set, many of whom would later become part of the Reagan Kitchen Cabinet.

I campaigned cross-country for McGovern while my father took to the stump for Nixon. He saw my support of McGovern as senseless and self-destructive. How could I back a man whose programs were so socialistic? A 50 percent inheritance tax! Didn't I see that I was only spiting myself in the end? Did I just want to throw away my inheritance? Cast it to the liberal wind?

My politics were now indivisible, in my parents' eyes, from my relationship with Robin. They could not appreciate my arguments on his behalf. My mother swore, the one time he came for dinner at their house, that he spent the whole of it gazing at his reflection in the mirror opposite him. And when, on the phone, he called her "Frannie" and urged her to "go with the flow," she cast her vote as an emphatic "No."

My father, never much good at names at the best of times, blocked Robin's completely. "That producer fellow" was the closest he ever came. They were enemies in each other's eyes, and where I was concerned, either side was the losing side. If I sided with one, I lost the other. And I felt torn between the two.

In the two years I lived with Robin, I never announced my change of residence to my father. My mother knew and disapproved but, as in the past, protected me. Not only did I not tell my father; I implied otherwise, inviting my parents to dinners at the Aviary, where I rarely went now, to indicate that in spite of my relationship I had not strayed but had stayed close to home. That, no matter what, my heart belonged to Daddy.

Robin wasted no time in nailing me on it. "Why do you have to play such childish games? You're being dishonest. This is where you live; have them to dinner here." Which, in order not to incur increasing disapproval, I reluctantly did, frantically straddling both sides of the filial fence.

Robin's attitude toward my father, his pressure on me to come clean, were sometimes unbearable, but at other times productive. One night, as I was saying goodbye to my father on the phone, nicely but stiffly, Robin called out casually from across the room, "Tell him you love him." The suggestion was so startling that, without thinking, I suddenly stammered, "I love you, Dad."

After a short but stunned silence, my father said quickly, "Well, that's nice, Monstro, I love you too"; and, pleased but embarrassed, we hurriedly hung up. It was a milestone for me and I was ecstatic, amazed at what I had done. It was the first time either of us had ever said "I love you" to the other—even if it was on the phone. We could never have managed it in person.

When he turned forty, Robin dissolved his company, decided to devote himself to radical politics and set about making his life an extension of those beliefs. A midlife shake-up, some might call it, but he preferred to think of it as yet another step in the process of nonattachment, the endless expedition of Living in the Now.

"Monogamy is a bourgeois concept, a middle-class constraint," was a line I heard a lot. "I think I'd be happiest living in a commune, in a collective of all my friends. Everybody living, being, together. I'd like to try that someday."

"*Living in a commune?*"

"Um-humh."

"When, exactly, were you thinking of trying it?"

"I don't know. Soon. The idea seems so natural, so loving, so whole. It really appeals to me."

Clearing of throat. "I kind of like the *two-person* commune myself. I don't want to live with anyone else, in fact, I'd hate it. I hardly like when people come for dinner."

"Look, Bergen, we're very different animals. You're basically a very guarded, closed person who enjoys her time alone. I prefer being with people. Being alone is painful to me. I need that human connection."

"So?"

"So, if you want to go away to work on a story or a film, you have to realize I'm going to be seeing other women. Living in a more communal structure, with friends, would obviate that need. But for now, if, say, you leave for any period of time—for your *own* needs, which are fine—just accept *my* needs for company during that time."

"But work is different from—"

"Bergen, we each have our own needs, our own pain."

But I . . . but you . . . but wait . . . isn't this what they call blackmail? Just my luck to creep out from under the rainbow to slam slap into the Commander Perry of relationships, exploring the frozen tundra of sexual freedom.

He was impatient to explore and experiment with life on all levels. And he wanted to do this with me. Because I appeared to be the kind of partner he was looking for. Because I was an explorer myself. Except now, because of him, what I wanted to explore was all the things he wanted to break with.

His case was so convincing—based on total honesty, sharing,

greater intimacy, trust and conquering old conditioning of posses-
siveness, jealousy and fear—that I couldn't, beyond wild-eyed and
incoherent weeping, come up with one of my own.

His needs for "human connection" seemed a high price to pay
for my needs to travel and work; but when he showed signs of carrying through his policy, I did the only sensible thing—I never left.
After all, I had my principles; I just didn't know how to hang on to
them. I may have been twenty-six, but I wasn't grown-up enough to
hold on to myself.

I got an offer for a film. With Paul Newman. In Malta. For
twelve weeks. Twelve weeks is three months. Three months is
ninety days. Ninety days away, leaving the Love Object alone. For
ninety nights.

My agent was waiting for an answer. "Uh, Sue? I think I'll pass.
Yeah, I know I haven't worked in a year. Sure, I know it's Paul Newman. Right, you told me John Huston was directing. I agree it's
good money. Well, it's not something I can put my finger on exactly.
I just think . . . the material is too risky."

When it came to choosing me or the relationship, there was no
question. Already, there was little enough left of me; soon, there
would be nothing left of the relationship.

In 1973, in the afterglow of Nixon's first trips behind the Iron
and Bamboo Curtains, a New York newspaper called the *Guardian* announced that it was going to sponsor a group of twenty people on a tour of the People's Republic of China. Robin had been
approached about joining the group and suggested me as well. The
only credentials required were participation in some area loosely
defined as "the arts" and evidence of liberal political leanings and
activities.

It was one of the first American groups to go to China since
Nixon's meetings with Mao. The trip would be unofficial and we

would travel without State Department approval or protection. "Red China," as it was still called then by all but the liberal cognoscenti: mysterious as Mars; Gang of Four, Red Guards, Long March, Great Wall—800,000,000 people marching around in Mao jackets with no makeup. It was not the American Way.

The *Guardian's* intention was to assemble a representative group from different racial, geographical and financial backgrounds. The final group was twenty-one: nine men, twelve women; sixteen whites, four blacks, and one Chicano; or five hard-core Marxist-Leninists, three soft-core, six old-line radicals, two young radicals, one black Muslim, one feminist, two committed vegetarians and one McGovern Democrat (guess who).

The *Guardian* advised specificity in the visa application. If you'd made films, for example, list titles. Give examples of political activity, etc. It was implied that my political credentials might be substandard. So I synopsized some of the films I'd been in: *The Sand Pebbles,* a story of American imperialism in China; *Getting Straight,* about the student revolution in America; *Soldier Blue,* the white man's genocide of the American Indian; *Carnal Knowledge,* which dealt with the oppression of women in America. I left out *The Adventurers.* It read like the most radical catalogue of films ever to hit the screen. It made Jane Fonda look like Sandra Dee. I got in.

When we were sent our itinerary, it was addressed "Dear Cultural Worker: You will be visiting the following cities in China: Canton, Changsha, Shao-hsing, Peking, Soochow and Shanghai." What in God's name was a Cultural Worker? I was the only one in the group who had to ask. A Cultural Worker, in Marxist terminology, is someone in the arts. For the next month, I was to be one.

I wanted to see China as a tourist, not as an architect of the Revolution, and in a group whose Marxist commitment ran high, it was clear I was just along for the ride. I sat in the back of the bus taking notes for an article I was writing on the trip for *Playboy* (not a Marxist publication) called "Can a Cultural Worker from Beverly Hills Find Happiness in the People's Republic of China?"

In our traveling collective, day after day the dialectical debates grew more heated; ideologies were argued, cries of "counterrevolutionary," accusations of "revisionist" could be heard. The Marxist leaders complained about the level of commitment to the Movement.

With a guide, we discussed sexual morality in China. Premarital sex, we were told, does not exist in the People's Republic. Yeah, but . . . There are no buts; buts also do not exist. Still, I persisted, "What if a boy and girl want to . . . ?" "They don't," I was told firmly. After three weeks in China, I believed her. There was a total absence of sexual energy. I felt as though I had been neutered. The very idea of sex was redolent of bourgeois self-indulgence. In China, marriage is called "class friendship." We asked what qualities people looked for in a "class friend." "Political ideology" was the reply. Well, I knew that story.

Robin and I were engaged in a class struggle of our own through most of China. Still as impatient with my incessant insecurity as I was aggravated by his dogmatic self-assurance, he hammered at me to see myself—the light side and the dark—and to try to change the parts in me that held me back. Certain dialogues were doggedly constant with us, the subtext steadfast: "interior space," "ego needs," "feel my pain," "overcommunicating," his "frontal attacks," my "sneak assaults," my self-doubts, his inordinate rage, my manic evasion of his compulsive confrontations, my neurotic need for "positive feedback," his manipulation of my fears, my refusal to accept responsibility for my behavior. On and on and on—red-eyed and tight-lipped—the Red Guard and the Revisionist . . . see them cut a swath across the People's Republic in a tale of Revolutionary Romanticism.

Our last day in China was May 9, my twenty-seventh birthday. I felt much older. Three weeks after we had left, we returned to

Hong Kong, where we left the group to check into a suite at the Peninsula Hotel and the next day fly home—first class.

There was a party the night we got home from China, given by some of my friends, not Robin's. Nice people, old friends I liked, and over the last two years had missed seeing. After three solid weeks of dialectics, I wanted conversations without class struggles. A little capitalist companionship, lighthearted laughter, yes, even frivolity. And, like Marco Polo, I had wondrous tales of the Orient.

Robin refused to go. Finally, I went alone, promising to stay only a short time and to be home by eleven.

Time, as you know, flies. It was a fine party, and when the hostess called me to the phone, I looked at my watch with dread. It was one thirty. I was in for it.

"Get home immediately." The voice was trembling, tight with rage. And then the fear ball, when you can't find your stomach: you seem to have dropped it somewhere and suddenly you are four years old and really scared, and you edge stiffly out the door, knowing you're going to get it.

He was sitting on the bed, shaking with anger; his speech was slurred but deliberate. There was a tape recorder in front of him. He pushed the red "record" button, explaining, so slowly, that he was going to tape the dialogue of this argument for my benefit so that, at a later date, I could replay it and possibly understand my behavior in these situations. This was going to be a big one.

And then—for two hours—he proceeded to talk, clenching and unclenching his fists, about how this was yet another example of the ways in which I tried to undercut him, tried to destroy the relationship. Of my constant subconscious manipulation designed to keep control.

I was silent, weary, watching. Yes, I said I'd be home by eleven.

Of course, I should have called. You're right, it probably is indicative of something larger on my part and I will try and confront my anger. Head hung, humbled, penitent before my confessor and his Sony. God, he was good. In countless little ways, I always asked for it, but the overkill could drive you crazy.

It was 4 A.M., he was still going; when was I going to get in touch with my behavior? Why couldn't I stay conscious? I was irresponsible and cruel. I was a killer. He was screaming now while I shook with the traditional defensive sobbing. Suddenly, he picked up the television at the foot of the bed and hurled it into the next room, where it shattered on the brick floor. I was terrified and also awed: it was our most significant breakage so far, and on some level fairly impressive.

After that, our fights remained at fever pitch; the arguments grew increasingly violent, until I felt like a stewardess, ready to leave at a moment's notice. The house was often scattered with our debris the day after a fight. Bewildered gardeners would find the pool furniture—appropriately—at the bottom of the pool, where we had flung it the night before; metal gates were wrenched off their hinges, doors hung askew, assorted windows were cracked or broken. I was glad these fights took place at Robin's house instead of my own. Appearances would have indicated that its tenant was The Incredible Hulk. One of us usually nursed a cut from all the glass we broke, flashing Band-Aids like seals of long-suffering. I would drive violently. He would drive violently. Clutches were replaced routinely and carpenters came and went on a monthly basis. It was a wonder either of us was alive to complain about the other.

A Los Angeles day: relentlessly sunny, a toasty 78 degrees, the city lightly browned by smog, and I am alone, lying outside by the pool in a state of semi-coma that is now familiar and fairly common. I am also crying. Of course.

What a fine figure of a woman I present—slumped, with the

spine of a soufflé. Sniveling, I look over, through tiny red eyes, at my house: bright yellow awnings flapping gaily in the breeze, bougainvillea tumbling down the wall, sun searing through the stained-glass windows. I love my house. I miss it.

In the beginning, I was so reluctant about it all—leaving my house, moving in, sharing a life. Reluctant to lower my defenses, but finally thrilled to give in. And when I gave in, I somehow gave up, misplaced myself. I seemed to have disappeared.

Naturally, all this would tend to close in on a guy, put the squeeze on him, give him a cozy dose of claustrophobia. Now, this man who had wanted so much to take care of me, who was so enraged when I resisted—now when we talked, he was contemptuous of the dependent creature I'd become. And I was paralyzed. I knew I should leave—and lose Robin. I knew I could stay—and lose myself.

What am I waiting for? An exit visa? What more does it take for me to leave? One night, I am in the kitchen; Robin is in the next room talking on the phone. He seems to be saying something about a woman. Yes, he's talking about someone who is no longer the woman she was when he met her. Someone he thought was sure and independent, committed, an explorer. Now she's lost her strength, become weak and vulnerable; one of her problems is—she's hung up on her father. . . .

Hung up on her father? *Me?*

Robin and his friends with backgrounds in analysis from the East had been the first people ever to ask me pointedly what it was like growing up with a father like mine, with a dummy as a sibling. I was surprised by their interest and dismissed their questions lightly, cavalierly. I had never paid it much attention; it seemed normal to me. Psychological impact? Traumatic effect? A *dummy?* Weren't they carrying Freud a bit too far? Frankly, I never paid much attention to him—ah, *it.*

The point, I now saw, was not that I had grown up with a

dummy; it was that I had grown up with a dummy and his ventriloquist—the very metaphor for manipulation. From those early mornings in the breakfast room, Charlie on one knee, me on the other, my father's hand squeezing my neck, his voice putting words in my mouth . . . who better than Robin for a girl schooled so literally in manipulative relationships? Wasn't he another ventriloquist in kind?

In being a rebellion against my father, the relationship was all about him in the end. Beneath the rebellious daughter was the devoted and dutiful one. The little girl who longed to please her daddy. The girl who was "her father's child." If I feigned indifference to, even provoked, my father's disapproval, it was because I still needed it so deeply, and had turned to Robin for his in its stead. Robin, who brought me to life the way my father animated blocks of wood. Squeezed my neck. Pulled my strings. Supplied my dialogue. Grew impatient when I failed to perform. Everything short of putting me on his knee. But all he had to do was ask. . . .

Our breaking up was anticlimactic in contrast to what had come before. There was no final decisive battle; we had been breaking up, skirmishing steadily, for the better part of two years. Our first few months had been idyllic, but it was not for nothing that I was sleeping under the rainbow when we met, adrift in a sea of dreams; and it was not for nothing that he was a brand-new bachelor, cresting the wave of change. Our needs were great and opposing, and had begun, after a few months, to overwhelm a relationship that sank beneath their weight. The battle had been lost in the beginning, but neither of us had wanted to admit we couldn't win.

I moved out and kept moving. I didn't want to—couldn't— look back, and to make it easier, I put as much distance as I could between us. The Aviary was too close for comfort; I put the house and most of its contents up for sale, and I never slept under the rainbow again. I wanted no things to tie me down, but to start fresh, free and clean, with not much more than I could carry. It was back to traveling light and traveling fast.

It was no longer a problem of whether I would surrender myself in a relationship. Now I was faced with finding the self I had already lost, reclaiming it and establishing sovereignty over it, so that I would not be so quick to give it up again.

Starting Over

13

D. H. Lawrence once wrote to a friend about travel:

It only excites the outside. The inside it leaves more isolated and stoic than ever. It is all a form of running away from oneself and the great problems.

At the time I came across this quotation in a newspaper, it incensed me, and yet I clipped it out and carried it with me for years. Carried it to Nairobi, carried it to Cairo, to Dar es Salaam, Rio de Janeiro, Kyoto, Teheran . . .

The first ticket to cross my palm came courtesy of a travel magazine that assigned me two stories: a piece on Ethiopia, to include, if possible, an interview with Haile Selassie, and a report on the Masai tribe in Kenya.

On the plane I watched, a little unsteadily, as L.A. disappeared below. Back to Africa, back on my own. How do I do it? I forget how you do it. Alone. I look at my ticket: L.A.—London—Rome—Nairobi—Addis Ababa . . . *Addis Ababa?* Am I insane?

Then, softly, tiny whispers in my ear—oh yeah, oh yeah, it's all coming back to me, right, I remember now. I forgot about all the options open out there. Traveling, exploring, nosing around on my own. Freedom. No commitments. Belonging to myself.

Once in Addis Ababa, I applied for an audience with the Emperor, then went north to travel the country until my request was approved. The peak of the trip was Harar, straight out of fairy tales and fables. Behind its high walls, in the Moslem marketplace, were faces and costumes from every tribe—Gallas, Tigres, Somalis, Cottus: faces that gave you just a glimpse, each one more beautiful, more exotic than the last; costumes of spectacular color—magenta, emerald, crimson, tangerine.

The women fascinated me most—Cottu women wrapped in black with dark, striking faces, amber at their throats; Galla women with ruby-studded nostrils, a Tigre woman who shone like the sun in a dress of spun gold. They wove colors into baskets and sold spices in brilliant pyramids of saffron and mustard.

Down a cobblestoned street, Rimbaud's residence crumbled like an old gingerbread castle; wiry, wizened men, delicately bearded and swathed in cloth, padded silently by, taking no notice of this romantic shrine, or of the blond American who gaped at it.

Since there wasn't a lot to do in Harar after dark, the entire nightlife consisted of going to the edge of town to watch the "Hyena Man"—a man who called the hyenas that lurked in the hills and fed them by hand. He was said to be the only man to succeed in getting wild hyenas to take food from a human being.

The night before I was to return to Addis, I went to see for myself. About twenty huge hyenas skulked around him, casting furtive looks, and crept up edgily to snatch strips of meat from his hand. Their jaws were strong enough to snap an elephant's leg in two. Suddenly he motioned to me and handed me a femur (of what? I wondered). I held it out to them—obviously a part of the floor show—until one came up and took it daintily from my fingers. And for the finale, one slunk up and gingerly took a bone the Hyena Man held between his teeth. Frozen nose to nose: a moment of trust between two creatures trying to make a living.

• • •

The Emperor's offices were in King Menelik's old palace, built before the turn of the century; caged outside the entrance were two decrepit dozing lions who looked to be from the turn of the century as well. A faded tomato-colored carpet was unrolled and I turned to look for a dignitary, but it appeared to be for me. The tall doors opened and I was silently shown into the vast reaches of an office.

Facing me were an elaborate carved desk flanked with flags and a marble fireplace banked with a huge polar-bear rug upon which quivered a tiny bat-eared Chihuahua. On the left was a cluster of chairs—one of which was grand, gilt and brocade, topped with a crown and the imperial insignia—apparently a throne. The Emperor was in it.

His Imperial Majesty Haile Selassie I, Emperor of Ethiopia, King of Kings, Elect of God and Conquering Lion of Judah, silently and slowly rose to greet me. A little man with a lot of medals. A hero for millions of people around the world, a villain for millions of others, he was the last in a league of great world leaders, having survived his contemporaries: Churchill, Roosevelt, de Gaulle. We shook hands and I dipped into a shaky curtsy.

His Majesty, who was eighty-two, had just finished meeting with all his ministers; his son, the Crown Prince, had recently suffered a stroke in London; Princess Anne was visiting Ethiopia. And some actress from America wanted an interview for a travel magazine.

I plunged ahead guiltily with the help of a translator in Amharic, stuck with the prosaic questions I had submitted for approval in advance: how he felt about the achievement of the Organization for African Unity, his personal project; were education and health care the primary thrusts for development? What was his attitude toward America at the present? I got the kind of programmed answers I deserved.

He was very patient but seemed wooden and weary. His face was extraordinary, piercing and fierce, and I wanted very much to photograph him, but had the nerve to take only three shots. I felt my visit was a frivolous imposition on a tired old man trying to run a country; I thanked him for his time, shook hands and said goodbye.

For the piece on the Masai, I returned to Nairobi, where I'd heard about a Masai witch doctor, a *laibon*, rumored to be the greatest of them all. Like many famous, successful doctors, this one was immensely wealthy—translating, in his case, to an eight-hut *boma* (or village) instead of a six-hut one, eight wives and many fine cattle.

His village was a half day's drive from Nairobi, isolated in the middle of the vast Rift Valley. I carried with me, as instructed, bags of tea and sugar for the *laibon*'s wives, gallon cans of liquor for him, candy for his multitude of children, and, for myself, a young Masai named Paul to translate. Since I wanted to watch the witch doctor perform—casting spells, throwing stones—he had suggested I spend the night as, like so many creative people, he performed best when drunk.

I arrived at midday and met the *laibon*—a striking old man with opaque eyes, draped in a *shuka* and carrying a spear. We walked through the *boma* and, through Paul, he explained that there were good and evil *laibon*—altruistic witch doctors who helped people and malicious men who specialized in evil spells. He was of the former category, catering to a clientele whose most common requests were for health, wealth, popularity and fertility. Like most faith healers, he asked no fee. And like most faith healers, he had more riches than he knew what to do with. People paid what they could afford; in this case, cows were graciously accepted.

A *boma* is a group of huts made of sticks and dried cow dung, arranged in a circle and protected by a shoulder-high wall of thorn-tree branches, forming a kind of corral. I spent a slow and fly-filled day in the *boma* and, at sunset, watched the tribesmen herd their goats and cattle back inside the compound for the night, carefully closing up the entrance to protect the herd from lions, cheetahs and other predators.

Once the herds were safely inside, women and children, clutching pans and gourds, scurried around inside the compound milking the animals for dinner—usually two to three quarts of milk, sometimes mixed with cow's blood. The *laibon* beckoned for me to join him outside his hut, pointing to a tiny tripod stool. I sat and he graciously gave me dinner: his personal gourd, or calabash, washed with cow's urine and filled with fresh goat's milk. Because of the arid land and lack of water, the Masai use cow urine to wash their utensils and as a preservative. I drank a little more than half the contents—Paul's estimate of the minimum necessary to avoid offending the *laibon*.

Next, a bunch of leaves appeared before me and Paul told me to chew them, explaining that they grew at the base of Mount Kenya and were called *bhang*. "They're not strong," he said. "They take away sleep and hunger." We sat in the moonlight chewing twigs until my tongue withered and my teeth were full of bark.

Eventually the *laibon* stood up and disappeared into his hut to drink the liquor I'd brought and get in shape to demonstrate some fancy spells. But perhaps I'd brought too much: he didn't come out till morning.

The women and children were now singing gaily, dancing gracefully as they do each night—tiny voices piping cheerfully off-key, everyone laughing and enjoying it all. I thought that I had never seen happier people.

I threaded my way through sleeping cattle and watched the silhouettes of smooth, shaved heads bobbing rhythmically in the moonlight, sharp arcs of steers' horns curving above them. When I sat down to rest on a rock that turned out to be a sleeping cow, the women burst out laughing and motioned for me to join them. They started me singing with them, stopping sometimes to check my feeble warbling, "*Hi yee hi yo,*" then collapsing in hoots, and urging me to try again.

Then one of the girls pulled me up to dance with her. I tried to imitate her smooth, swaying shuffle but finally showed her instead how to lead in a basic box step that brought the house down.

They were insatiably curious about me, both women and children, running their hands through my long, light hair, comparing the tiny pierced holes in my ears to the elongated two-inch openings in theirs. They felt me all over my body, cheerfully unbuttoning my shirt and gently touching my breasts. For one so modest in movies, I felt curiously comfortable under their scrutiny.

When all had drifted off to their huts, I guessed I ought to do likewise, but I had some apprehensions. To enter the hut, you had to crouch and crawl through a low, twisting tunnel; once inside, you had to stoop to stand up. There were no windows for ventilation, and the fire in the center had died out and now gave off smoke, not heat. It was like sleeping in a barbecue.

I groped my way around the hut, through the fire, and finally felt the cowhide platform that was to be my bed. I also found Paul, a baby goat and an old woman curled up in a corner. I lay down on the skins, wedging my nose next to a tiny hole I found in the wall, and tried to suck in some air. Within minutes, my body was a festival of fleas. It was going to be a long night.

I lay there in the pitch blackness trying to hold off a mounting attack of claustrophobia, struggling to breathe, concentrating on the sounds around me: the shuffling of some cows who couldn't sleep either, the laughter and low voices of the warriors guarding the herd. The sound of Paul's breathing next to me was growing heavier and was followed by the noise of a zipper opening.

Sex among the Masai has little ritual; there is no dating period, no dinner and a movie. It is fairly straightforward; so was Paul. I suggested nicely that he spend the night in the unmarried women's hut, and he apologized politely and crawled outside.

I lay awake until finally, on hands and knees, I felt my way through the hut and back out the tunnel, rolled up on the ground in my hotel bedspread and fell asleep. I was awakened at sunrise by a calf licking my hair.

Often, later, I thought of the Masai, and imagined what they must be doing. The herds are in safe for the night and the Masai have milked their dinner. The women and children are singing and laughing and the *laibon* and the elders are sitting and talking, drinking honey wine. There will be sleep, then sunrise. And the women and children will pray to Venus, the morning star: *I pray to you who rises yonder to hear me. Keep my cows alive. Take care of my people.*

By the end of my magazine assignment I was not only reacclimated to the joys of travel, the stimulation of constant change, the simplicity of solitude; I was hooked.

Next, Teheran, to Shiraz, Isfahan, Mashad, the Caspian Sea. The farther away from home I got, the more buoyant I became. Avoidance through adventure: the longer I stayed away, the more level my mood remained. Where once traveling had been exploration, it had now become an escape.

It was the return trip I had trouble with. No sooner did I board the plane than my spirits abruptly sank; I became low and listless. They were the true symptoms of a travel junkie, and for the next two years there was always the rush of another assignment, another trip, another location.

In the spring of '74 I signed to make a film in New Mexico. *Bite the Bullet* was a Richard Brooks film co-starring Gene Hackman and James Coburn. It was a film about a cross-country horse race, and the character I played was one of the contestants. I was confident about my riding skills.

Not so about my acting skills. Here was a triumph of miscasting by any but athletic standards: I was to play a voluptuous, tough-talking, two-timing prostitute. But it was beginning to dawn on me that I might take *some* responsibility here—might at least try to remedy my insecurity about the role.

I decided to ask a woman I knew slightly, a dedicated theater actress, if she would help me with my part. She came over to my rented bungalow and we read through the script.

When I told her that one thing bothering me especially was playing a character whose main attributes were large breasts, she suggested an exercise in which I fantasized large breasts of my own, stroking them, caressing them so that I could experience volup-tuousness. Walking around the living room, eyes half-closed, trying to ignore the gardener, who had stopped working and was staring at us through the French doors, I held my hands a foot in front of my chest, fondling my huge imaginary cones while she, with long, lacquered false nails, squeezed her real (and considerable) ones, moaning softly, "*Feel* your breasts, *feel* them, feel the *fullness* of them, their *smoothness, love* your breasts. . . ."

Here my resolve abandoned me completely, easy victim to my embarrassment. The exercise over, I thanked her and locked the door behind her, sure there had to be a better way. So I left for New Mexico with the same old baggage—the same shaky attitude toward my work, the same insecurity about my acting ability, the same tendency to turn my terror into criticism of everything around me. It wasn't, I implied frantically, that I didn't know what I was doing, could not hold up my end, but that I had been undercut by bad writing, miscasting, overscheduling and underbudgeting; the entire production, it would seem, had conspired to sabotage my skills. It was not my fault if I could not bring a role to life; it was everyone else's. Especially the writer's. Since I had no idea how to analyze or break down a script, I criticized it instead, unconsciously trying to camouflage what I was sure would be bad work.

But on *Bite the Bullet* there was a moment of truth. I found—the hard way—some of the responsibility I'd been groping toward. One morning, heading for location in one of the fleet of station wagons, with a taciturn New Mexican teamster in cowboy hat, denims and silver-tipped boots at the wheel, steadily negotiating the rutted dirt road, I fired a small salvo on the dialogue to the other actors in the car: mine sounded like Tonto's. "I can't say this stuff. It's like an anthology of cowboy clichés; Gene Autry had better lines, for God's sake, Roy Rogers—"

Suddenly, Gene Hackman, who had been sitting silently beside the driver in the front seat, swiveled sharply and turned his fury on me full force. "Shut up about the dialogue!" He was sick of my complaining. If I had such strong objections, then I should keep them to myself because he had to *play* the script I was so furiously dissecting. He—actors—had to find a way to make those lines work and "I don't need to hear any more of your wisecracks about how it can't be done. My job is to do it."

Silence. You could have heard an ant sneeze in that station wagon as we bumped along the rest of the way. There was nothing to say. Gene was right, of course, in all he said. Even when you think people are wrong, it is easy to tell when they are right. When they are right about something you are trying very hard to hide from others and yourself, you know they are right because you want to kill them. They have hit the bull's-eye, and you react with the righteous rage of someone trapped and wounded. The adrenaline bolts through your body and your face flushes and you break out in a slight sweat, but underneath, down in the depths of you, the temperature changes abruptly and it feels very cold. Simple acts like swallowing become monumental tasks. What are you trying to swallow there in your tailored cowgirl outfit bouncing along in the backseat blinking back the tears? Are you trying to swallow the truth?

Gene Hackman is the kind of actor—a truly brilliant actor—

who loves what he does for a living. He didn't give a damn about what anyone thought of him, never wasted his time buddying up to the crew or getting chummy on the set. He funneled his energy fiercely into his work, and he did make bad material good, mediocre writing great. Made magic. An actor who worked with intelligence, honesty and passion, he was the first person to give me a sense of respect for acting, some real understanding of what was involved. *Bite the Bullet* was our second film together; he had shot me in the stomach in our first one, *The Hunting Party,* in Spain, and he got shot in the back in our third one in Mexico, an unfortunate film called *The Domino Principle.* That film (in which I wore a short, dark wig that prompted one critic to remark that I was beginning to resemble Shelley Winters) was a fiasco, but Gene and I finally became friends. He worked with me, made suggestions, explored the scenes, taught me exercises, told me tricks, encouraged me and coached me; he shared with me his sense of joy in what he did. By then I had been making movies for ten years; that was the first time I began to see the complexity, the infinite challenge of my profession.

I turned twenty-eight during *Bite the Bullet*—a birthday of no particular significance except that it edged uncomfortably under the shadow of thirty and nothing had changed. Here I was closing in on thirty, as puzzled, as self-pitying as I was at twenty-five.

Back in Beverly Hills, I began going to an analyst, a respected man, distinguished in his field, who had started conducting group-therapy sessions with his many illustrious patients. I enrolled in group and we began meeting twice a week in the art-lined, leather-upholstered office for what turned out to be a pleasant ritual, not the painful one we hoped and expected it would be. We began to look forward to it as a convivial and comforting gathering at the end of the day—a clubby Gestalt cocktail hour whose regulars included two heads of major motion-picture studios, a famous film star of the fifties, a prominent surgeon, the wife of a celebrated director, a conceptual artist and me.

Most of us had known each other socially before the group was formed, and it seemed an easy if unorthodox selection. Conversations orbited around show business; there were epic anecdotes about famous figures, firsthand accounts of historic encounters rich in imagery and detail. The studio heads would lament low grosses and high losses, tackle test-marketing techniques and discuss production and distribution.

Discussions were lively and quick-witted, informative and entertaining. Occasionally we would grapple and hold each other in an emotional hammerlock, but basically we enjoyed ourselves and drove home happy, comforted by the contact.

Of course, we suspected that comfort wasn't enough. *Other* groups, we'd heard, had things called breakthroughs, psychodramas. *Other* groups, *real* groups, were painful and intense. Ours was too much fun.

What we wanted was legitimacy, and the way to get it, we decided, was to have a marathon. Other groups had marathons—extended sessions that often lasted twenty-four hours, or even a weekend, and produced, through prolonged encounter and the vulnerability of fatigue, dramatic results.

Flushed from the exhilaration of that decision, we tackled the next: where to have it. The office was an obvious choice but seemed too confining for so lengthy a set-to. The artist had a studio high in the mountains, but that was vetoed as being too far away. The wife of the director had a vast and elegant house in Bel Air and she offered to have it there, planning the menu as she spoke—a light meal of cold poached salmon with dill sauce, cucumber salad, white wine and fruit. No, no, we said, this was a *marathon,* not a buffet; be serious. The environment should be simple, impersonal, austere. So it was with great relief that we reached what seemed the perfect solution: a bungalow at the Beverly Hills Hotel.

And it was there we found ourselves, two days before Christmas, variously attired in jeans, Ultrasuede and surgical greens, sitting uneasily in the living room, waiting for the waiter from room service to arrive with the drinks, tense, ready for combat, determined not to trivialize this experience, hell-bent not to have fun.

Well-heeled, well-intentioned explorers, we set out to discover our feelings, expose emotions and slay our mental dragons. Hoping for a hero's return home at Christmas, we trekked valiantly through the night, stopping only for a brief rest and room service, and continued on wearily until dawn eased over the palms.

In the early morning light we eyed each other uncertainly, like first-time lovers edgy about finding ourselves in such intimacy, disappointed after having expected so much. We had waited and hoped for something to *happen,* and none of us knew for sure that it had. Perhaps we felt some sense of pride in simply having stayed up all night. As morning broke and the birds started up again, we filed out past the ferns, feeling exhausted and incomplete. Smiling bravely, hugging gamely, we wished each other Merry Christmas, sealed ourselves in our cars and drove slowly home.

The party in Bungalow 5 had checked out.

That summer I went to Spain to do a film with Sean Connery called *The Wind and the Lion.* Almería was the "Western capital" of Europe—a vast backlot. Its dun-colored, dry, rocky landscape and unexpected patches of sand dunes served as a convenient and economical substitute for the legendary geography it so handily resembled: the Arabian desert and the great American West.

So many films had taken advantage of this similarity that

Almería had the character of an eerie archaeological site. The area was littered with primitive facsimiles, layered with conflicting civilizations. Western towns bordered Moorish villages; Mexican pueblos dotted the plain. You could crest a sand dune and find cartridges spent on *Lawrence of Arabia*, arrows from *One Hundred Rifles*, tombstones from *A Fistful of Dollars*, water gourds from *The Good, the Bad and the Ugly*. Fossils for film buffs. Explorers from the future who stumble onto this barren land will be baffled by these ruins, overwhelmed by this cultural windfall.

And now we were about to leave another layer of our own. *The Wind and the Lion* was based on a historical incident between Teddy Roosevelt and the Great Raisuli, Lord of the Riff, which took place in Morocco. Some of the film was shot in Madrid, Seville and Granada, but most of it in accommodating Almería, its chameleonic country taking on the colors of the Riff. Old Moroccan villages sprang up overnight, centuries of whitewash gleaming in the sun; ancient abandoned forts were spread with Oriental carpets, filled with flowers and, for a few days, given new life.

The film was a sweeping historical epic—spectacular in the old Hollywood sense, wonderfully written by its director, John Milius. Sean Connery played the great desert leader; Brian Keith, a truly bully Teddy Roosevelt; and I, an American widow in Tangier taken into the desert as hostage. My dream come true. Every day on the set was like walking into a book by Lesley Blanch: Berbers on horseback, herds of camels, Moorish palaces and black camel's hair tents piled with pillows, hookahs, camel saddles and silver trays of dates. It was the most romantic location of my life.

While signing a Scot to play a legendary Berber chieftain seemed to some a quirky piece of casting, Sean gave an effortless performance: strong and dashing, witty and wry. He had that same wryness in life—a laconic sense of humor, an easy sense of fun. But what struck me as most unusual in a star of his stature was his lack of vanity, his comfortable sense of assurance. There was an honesty and directness about Sean, a wholeness, a manliness, that stardom had not eroded.

That in itself may not sound worthy of scientific study, but it is rare enough: I had discovered, over the years, that insecurity was not, as the stereotypes had it, the exclusive province of female stars. And I had met few men who had escaped the business of being movie stars unscathed, with their integrity and masculinity intact. For men, as for women, stardom often involved long journeys of obsessive self-involvement. Anxious, frequent mirror checks: makeup, hairpiece. Am I there? But our culture forgives this kind of behavior less readily in men than in women; so, most often, do the men themselves.

The ones who survived it were either the rare, dedicated, unpretentious ones like Sean and Gene Hackman, or those who enjoyed—even reveled in—the dramatic facades they created off screen. Like Tony Quinn. On *The Magus*, his arrival on the set had been announced by his Spanish valet descending the steps, bearing a handsome leather director's chair with ANTHONY QUINN in huge, elegantly hand-tooled letters. Funny, ferocious, childlike— and probably a pistol to live with—Tony was a giant: one of the handful of movie stars who are as large in life as they are on screen. His tall, solid frame filled a room and his expansive spirit left little space for anyone else. He loved every minute of it and I envied him his enjoyment of who he was.

If I sound like a maven of male behavior, it might have to do with the number of Westerns I made. All locations are illusions, overnight universes where ordinary laws are suspended so that people can do whatever it takes to get the job done and go home. No one is held accountable for his actions; the citizens of this world have a slim chance of ever meeting each other again. So a sort of stag-party sensibility prevails, and sometimes the locations are more entertaining than the films themselves, rife with swift and shifty shipboard romances, liaisons unlikely and short-lived.

But if all locations are mirages, Westerns are the most bizarre. Traditional male havens, they seem to induce some sort of strange childhood regression. Grown men return to being little boys in backyards, playing glorified games of Cowboys and Indians. Actors prowl the set twirling pistols, quick-drawing, smooth-holstering, hotshot mounting, drinking hard and riding reckless. Whipping their overworked horses into a gallop between takes so that when it comes time to shoot, the animals are lathered, winded and half dead.

On most sets, slow-talkin', fast-movin', hard-ridin', steelynerved, roll-your-own stunt men watched those overpaid bozos silently through squinty eyes, their lips curled softly in a condescending grin. They made scant effort to conceal their contempt for certain actors they saw as pretentious pansies—big men who bullied little ones in bars after work, who tested their toughness on tired horses. Men who pretended to do what stunt men did best. Men who pretended to be men.

There were some few actors who refused to use stunt men—made the refusal a point of honor, a declaration of their very manhood. They had guts, by God; they had spine. They had *balls*, let's face it. They took their own falls, threw their own punches and bragged about it on talk shows later. I may be an actor but I'm a *guy*. Men certainly don't make it easy on themselves.

Locations also served as handy crash courses in language: I'd improved my French with Lelouch and his crew, picked up some Italian in Rome, and learned Spanish on Westerns shot in Mexico and Spain. But it was a quirky kind of Spanish learned from Spanish stunt men, Mexican wranglers—a cowboy's command of the language. I could say, "Please lower the stirrups" (*¿Se puede abajar los estribos?*), "My cinch is loose," "This bit's too tough," "Have you seen my spurs?" "Is this your arrow?" "My horse is lame," "My shotgun's jammed," and "I have to reload my pistol." Short of a bank robbery in Baja, I had no call to use it.

• • •

When *The Wind and the Lion* was over, I was sad to see it end.

Leaving a location was always hard for everyone concerned: readjusting to family life after three or four months away; or, for those without families, returning home to an empty house after working intensely, intimately, in a group. As sets are struck, cases packed, and trucks loaded to leave, the months of close camaraderie are already fading. Hard on everyone—and, for me, getting harder all the time.

14

Twenty-nine. Almost thirty. Traditionally a significant year. In the sixties, crossing that line had meant being banished forever to the establishment along with all of your peers. In the seventies, thanks to the women's movement, "thirty" had ceased to be a social stigma and women were no longer branded and sent into the snow to die. Still, there was no denying that it was a milestone of sorts.

I marked the occasion by moving back to New York; it seemed a more appropriate place than Los Angeles to live out the autumn of my years. A mature choice for a mature woman. A place for serious pursuits. And I bought an apartment overlooking Central Park, conspicuous in its lack of a rainbow. A mature apartment.

In New York, I was offered a job by NBC's *Today* show to produce a series of photo essays on subjects of my choosing. It was a dream job and I jumped at it. I crisscrossed the country from Camp Pendleton to Pittsburgh, Venice to Baton Rouge, photographing women Marines and women coal miners, blind beggars, body builders, Muhammad Ali, Joe Namath and the Ku Klux Klan; writing the accompanying copy, which I read over the series of stills. I loved it.

Sometimes, arriving at NBC as dawn was breaking, I passed

rumpled, red-eyed kids leaving the lobby; people whose day was ending just as mine began. They were writers working all night on a new late-night comedy program called *Saturday Night Live*; their first two shows had had George Carlin and Paul Simon as guest hosts. But few people had heard of the show or seen it when Lorne Michaels, the producer, asked me to host the third. When he showed me the tapes of the first two, I said I would follow him anywhere: it was everything you wanted television to be. In all, I hosted three shows over a year, with a rush of exhilaration and terror. Lorne said that the first time the camera cut to me as I was introduced to the live audience, my expression was "like Patty Hearst opening the door to find the SLA."

In 1976, when America was celebrating her two-hundredth anniversary, I was preparing to turn thirty. I took out a new passport—a jaunty Bicentennial model with Liberty Bells blanketing every page and an American eagle embossed on my face—and gave an interview in *Vogue* trumpeting my new maturity:

> . . . I am now thirty and have begun, like other women I know, to hit my stride, so to speak, to really come into my own. And while at times it's confusing, uncertain, and often lonely, I wouldn't have it any other way. There may be a point of diminishing returns but, for now, it all gets better. . . .

Then I went into a coma. Perhaps it was premature midlife crisis; whatever it was, the symptoms were unpredictable fits of weeping: suddenly, at dinner with close friends, I would inexplicably burst into tears. Probably just part of "hitting my stride," I supposed, but it left me embarrassed and bewildered. Then, apologetic, polite even in crisis, I would bring my weeping under control, smile weakly and wait for the next attack to come. Perhaps it had to get worse before "it all gets better. . . ."

The person so recently described in *Vogue* as "a 1976 woman who can shape, sustain, and enjoy life on her own terms" was now to be found wrapped in a flannel robe in a rocker, staring out over the park or religiously watching *The Bionic Woman* and whimpering softly to herself, "What's to *become* of me?"

Life was not proceeding according to plan. By my calculations, my life was meant to be in order by now; from the passport I took out at twenty-five to its Bicentennial replacement at thirty, everything—marriage, a family—should have fallen into place. I had not anticipated the sweeping changes that had occurred around me, sudden shifts in the social wind—and had failed to take them into consideration.

I had traveled the feminist circuit faithfully for a time, speaking at pro-abortion rallies, equal rights meetings, women's caucuses, campaigns for female delegates; but I had realized, more quickly than I admitted, that I couldn't match or even truly comprehend the fervor, the sometime fury, of the movement. In truth, I was a special case—a woman lucky enough to lead a man's life in a man's world, who had functioned freely, profited handsomely by the system; who had not been penalized by my sex but rewarded for it. I worked for and supported "our" rights because "mine" had never been denied to me.

Certainly, the women's movement dramatically expanded women's options. And it made many of my choices easier. But ironically it wasn't until the late seventies, when women were coming to terms with the movement's promises, that I discovered common cause with some of its staunchest supporters. Many women (never mind the men) were well confused—especially those my age, in whom twenty years of traditional thinking clashed with ten years of feminism. Were women meant to do everything? Work *and* have babies? Were love and marriage to be discarded completely? What was "a 1976 woman who can shape, sustain, and enjoy life on her own terms" supposed to do? To want? What *were* my terms anyway? Frankly, I hadn't a clue.

If my thinking had changed radically, my conditioning remained the same: I wanted a man to share my life with. Yet, for all this seemed to matter, the recent relationships I'd involved myself in were perversely unlikely: liaisons with men on distant continents with whom I spoke no common language. The greater the guaranteed distance, the greater my interest. Curious choices for someone with a hankering to settle down.

In Europe I'd met and been pursued by a pleasant, if improbable, man, affectionate and insistent, charming. A man whose relentless devotion was reassuring after the battle fatigue incurred with Robin. It was a manageable mismatch whose main attraction was the avoidance of pain; unlikely to get messy or out of hand. But it was not a relationship in which I belonged, and I was tired of not belonging.

Ironically, in this imbalance of affections, as I remained uncertain and unconvinced I began to behave like a man in a similar circumstance: withholding commitment and dictating my own terms. Though I accepted the unconditional affection that was offered, I felt guilty for not repaying it in kind and, when the need arose, played the role of provider instead, in exchange for the freedom to do as I pleased. The ancient male maneuver of control.

I enjoyed it for a time; it felt good to be in charge, to be the one to hold the reins, to be at my liberty, to pick up and leave. But gradually I began to sound like so many men whose behavior I deplored: talking in controlled, condescending tones; smiling patiently, patronizingly; speaking in simple language as if to a child. Sounding like all the men I knew who were in relationships with women for wrong reasons: uncomplicated companionship, "low maintenance," the absence of pain. Who assumed financial obligations instead of emotional ones.

I quickly came to hate it—and myself as well. Some men did it so often, so easily—suffering adoration in silence and smug superiority, pausing to stroke their partner like a pet. But I found myself glancing over furtively, wondering what I was doing with this person with whom I had nothing in common, to whom I had little to say. Was this better than being alone? And I came to resent this man for loving me, and myself for not loving him and for not leaving. What was once comfortable soon became unconscionable. Avoiding pain was one thing; inflicting it was another. If this was life on "my own terms," I wasn't having any. And so I moved on.

To South America. "It's no accident he lives five thousand miles away, Candy," a wise friend said to me after I had just gotten back from another trip to Brazil, where I went, like a South American shuttle, to visit a man with whom I was having an affair. A dashing, self-destructive man. A journalist who had been with Ché Guevara when the rebels entered Havana; a Communist who had been a political prisoner, put in solitary in Brazil; a declared "enemy of the state" who had spent years in exile. A man without a penny to his name who would give you the shirt off his back. A man with a giant spirit and a death wish to match. A man who liked hard drinking and handsome women. A South American man.

And in Brazil, I found an intensity of feeling, a crazy connection that was food for my cool North American soul. This man and his friends lived so hard and fast that at times they threatened total burnout. I could tolerate the sensual siege, the relentless pace only for short periods before I had to fly back to New York, wrecked and ruined, relieved to recuperate and recover.

I spent one Christmas on a coffee plantation north of São Paulo with kind and gracious people. But suddenly I missed my family.

My friends. Why wasn't I spending Christmas with them instead of wandering among the coffee trees like Juan Valdez?

I was getting a little long in the tooth for this sort of thing. Romance with the safety of a six-thousand-mile separation. Conducted in Italian as a common language. I no longer had time for flings with no future, for flights down to Rio. If I was going to have any relationship at all, it would be one for keeps on shared soil.

What I wanted was the part where you read in bed, rub feet and watch TV together. No Latin love themes or tangos on tropical terraces—just to be with someone with whom you don't have to hide anything or pretend to be better than you are. But I had acquired habits of selfishness and solitude and wondered if it was too late.

Turning thirty was harder than I thought.

What made it easier were friends. My friends were my extended family: true-blue, old-shoe, longtime friends like George-Ann and Peter Hyams and Marty Elfand. Friends with whom nothing-sacred, no-holds-barred behavior prevailed: dressing in gorilla suits, pelting each other with pies—there was very little we wouldn't stoop to to make each other laugh.

Ali MacGraw was a true-blue friend. We had met my first summer modeling in New York when she worked as a photographer's stylist. Dashing off drawings, collecting accessories, bringing her instinctive sense of style to the set, she radiated intelligence and vitality. Sassy and classy, she could charm a snake if she chose to, and I was drawn to her generous spirit. But it wasn't until years later, when we were both in films and living in Los Angeles, that we became close friends, spending long evenings by the fire at her house at the beach, catching up on changes—or lack of them—in our lives and occasionally weathering rocky reviews together.

And Kitty Hawks—"The Hawk," I called her—was one fine,

fierce friend. Tall, elegant, slender, she wore her hair in a braid that grazed her waist and swayed to a languid, giraffe-like gait. Uncommonly articulate, she was a woman whose opinions I respected and whose friendship I cherished.

And there was Connie Freiberg, with whom I was closer now than when we were a team in high school; Tessa Kennedy, who included me in her English country Christmases; Ann Sterling, a strong, savvy woman who worked in fashion and gave me infallibly caring advice on everything from knitwear to life; Carol Ryan, a tall, exotically beautiful lawyer who was funny, loving and wise; and Rusty and Mary Ellen, of course, with whom I continued our ten-year tradition of lunches at the Russian Tea Room. Rusty, recently divorced, with a young daughter, was working as an editor for *Rolling Stone,* and Mary Ellen was always just back from someplace and on her way to another: Bombay, Manila, Tangier.

Like so many other women, I was finding an increasing sense of connection—even a sense of wonder—in the comfort of female friendship. If, after the women's movement, relations between men and women had grown fraught, friendships between women had never been tighter. Suddenly, we were seeking out, celebrating each other's company, and it was odd to remember that only a few years before, women had shunned each other's company at parties, preferring that of men.

It was my friends who gave me a sense of proportion about my attacks of Premature Midlife Crisis, and who steadily kidded me out of my coma. It would appear that I am a slow learner, but when I emerged from my cocoon, the lessons seemed clear at last. There is a price to pay for our choices, a simple law of cause and effect. A choice of college based on an ivy-covered campus. Of men for shoes. Of films for locations. Of travel in the name of avoidance.

I now saw my periodic months of absence as an abandonment of my family and friends. I was devoted to them, indebted, and I wanted to be as available to them as they had been to me.

My appetite for travel diminished. Gradually, I began to elimi-
nate excess in my life—people, parties, places—and to choose
silence over noise, contemplation over distraction. Where once
the very concept of responsibility had instilled terror if construed
in any but the narrowest sense, I now began to welcome it. From
acknowledging my responsibility to my extended family of friends,
it was a short—if halting—step to acknowledging responsibility
for my own life.

I arrived in Kansas City in midwinter, rented a green Granada and
drove through three hours of frozen farmland to Roscoe, Missouri,
wondering who I would find when I got there.

For my first ten years, the one constant in my life had been my
governess, Dee. The last time I'd seen her was ten years before,
when I was just back from filming in the Orient; I had gone to visit
her and her husband, Don, at their California farm. Soon afterward
they had moved to the small county in Missouri where Don was
born and raised, and we'd kept in touch by cards and occasional phone calls. In the years that followed, preoccupied with the
business of growing up—or avoiding it—I had underestimated the
strength of the bond we formed. Now, in the small step back I had
taken from my life, I had a sudden longing to see once more the
woman who did so much to raise me.

Theirs was a simple two-story house with a weathered red
barn in back. The moment I pulled in, they came out the door—
looking like strangers, and yet seeming exactly the same. They're
old, I realized with a shock; the difference is they've gotten old.
We hugged each other awkwardly, Dee and I holding back tears,
feeling more emotion than we were yet comfortable sharing. It
was a sweet and sudden reunion, charged with sentiments of a
childhood long since gone. Seeing them made me even happier
than I'd imagined.

We went inside and eased in with each other. Dee, always small and delicate, had thickened some; her face was deeply lined now and her head shook slightly in a steady small nod. But it was Dee, all right; it was still Dee.

She had on a double-knit slack suit and wore a short wig some- one had given her for Christmas. "I have to wear a wig, Candy," she said. "I'm so short it gives me height; it makes me look better."

Don was in overalls, plaid wool shirt, high-topped Wellington boots, a pocket watch hooked on his suspenders. The farm boy come home to roost. He wore thick glasses now. "Since his cataract operation," Dee explained, "without them he's almost blind."

The house was small and cozy: a fourteen-year-old living room set, a roll-away bed for me, plastic horses on the mantel, a stereo. "We finally bought a stereo set but we haven't bought any records to play on it yet," Dee said. "They're so expensive. Six dollars apiece. Oh, we do have *one* someone gave us for Christmas—Loretta Lynn."

After the house, we toured the farm. A horse and cow dozed in the barn in the back and in the shed nearby was a cellar for shelter from tornadoes; one had flattened the barn across the road last year. In the cellar were shelves lined with Mason jars filled with homemade preserves, jams, jellies, vegetables and fruit from the garden. They were selling the farm, they explained, to move to the little town nearby in order to be nearer a hospital, a clinic, a doctor—"in case something happens." They'd sell the cow, too, and maybe the horse. "I want to keep my horse but my wife won't let me," Don said, a little bitterly. "She's very economical, too much so." "He's too sick to care for her, Candy," Dee whispered to me, adding ruefully, "We're senior citizens, now, you know."

Dee sat, staring at the fire, her tiny head softly bobbing. "You know, we lost all our savings when the bank failed a couple of years past and it set us back something awful." She looked up at Don. "We can talk about it like this now but the day it happened we just came home and sat in the living room and bawled. At our age, we had to start all over."

Conversation changed at dinner. Random chatter, catching up. "Don," I asked, "whatever happened to Teddy, the collie? He was some dog."

There was a pause. "Well, Teddy turned queer on us," Don said, chewing quietly.

"Queer? A *collie*?"

"Yup. I guess he'd never bred a female and he started becoming insane for sex and all we had were chickens on the farm and he started having sex with the hens and he killed a couple of 'em. Just plain wore 'em out. So we had to have him put to sleep."

And gradually the conversation spiraled around to all the subjects we'd never discussed before—that only an adult can ask about the childhood that was.

"What was it like, Dee, at those parties we used to have? When the governesses stood behind the kids while we were eating our cake (and having it too). What did all of you talk about together?"

"Oh, we'd make dates to have lunch together, to meet in Beverly Hills, you know, and sometimes we'd gossip a little. Do you remember Dottie, Betty Hutton's governess?" I didn't, but I nodded yes. "Well, Dottie used to tell me that Betty Hutton walked around the house all the time nude and Dottie threatened to quit if she didn't stop it. I think that's finally why she did quit, too, but she also said Betty Hutton wouldn't let her children kiss Dottie good night, and Candy, they *wanted* to. They loved Dottie but Betty Hutton said no: that children should only love their parents."

"It's a good thing your parents didn't feel that way," Don chuckled, scraping the ice cream off his plate. "You wouldn't go to *anyone* if Dee was around. You'd just hang on to her and wouldn't let go. The only one you asked for was Dee; once, your mother joked and told her, 'Sometimes, I wish you'd change your name.' I think she was a little annoyed."

"Oh, gosh, once we went to New York, just you and I, when you were fifteen months old," Dee said, shaking her head. "You'd just learned to walk. Your parents had been away in Europe three months. They met us at the station when we arrived and you wouldn't let go of me—you didn't know them. You cried when your father picked you up, so I walked away a little, just to let you get used to them, and then it was okay. My goodness, you would just cling to me. You didn't trust anyone."

After lunch the following day, Don went to check on a new calf while Dee and I sat, talking, at the table. "You know, Candy," she said slowly after a while, "Don just isn't the same anymore. He forgets things now. He came into the house last week and couldn't remember where he'd been or where he was or what he'd been doing. I said, 'You're standing in the living room by the TV, Don.' He said, 'Where did I come from? What was I doing?' So, he's afraid to be alone now. It's his heart, his blood pressure." She stopped, her hands lying limply in her lap, and stared out the window. "You know, he used to be so good at figures and now he makes mistakes. But I never say anything." She shook her head slowly. *"Never."* Then, as if she read the question in my mind, she began simply, "If something happens to Don, I want to go back to Oklahoma. To my family. I want to be buried in the Catholic cemetery there."

We spent the rest of the afternoon in the living room before the fire while the wind whipped and whistled outside. Dee brought down boxes of photographs from the attic and we pored over them wistfully. Photos of Dee when she was young and sassy in Oklahoma, photos of them together at the start of their courtship—just after they'd met on the floor of the Aragon Ballroom—looking smart and spiffy, large expensive prints of her and me and my parents, the birthday parties, the sprawling hacienda on the hill, the turtle funeral, the lush "at home" layouts with Charlie.

We went over our lives, sitting there toasted by the fire, Dee's head gently bobbing as we reminisced and she talked of Holland

and Oklahoma and Beverly Hills and Roscoe; of wanting to travel. Of feeling old. Of feeling young.

That night, after dinner, Dee went outside to check on the horse and the cow. Don sat back and ran a hand smoothly over his bald head. "It means a lot to us that you're here, Candy. We never had any children and we consider you like one of our own. It means a lot to us."

"It means a lot to me, too, Don. I wish I hadn't waited so long."

We sat silently for a while and then he sat up and, resting his elbows on the table, hunched over his plate. "Candy, do you notice how Dee's slipping a little?" He looked anxiously toward the door. "She's not what she used to be. You know she's seven years older than I am, but she looks better for her age than I do."

"I thought you were the same age. She told me she was seventy."

"Nope, she's seventy-seven. She lied on her birth certificate from Holland." He chuckled. "She was born in 1901 and she changed the one to an eight but when she applied for her retirement, they sent to Holland for her birth certificate and they found out. She was really hot under the collar, but she needed her retirement." He leaned back, smiling. "But she looks better than I do and you see the way she drives around and takes care of the farm and she always protects me and takes care of me. But she's seventy-seven, all right."

I had come to Roscoe hoping for insights on my own life from two people who had done so much to nurture it, and found, instead, that they wanted to share theirs with me. What I'd seen, in two short days, was more loyalty and friendship, generosity and trust than I'd ever thought existed. Two people who kept an extraordinary commitment to honor each other for a lifetime, faithfully, richer or poorer, in sickness and in health. That was love, that was marriage. It took them to show me I'd completely missed the point.

The next morning I was leaving for the airport in Kansas City; we decided I should start driving by 6 A.M. They were both worried about the weather and offered to drive in with me and take the bus back. My leaving made all of us sad and we stayed up late talking, holding on to as much as we could of the last two days.

Later, lying in my rollaway, I heard Dee, the old diehard, snappily patting cream on her face—a fragile, feminine blonde of seventy-seven. None of us slept much that night; Don was up and down checking for the approaching storm, and I heard the two of them talking in concerned voices throughout the night. By five o'clock, Dee and I were both in the kitchen; I was eating a new crunchy cereal that she had highly recommended. "Candy," she asked as I crunched, "do you use Crest?" "Nope." "You *don't*?" She sounded shocked. Old habits die hard.

She handed me some homemade bread and jam to take to my mother. I saw by the clock on the stove that it was time for me to leave. Dee went in to wake Don, who had fallen asleep again, and he shuffled out in his wool robe and slippers, without his glasses. "Without them he's almost blind," I remembered Dee saying. Don told me to come back soon. "The mare's due to foal and I don't want you to miss that little colt. He should be a beauty."

"Yes, Candy," Dee joined in, holding his arm. "Come back soon—when the weather's nice. The springtime's beautiful here."

"Well, I'm not sure when I'll get back but I'll come as soon as I can."

"Oh, please do, honey. Don't leave it again for too long."

"I won't, Dee. It's been so good to see you both; I'll really miss you."

"I love you, honey," Dee said as we hugged each other tightly.

"I love you, too, Dee." We were starting to cry again. "Don." I turned to him standing a little unsteadily next to her, wiping his eyes with the back of his hand. "Don, I'll see you soon, okay? And

I'll call you both as soon as I get home." We hugged each other clumsily, patted each other awkwardly, wanting to say, "I love you," but not quite getting there.

Light was barely breaking as I got in my car. As I drove away it was beginning to snow.

15

My father grew old suddenly. He seemed almost to age overnight, soon after he turned seventy-five. He didn't like it much; none of us did. It was apparent in his attitude, not in his appearance. Outwardly he remained unchanged. He had never been "boyish" to begin with, his years as "youthful" had been few. Early hair loss and a remote demeanor gave him, from the age of forty, the distinguished aura of an older man.

The place you saw it first was in his eyes, wide now, and nervously darting, alert and watchful, full of fear. That was the difference—the sudden fear. He was frightened of things going on in his body that he didn't understand and couldn't control—his blood pressure, loss of memory, deep fatigue, and especially his heart, which had hospitalized him once and now demanded a battery of medications. He was more short-tempered than usual, even more distracted—perhaps his most characteristic state—and it was hard to catch his attention. Never the most direct of men, he seemed not to look anyone in the eyes but to constantly shift his gaze, avert his glance, as if to avoid being face-to-face with what he knew was coming.

Ventriloquists, even great ones, were now truly shelved as odd-ball relics. If offers came in, they were small potatoes—out-of-state conventions, country fairs. At one time he would have been glad even for those—any excuse to be entertaining—but, now, his health steadily declining, he could hardly trust himself before an audience. He stumbled through routines he'd done for forty years, forgot his lines, became confused, and left the stage embarrassed and bewildered.

My brother often traveled with him on these bookings—my brother, now almost a man: driving him, cueing him on his lines, dispensing his medicine, carrying his dummies and the names of doctors to call "just in case." Loving, patient, dedicated to his dad, he once phoned my mother from Arizona in tears, pained for his father who, while telling a story to local reporters, had suddenly gone blank, the thread of what he was saying snapped, the words refusing to come.

When my father was home and restless, not working, it was my mother who distracted and amused him, kept him busy by inventing projects that needed his attention and encouraging his enthusiasm for a planned autobiography, carefully concealing with artful gaiety the stress his illness placed on them both.

And still, at times, he would turn strangely silent. Who knows what was fixing his stare, holding his tongue? The sighting of his own death, about which he professed to have no fear? Before our eyes he was pulling into himself, like a pale turtle, staring warily out of his shell.

For the better part of a year, when his health began to fail him, I spent most of my time in Los Angeles in order to be near my father. His condition was precarious enough that I avoided taking long or unnecessary absences, and when I was away I was careful to keep in contact.

I felt the urgency of remodeling our relationship before time ran out and the end closed in, of conquering our fear of each other, bridging the distance between us; of making one last try at being the daughter he wanted, proving to him that I loved him, convincing him to love me.

It didn't go smoothly; we had lost a lot of ground. I was entirely at fault. The year before, I had given a lengthy interview in *McCall's* and had said too much—much too much. Especially about my father, lamenting the distance between us, his postponement of my inheritance, which I interpreted as a refusal to grant me approval, the fear that I always felt of him, the sense of frustrated affection.

It was a strangely compulsive confession and I was later horrified to read what I had revealed. But it was entirely voluntary; the many words were mine. Here were feelings I never knew I had.

The interview hurt my father; my mother told me this. She had tried to keep it from him but too many people had read it, too many friends were calling wondering why I would want to say such things. And so my mother read it to him while he lay in bed, not feeling well. She read it all and he said nothing, just stared silently into space. Then he got up without a word and walked slowly from the room. It was never mentioned again.

Months passed and I tried furiously to make reparations, attempts at atonement, to no avail. He was polite but absent. When my parents came to New York, I served them supper at my apartment, then took them to see *Annie,* which had just then opened. *Annie*—the story of the love of a father and a daughter. *Annie*—where the sun will come out tomorrow.

In Los Angeles I redoubled my efforts, grateful for one last chance. In that year, I told him often that I loved him—face-to-face, not furtively on the phone—and truly tried to thank him for all that he had done for me, all that he had been. The time had come for me to give.

One night I asked him to dinner—just the two of us. We had not had dinner alone, he and I, for twenty years, not since those weekends when the two of us took wing. If I was nervous when I arrived to pick him up for this landmark meal, he was a wreck. When he realized that my mother was going out somewhere else, she told me later, and that my brother had football practice, and that left the *two* of us to have dinner alone—evidently something he hadn't understood before—he panicked and asked if she couldn't please come with us.

He looked unhappily resigned when I came in early, respectfully dressed for dinner with my father at Trader Vic's in white slacks and blue silk shirt. I looked nice; my father liked blue. But as I entered his dressing room, he looked me over and said, "Well, I'm glad you didn't waste too much time dressing. Is *that* what they're wearing now?" Nervous.

"Where would you like to go, Dad?" I asked, in case he changed his mind.

"Oh, let's go somewhere sexy."

We arrived at Trader's and he smiled at the captain, saying, sotto voce, "Don't tell my wife." As the captain showed us to our table, we passed family friends along the way who avoided him, averting their eyes from his "date" discreetly until one finally yelled after him, "I won't tell Frances!" The unspeakable is spoken.

My voice jumping to the octave level of Bambi's, I tried, once again, to apologize, to tell him I loved him, to make certain he understood. I explained that my regrettable mention of money in that interview was not about money at all but about what I saw as the long-postponed promise of his approval. Nothing more. Nothing less.

How was he to know? Anointing me was hardly his job, of course. He had enough to do without dispensing paternal seals of approval. If I believed life began with his benediction, that was my problem—a handy excuse to hang back till Dad's Decoration of Worth. On and on I went, while he said nothing, trying to unsnarl the mess I'd made, hoping that out of the ashes some fatherly phoenix would rise up to hug me again.

And then, for the first time, we talked—cautiously, politely. We talked about getting sick, about getting old, about dying. About why he said he wasn't scared. "I just feel it's ungrateful. It's unfair to be angry or afraid when I've been lucky enough to live this long, this well." But the fear in his eyes belied the nobility of his beliefs. "In the past six months, for the first time, I feel like an old man. I don't have the energy anymore, I've lost the drive. I have trouble remembering things—lines in my routines, appointments. Sometimes, I forget where I am, where I'm going. Just in the last six months. It happened so *quickly*."

And he talked about my mother. "When we met, in many ways, she was still a child; I felt she was too young. I sort of waited for her to grow up but I couldn't get her out of my mind. And now, I don't feel complete unless I'm with her."

And then, he talked about me. He was concerned about my rootlessness, my restlessness, he said, recognizing in it much of his own. "I hope you're happy in your life," he added, so quietly I knew he sensed that I wasn't, and also understood that it was more difficult than it seemed.

"I remember when you were six or seven," he said. "I came home at night and you were in your room and you called out—maybe you were feeling lonely—and I came in and lay down next to you and cuddled you and you said, 'I know the twinkling stars are the ones that burn gas, Daddy, but what are the other ones? How are they lit? And what's behind them?' And I just didn't know what to tell you because, of course, I didn't know the answer myself. You were always bothered by what was behind the stars, about what lay beyond."

We drove home slowly. My brother had come back and was

waiting for us at the door, grinning, to wrap his arms around his dad, engulfing him. A bear hug for his best buddy. We walked into the study together, and, on his desk, my father saw a letter from the Burbank Police Department. As he opened it, my brother and I peered at him anxiously, knowing what it was.

My father looked up, way up, at my brother—my father being five feet eight and my brother six feet two. "This seems to be a notification from the Burbank Police that you were booked for possession of marijuana at a rock concert last week. It says we have to appear in Juvenile Court." My brother carefully examined the rug. "Kris, you've been *booked* in Burbank? Before your sixteenth birthday you have a *record*?" My brother looked at him, his eyes big and blue. "What will become of you?" my father asked.

"Well, Dad," my brother said quietly, "all it really means is that I can't be a policeman in L.A."

Our father stood looking up at us. A seventy-five-year-old man with a thirty-one-year-old daughter arrested for obstructing a hallway in the Senate and a fifteen-year-old son arrested for possession of pot. He shook his head, bewildered, smiled ruefully, and gave me a kiss on the cheek, "Good night, honey," then put his arm around Kris, who hugged him back, "Good night, chum," and slowly shuffled off to bed.

EDGAR AND CHARLIE TO MAKE FAREWELL APPEARANCE
Bergen Announces His Retirement

In the summer of 1978, my father reluctantly called a press conference at the Brown Derby in Beverly Hills to announce his retirement, half wondering whether anyone would show up. He had not expected it to make much of a splash in anyone's pond and so was surprised when the press conference, packed, was carried on the evening news, and startled to find his picture with Charlie on the front page of the *Los Angeles Times*.

While it had been years since the pair had made America sit up and take notice, it had never occurred to people that Edgar and Charlie might not always be there. Since anyone could remember, they always had been there, and one assumed they always would be.

His final appearance, he announced, would be a three-week engagement at Caesars Palace in Las Vegas on a bill with Andy Williams. The engagement was a serious risk to the health of a man who, not six months before, had been hospitalized in coronary intensive care. But as soon as the offer had been made, he was hell-bent on accepting it, determined, one last time, to "play the Palace"—not between the trained-dog acts and the dancing girls, as he'd done for the past ten years, but once again featured on "the top of the bill"—*Edgar Bergen and Charlie McCarthy*—just like way back when. Here was an opportunity to go out in style—and one he could not refuse.

He was so dead set on the September engagement that my mother, with his doctor, agreed that depriving him of the appearance and confining him at home would put as great a strain on his heart as that of performing two shows a night.

My mother went with him to Las Vegas and they checked into a suite at Caesars Palace that would have made Liberace blush. Little chalk-white Venus de Milos and miniature Michelangelo Davids perched on pedestals in the red rococo living room and, in the bedroom, pale plaster cupids pinned back cut-velvet curtains on either side of the circular bed. Sunken in a raised marble platform, a giant Jacuzzi was visible in the open adjoining bath.

Lying in bed later that night, in the sleazy splendor of their suite, startled to find himself in the mirrored ceiling, my father chuckled softly and gently patted my mother on the head. "Well, my dear," he said, smiling up at her mirrored reflection, "it looks like I've brought you here too late."

•   •   •

On opening night, my brother and I were there to surprise him: Kris had come from Los Angeles and I had flown in from New York. We were sitting out front with my mother in the giant showroom as the house lights dimmed and the orchestra started up, hoping he would make it smoothly through the routines, terrified that he might lose his way in the lines and wanting so much, for him, for it to go well. Then the music was stilled, and from the darkness an announcer's voice boomed, "And now, ladies and gentlemen, Caesars Palace proudly presents—*Edgar Bergen and Charlie McCarthy!*"

Our eyes met for a second, the three of us barely breathing, as the orchestra led into "Charlie My Boy"—the familiar theme brought into America's living rooms by radio thirty years before. There were many there that night who remembered—people for whom Edgar and Charlie were old fireside friends—and, as Bergen walked from the wings with McCarthy at his side, the applause was long and alive with memories of the years of Sunday evenings when these two had made them laugh.

My father stood straight and proud on the stage, his right hand on Charlie's back, his left resting lightly on his knee. For this occasion, his final farewell, he had insisted on playing once again in white tie and tails. He was, after all, an elegant man, a man of manners. He looked splendid, I thought, the tears starting, as I watched him modestly acknowledge the prolonged applause, a poised and graceful presence commanding center stage.

Even in the outrageous, silly spectacle of "Circus Maximus," Caesars' garish showroom packed with people in open shirts and polyester, spearing frozen shrimp and sipping soup du jour, he shone as something special, reminiscent of a grace long gone from our lives.

"Well, Charlie—"

"Bergen, you old windbag, I'll kill ya, so help me, I'll mooowww you down—"

And they slipped into their old roles and routines, the familiar patter of a partnership that had lasted sixty years.

The routine went more than smoothly; it was flawless. Bergen reasoning, McCarthy razzing, the steady laughter of the audience, delighted, the frequent interruptions of applause. The two of them flying now, nothing could stop them; the audience was enchanted and asking for more.

My mother sat, still as a statue, her concentration locked on the man on the stage. Only her lips moved silently as she unconsciously mouthed the dialogue she had followed for thirty-five years like a mantra, as if willing it to come out right. Each of us knew by heart the lines of the routines that had spanned our lives; but there, that night, we heard them fresh, as if for the first time—perhaps because we knew it would be the last.

The act ended with a sound track from their old radio shows, a montage of Bergen and McCarthy memories: John Barrymore jousting with Charlie, Marilyn Monroe and Charles McCarthy announcing their impending engagement, W. C. Fields threatening to split him into venetian blinds—flashbacks of famous voices from the past, while, up on stage, Edgar and Charlie cocked their heads, swapped knowing glances and chuckled softly as they looked up, listening wistfully to their lives.

Then my father said simply, "In vaudeville, every act has to have an opening and a close, and I think, for me, the close has come and it's time to pack up my little friends and say goodbye. Good night, God bless, and thank you all for listening." As the orchestra played his favorite, "September Song," he picked up Charlie and gracefully walked offstage.

The three of us smiled and cried, trying to compose ourselves before the house lights came up. But Bergens were not the only ones moved. There were tears in other eyes that night, and I think everyone felt they had been a part of something special. At the end, the audience rose to its feet, applauding him with deep affection, grateful to share his farewell.

There were photographers in his dressing room backstage as we entered, and we had to press our way through the throng. He hugged Kris and my mother, then I came forth, wiping my eyes. We held each other tight and once again I started sobbing, so proud of him, so happy for him, so sad. Knowing somehow that it was a last goodbye. His to an audience, ours to him. We held each other tight for a few seconds while I cried. The love of a lifetime squeezed into those few seconds, surrounded by photographers, for once unaware of their presence.

My father seemed moved and surprised that Kris and I had been there, flattered by the popping flashes of attention, quietly content with his success. Yet, wedged in the corner between the crush of well-wishers and the floral sprays, he seemed oddly silent, conspicuously calm. Still in his stiff white tie and starched dress shirt, he sat, completely peaceful, distant and detached. Where has he gone? I wondered, and thought that I had never seen him so serene.

The reviews of the show were unanimous, effusive in their praise and appreciation. The next day's performances went just as smoothly again, with a standing ovation at the end of each.

It made no sense, then, to my mother that on the third day after the opening, she woke up feeling strangely weary and deeply depressed. Lately she was often up and dressed before my father, but that day she stayed in her robe and never left the room, offhandedly making excuses to him to cover her bewildering behavior.

That night's performances went just as well, and my father went to sleep in good spirits. My mother stayed awake most of the night and rose early, tiptoeing from the bedroom, dressing quietly in the other room and, going back in to wake him, proud of her head start on the day. She half opened the blinds and called to him softly. It was not for several moments that she realized he was dead. His heart had stopped; he had gone peacefully while he slept.

For my father, there could have been no better ending; it was one he might have written himself. And who can say that he didn't? That, somehow, he hadn't made his choice? There was the supreme sense of timing ingrained over sixty years of performing. Just as in vaudeville, he knew when to close.

I was in Los Angeles, where Kris was in school, but my mother was unsuccessful in her first attempts to reach us. Worried that it would get into the press before she could notify Kris or me, she called Pat Kingsley, a close family friend and my publicist, asking her to help keep it quiet until we could be found. It was Pat who reached me, hours later, and I heard it in her voice on the phone.

"Candy, your mother's been trying to reach you; it's urgent. Please call her right away."

Suddenly, I found it hard to breathe. "What happened? Is it all right?"

"It's your father. He's gone."

"Does Kris know?" I asked at once, worried about his feelings, deferring the panic of my own.

"Not yet. We're trying to reach him."

He was not home when I called and I went immediately to the house. They had notified him at school and he had arrived by the time I got there. I found him standing alone in the living room, his head bent, hands hanging helplessly at his sides, weeping. As we hugged, I began to cry.

That afternoon a friend provided a private plane to fly me to Las Vegas and bring back my mother. The pilot offered me a Scotch before takeoff and, while I hardly drank, I downed it, then another. By the time we landed in Las Vegas, it all seemed a dream.

My mother was waiting at the airport, looking delicate and dazed. While she'd gotten through the day on her own like a general, she now seemed like a little girl lost. We held each other, then quickly took off, holding hands on the way home. The shock of it had settled on her and she shook softly, telling, over and over, how she found him, the peacefulness of his face.

The days preceding the funeral were oddly energized, highly efficient, moving at a fever pitch. Family friends stuck fast and there was a gentleness about the house, a loving generosity, with welcome bursts of humor to puncture the tension. Undaunted by the tasks of organization, my mother and I instead found solace in them.

All my life I had dreaded the death of my father. That will be the Big One, I thought, uncertain that I could cope. But here it was happening, and for me it held no reality. I watched as from a great distance, concerned for others' pain while allowing none of my own. I was aware of the irony of my surroundings—the replica of the gates of Buckingham Palace at the entrance of the funeral home, the bronzed Bambi drinking at the Pool of Eternal Life; and I knew that somewhere deep inside that building lay the body of my father, which I did not want to see.

The moment had come, but I kept myself a stranger to it. My clarity and composure were unsettling to me and I felt guilty over the absence of what I always assumed would be crippling grief. In the face of this long-dreaded death, I felt emotionally defective and I waited edgily for the shock to hit. The clinical name for it could be "denial"; or perhaps, under constant public scrutiny as a child, I had learned too well to perform in public, to mask my feelings—even from myself—with crisp manners and an eager, even smile.

•   •   •

Hollywood funerals, like most of its milestones, are accompanied by the same flamboyance and flashbulbs that glamorize gayer occasions like parties and premieres. Here, even death is larger than life. The funeral is an ennobling event; there is the same indefatigable "the show must go on" spirit, and, hand in glove, the press is there to capture it, swelling the performer's self-awareness in his moment of mourning, snapping muted studies of grief. The church, while grateful for the publicity, has a hard time holding its own against such savvy icons, such golden gods, and it struggles—often unsuccessfully—not to be upstaged.

My father, though he called himself a religious man, was offhanded in the practice of his faith, which he would have described as Swedish Lutheran. Having always resented the lugubriousness of many funerals with their open caskets and dismal dirges, finding them mawkish and punishing for those in attendance, he himself wanted no such pomp and ceremony, preferring cremation and a memorial service that celebrated life instead of death, reflecting the spirit of the deceased rather than a religious recruiting campaign.

My mother and I well knew how he felt; we had discussed and planned the service, arranged for who would speak, and I went off with friends to All Saints' Church in Beverly Hills to describe it to the minister. I may have tipped my hand upon entering by announcing that we were "here to discuss the Edgar Bergen Show—sorry, *service*—" correcting myself too late and reminding myself that we were in a House of God, not Caesars Palace. (You can take the child out of Hollywood . . .)

Then I got down to business, cautiously broaching the subject of music, explaining that it was being taken care of by a friend of my father's who was himself writing the arrangements of music we had selected from my father's life. What hymns were we having? he wondered. Hymns? Well, we preferred *no* hymns, actually (they would sandbag the show). And the sermon? Oh, the *sermon*—was a sermon mandatory? He paled. Perhaps a *short* sermon, I ventured (and hold the brimstone). Why didn't we just hire a hall?

Then I named the four family friends who had kindly agreed to give brief eulogies: ex-governor Ronald Reagan, Rams owner Carroll Rosenbloom, Johnny Carson and Jim Henson, who would be bringing a frog. A *frog*? Well, *Kermit* the Frog, I explained. Jim Henson had created the Muppets and my father had been his inspiration (he later dedicated the first Muppet movie "to the magic of Edgar Bergen"); he was closing down production just to be present.

The minister took off his glasses and rubbed his eyes. There's no people like show people. What's a man of God to do? Nervously, he gave the go-ahead.

It was not until later that I realized how well I had been trained for this particular task. What I was giving my father, on the grandest scale, was the Turtle Funeral he had produced for me when I was six.

"Edgar bergen: voices stilled, Ventriloquist Dies in Sleep at Age of 75" was announced on the front page of the Los Angeles newspapers. "Charlie McCarthy will go to the Smithsonian Museum, the national museum in Washington, sooner than he expected. Edgar Bergen, the man who breathed life into him for 56 years to the delight of Americans of all ages, is dead." *Variety* ran a cartoon, bordered in black, of Charlie with a tear on his cheek.

The day of the funeral, my father had a full house. His was an ending others envied, and perhaps only a true entertainer could understand what it meant. At the service, well attended by his peers, one was overheard saying to another as they entered the church, "You know, I envy Edgar, he went out performing at his peak. I hope it can be the same for me."

The service itself went smoothly. The men spoke simply and affectionately, giving short, personal speeches with warmth and wit. Praising his gentleness and humor, Ronald Reagan said, "He was a puckish, pixielike destroyer of the pompous." Johnny Carson said, "He was probably the most unpretentious man I ever met."

Dominic Frontiere, who had begun his career conducting for my father, oversaw the music, arranging the medley of songs for strings—violins, cellos and harp. He conducted it himself, for my father, one last time: a Swedish folk song, the radio show theme, "Charlie My Boy," and "September Song," which was sung by Andy Williams. It was a loving, lavish tribute that left many in tears. It paid honor and humor to a man who gave amply to the world of both. It was the farewell he deserved.

After my father's death, I stayed a few days at the house with my mother. She was still in a state of shock, running on adrenaline, and it would be some time before the reality of it would hit. A closeness had sprung up between us that had only existed sporadically before, and we were easier, more intimate with each other than I could ever remember. One evening the two of us were stretched out side by side on the bed like two best friends at a sleepover—smiling, sharing secrets, reading over old love letters she had come across in my father's file. She found a packet tied with ribbon, a collection of her letters to him during their courtship; she was touched that he had kept them and surprised, in reading one to me aloud, at the spunk and humor of their author. "Gee," she said, smiling at a smartly turned phrase, "did *I* say that? That's pretty funny." And she slipped the letter back into its envelope, musing mostly to herself, "Maybe I wasn't such a bad kid after all."

We went through the family photographs Mary Ellen Mark

had, for some reason, insisted on taking, pestering me for months until we had arranged a sitting in June. They were for no professional purpose—she had made them as a gift—but looking through them you could see what had inspired her to persist. There were the four of us in the garden, the *five* of us; then, each of us, separately, with my father, me holding Charlie in my arms, and, finally, my father, alone, with Charlie, tenderly putting him to rest in his trunk.

My father had left the memorabilia of a sixty-year career stacked in his office storerooms, and it fell to my mother to sort them through. One day I went with her. She had warned me about the amount and variety of what waited there, but there was no preparing for it. The huge room was piled high with one man's past, and an eccentric past it was.

For the better part of a day we sifted through magic books, sleight-of-hand manuals, rabbits in hats, crystal balls, magic wands, steam-engine models, hand-tooled Western saddles, variety bills, vaudeville scrapbooks, high-school yearbooks, radio acetates and cases of cameras. There were steamer trunks of dummies' wardrobes: countless pairs of tiny (size 3) socks, Mortimer's Boy Scout uniform, Charlie's cowboy suit, his Indian headdress, a jeweled turban, an embroidered sombrero, and a Sherlock Holmes deerstalker cap and cape.

Strewn piecemeal about, as in the scene of some macabre crime, were odd and unattached wooden extremities: a small hand here, a foot there, loose legs, headless torsos—the surrealistic rubble of dismembered dummies.

My mother picked up a tiny turtleneck with a slit sewn in the back through which my father could reach to manipulate the mouth lever on the head stalk. We shook our heads, laughing, crying and marveling at it all—at this man, his life and all its crazy contradictions—and wondering who he was.

Clues to that mystery might be locked in the huge, heavy safe in his office upstairs. It was more of a vault, really—massive, well above shoulder height, with a combination wheel like the kind used in caper movies. There was no evidence of a combination and, short of a blowtorch, apparently no access to its contents.

My mother tried his old combinations—birth dates, addresses, phone numbers—but none of them worked. Rifling through papers and files for a clue to the contents, we found nothing. We were there for hours, like inept safecrackers, my mother racking her memory for ancient numbers, formulas, passwords, secret codes— none of which corresponded. The safe stayed sealed, impregnable, its mysterious contents a secret.

The very presence of the safe was puzzling, and curiously compelling to us both. The will had been read, the estate was being settled—what more could be locked up inside a safe whose contents my father had failed to mention? Inside a vault whose existence was left unacknowledged, unexplained?

Suddenly my mother gasped. "I have it!" Rapidly making notations on a pad, transposing letters into numerals, she looked at me. "It's Charlie!" she said, excited. "The combination is C-H-A-R-L-I-E! *Of course.* Why didn't I think of that in the first place?" Reading from the series of numbers as she slowly turned the dial, she paused and looked at me. "You know, your father and Charlie were the same person."

The combination clicked softly, the door swung easily free and we held our breath as the inside was revealed. Would it be stacked with neat new bills? Crisply lined with cash? Would there be treasure, secret documents, uncut stones? Living with my father had prepared us for virtually anything, yet my mother and I both leaped back when, at last, we looked inside.

There—spaced on a shelf on stands—stood three Charlie heads: the cocky, monocled, much-loved original; the angry Charlie, its face grimacing grotesquely; and the old Charlie, the red hair receded to a silver fringe framing the hearing aid, the once-sharp features faded and weary with age.

16

A month later I returned to New York to begin work on a film called, appropriately, *Starting Over,* in a role I'd been reluctant to take. The one I'd wanted was the starring, sympathetic, funny part that later went to Jill Clayburgh; the smaller role of the vain and venal wife of Burt Reynolds who goes down in feminist flames was the one they offered me.

I'd been dumbfounded, offended. How did they think that I, a person of substance, could even begin to play someone so silly, shallow and self-absorbed? How could I possibly understand such an abrasive human being? Not since Tony Curtis in *The Vikings* had there been such classic miscasting.

Jill's role, on the other hand, was wonderful. The Lovable Underdog. Witty, winning, charming, disarming. A woman of thirty-one who lived alone and tried to make a meaningful life without a relationship—both afraid of, and yearning for, emotional commitment. Now there was a role I could relate to. Not the simpering siren offered me—a parody of a character I found pathetic. That woman had nothing to do with me. Did she?

What if people concluded that I, too, was feebleminded and contemptible? I, who had spent my life insisting otherwise—even when no one was asking. Was all that work to go down the drain now? Worse still, would I be unmasked in the process? That was the problem, of course—the possibility that in playing a fool I would somehow be revealed as one as well.

But as much as I disliked the part, I loved the script and had always wanted to work with the director, Alan Pakula, whose work (*Klute, All the President's Men*) I respected and who had a reputation for getting fine performances from his actors. In keeping with my new resolve to start selecting work for the work itself—not for salaries or locations—I convinced myself to look upon *Starting Over* as a challenge. Reluctantly, I agreed to do it.

In the role of a woman who abandons a happy marriage to pursue, with a singular lack of talent, a recording career, I was called on at two points in the script to sing. Very badly. This in itself was not a reach for me, as I sing very badly under any circumstances. But as I worked on the songs in the weeks before shooting, I realized with a sense of dread that in order for the songs to work and be funny I had to be willing to make a complete fool of myself. It only succeeded when done honestly, with no editorializing, no holding back. The second I worried about seeming stupid and pulled back in fear, it fizzled. *Pretending* to sing badly was not only redundant; it was hedging my bets. I could not sit back, wink at the audience and disclaim my character. I had *done* that before. Here, I saw that as soon as I played it safe, I was sunk. I had to be committed and unself-conscious. Committed, in this case, to unmasking the fool in myself. Nothing less would do.

Once I understood this elementary lesson, I began to sing like a bird. *Some* kind of bird, anyway. A monster had been created, and once I started, I didn't want to stop. I arrived at my lessons early; my coach graciously braced himself for my exuberant braying; and when, during these sieges, he quickly shifted his look from the sheet music and took a sudden interest in the papaya stand across the street to conceal his laughter, I knew I was on the right track.

Once I had dreaded the first day's shooting because it was then that I was meant to sing my first song; but when the time came, I burst on the set like Ethel Merman, eager to strut my stuff. Worried earlier about the abject humiliation such a display before the crew would bring, I now shrieked happily while they grinned—holding pillows over their ears—and waited good-naturedly for me to stop.

I had two scenes in the movie with Jill Clayburgh, and had anticipated feeling intimidated to work with her: I'd seen her in *An Unmarried Woman* and been so struck by the sureness of her work that my first impulse was simply to back off, to say, in effect, "Oh, never mind me—*you* just go on ahead." But I found that I had an unfamiliar confidence: Wait a minute, I'm here too. I've made movies for more than ten years, for Christ's sake—I must have learned *something*. Alan and Burt, in turn, provided a safe place to take chances, a safety net of security and goodwill. I had never worked with an actor more generous or supportive than Burt, who worked as hard for my performance as he did for his own. And working with Alan was its own reward; he was everything I'd hoped. It was a set that gave you courage to stick your neck out. And so I switched from "absent" to "present," and threw my hat into the ring.

I had been afraid that people would laugh at me. Instead, I found the joy of making people laugh. And I was willing to sacrifice people's opinions for the freedom that came with my unmasking and the relief of *admitting* it: Finally, I could stop worrying about whether people thought I was a fool or not. And with the freedom from fear came great exhilaration—the pride of having fought a phantom and won.

The windfall was that it worked. Reviews of the movie were mixed, but most agreed that as an actress I'd come of age. Wrote David Denby in *New York* magazine, "She seems finally to have understood what people have always resented in her—the glacé perfection—and she parodies herself mercilessly." Backhanded at best, but considering my record, this could be construed as a rave.

When, the following year, I was nominated for an Oscar for Best

Supporting Actress in the role I'd agreed to play so reluctantly, it was an overwhelming reward. My father would have been so proud, I thought; but more important, so was I.

Slowly I was becoming more satisfied with myself. The process of settling, of eliminating, of taking responsibility that I'd begun at thirty was continuing and paying off. Increasingly I had felt I was the embodiment of the dilettante—jack-of-all-trades, master of none; and I finally decided to do something about it. To begin, I shed those things I hadn't the discipline to do seriously.

First to go was photography. It was a perfect example of the half measures I took, of the things I would no longer do if I wasn't willing to make them count. It was not that I didn't love photography; I did. But if I wasn't going to make the commitment to master the profession, I had no business taking assignments I didn't deserve. And so I put photography aside—except for occasions with friends and family, snaps without professional aspirations—until the time when I could return to it and devote to it the attention it required.

I became clearer about carrying out my professional commitments. My attitude about a long-term endorsement contract for Cie perfume—once that of a put-upon *artiste*—was now one of gratitude for continued creative participation and a salary that afforded me greater discrimination in my choice of films.

One of the first to gauge my growing up was Pat Kingsley, who had been my press agent since I was twenty-one. She was a maverick in the profession—a publicist with principles, with politics, opinions and convictions. She was also a trusted and unflagging friend. As one who believed in me long before I did and who tried, for ten years, to protect me from myself in the press, she was especially relieved to witness my increasing professionalism, to see ambivalence replaced by appreciation. "You know, kiddo," she said to me, in a compliment I could finally accept, "I always knew you'd come through."

Most importantly, at thirty-two I began to study. I took classes in acting and script analysis and started—after fourteen films—to learn basic techniques. I vowed never to accept another shoddy movie for expedient reasons but to look for roles that involved taking risks. I was finally finding my way in films and I was finding it—as my father had always hoped—in comedy. It was he who had first urged me in this direction, perhaps contrasting the stiffness of my performances to my bawdy humor at home; perhaps because he saw me, like him, find freedom from self-consciousness through comedy; and perhaps because underneath our shared reserve were clowns eager to be called to play.

I had always wanted to do comedy, but with my "glacé perfection," I was frozen solid in the "Ice Queen" category. Until Alan Pakula cast me in *Starting Over*, I was considered an unlikely candidate for comedy roles. But *Starting Over* wasn't idly titled. *Rich and Famous* followed, in which I costarred with Jacqueline Bisset. A witty, bitchy comedy about the warfare between two best friends, the script, by Gerald Ayres, was tailor-made for the director, George Cukor—eighty-two and still the master of high-style comedies.

I played a Southern belle named Merry Noel: ambitious, over-dressed, occasionally endearing, somewhere between Scarlett O'Hara and Eva Perón. Now, thanks to class, I knew how to break down and prepare a script; and this time I did my homework, stalking women on sidewalks and in department stores for inspiration, accosting strangers with quirky Southern accents, reading books about Southern women and by Southern women. By the time I was done, I knew her inside out and under.

I loved every day of *Rich and Famous* and couldn't wait each morning to get to the set. I loved the script, the work, my co-star and crew, and respected my director, whose constant refrain was "At a good clip!" Never had I felt such security, such confidence, such joy in my work in films. Much of this was the comfort I felt in comedy, in playing a well-drawn character role. A lot of it was Jacqueline. Hollywood wags who had predicted fireworks on a set that featured two female stars were abruptly brought up short, not having reckoned on Jackie's generosity, her maternal instinct toward the cast, and her lack of competitiveness toward other women. We were in instant sympathy with each other: long typecast for our looks and ready to break out of our restrictive roles, we worked closely with each other throughout the film, a tight two-woman team, and our friendship was reflected in our performances.

George Cukor also taught me a thing or two about comedy, intent as he was on fast pacing, alert to the rhythm. A friend and fan of my father's, he declared that comedy was in my genes. Yet when my new sense of professionalism asserted itself in one request for a retake, he found it not so funny: he glowered at me fiercely and sputtered, "You *Swedish fanatic!*" To me, it was high praise indeed.

At last I was approaching work with honest ambition; shelving the suspicion that what made you good at acting made you bad at life—finding, instead, the self-knowledge that can come from living with a role, and discovering a thing or two about the character arcs that had so mystified me in the beginning: above all, I'd put into action my belated perception that acting—good acting—takes courage and commitment.

I had learned—determined—not to pay attention to reviews, good or bad. I seldom read them and had been conditioned to expect the worst. When someone dropped a copy of *Time* onto a table before me, I braced myself as I began to read. ". . . and this once bland beauty has become one of the screen's most arresting comedians." I blinked and read it again. And again. And I smiled and thought, Well, well.

It was only ignorance (or arrogance) that ever made me think acting was easy. If I hit my stride in one film, I lost it in the next. In the small cameo role in *Gandhi* that Richard Attenborough had asked me to play fifteen years before, I was a wallflower among British virtuosos, awestruck by the agility of the actors around me, earnest but uneasy with the dialogue. My discomfort clearly showed, and I was briefly discouraged at losing some of the confidence I'd finally come to feel.

But now, at least I know enough to find acting frightening; I can finally admit my fear of failure, my dread of appearing foolish. I know I love making movies—making magic—and that I want to serve them well. I know, too, that working, not wishing, makes it so.

The spring after my father died, I took my mother with me to London, a city she had visited often with my father. This was the first time she had been there without him. The trip, which I had hoped would distract her for a time from her loneliness at home, only seemed to emphasize it more. Emotionally raw, physically fragile, she seemed lost and shaken, like a child who finds terror in familiar places when separated from a parent. It was as if every cell in her body were railing against the loss.

My brother, too, had been devastated by the loss, two weeks before his seventeenth birthday, of the person he loved above all else in the world. Theirs had been an extraordinary connection, exceptional in its closeness, and he was manful and moving about his sorrow, open and unself-conscious in his pain. But as deeply as he missed his dad, he did not see it as the death of their relationship. Though they were no longer together, he continued to feel their closeness as a constant comfort and support. "I am my dad," he said to me quietly, a few weeks after his death. "I look in the mirror now and that's who I am." And in some ways he was. Suddenly more mature, more silent, thoughtful, restrained, polite. A seventeen-year-old who had become a gentleman before his time.

In London, as my mother's distress increased, I found it harder to comfort her. I was frustrated at my inability to relieve her pain, ashamed of my emotional ineptness. But my mother and I were new at direct expressions of affection and our vocabulary was still weak.

In our suite, the beds were side by side. One morning, my mother was smiling. She told me that during the night, in my sleep, I had reached out and held her hand.

When Charlie was put on permanent display at the Smithsonian museum, our family flew to Washington for the installation ceremony, arriving early to check the exhibit.

A young man was propping Charlie on a stand, casually adjusting his head, which suddenly began to sag and topple. My hand lurched out—instinctively, protectively—and I jumped to steady him. Hold it, fella, that's no way to handle dummies; *I'll* tell you how to handle dummies. I was as indignant about the absence of respect (reverence, even) that Charlie had always commanded in our house as over the indifferent handling.

You see, you steady the shoulder with your left hand as you insert the head with your right—very carefully . . . never let go of the stalk or the head might fall. With your hand inside the cavity in the dummy's back, keep a firm grip on the stalk, always holding it securely. . . .

Stepping back from Charlie, I checked his appearance: The familiar brown eyes that for fifty years had shot sparks and flickered famously now stared past me stonily into space, strangely dull, glassy, dead. There was no sign of life; worse, no recognition. *Hey! It's me, Charlie—it's Candy!* I waited for the wisecracks that would never come, the throaty chuckle, the clipped movements. I was shocked at his final silence. My father made the magic and the magic was gone.

• • •

Now, it was for me to make my own.

It had not escaped my notice that it was only after my father died that I summoned the courage to commit to my work. Was it relevant that my father himself, for all of his genius, had been the ultimate master of playing it safe—a performer who had more than a consummate facade; who had an alter ego? Was it that acting was such an obvious—an inevitable—choice for a child whose father made her talk, supplied her dialogue, literally manipulated her; that her terror at growing up to find no hand squeezing her neck, no voice but her own, receded only when all hope of rescue was irrevocably gone?

The approval I had sought so ardently—and perversely—was somewhere between a snipe hunt and the quest for the Holy Grail. I had spent so much of my life pursuing it that the impulse persisted even though the withholder had died.

Before I could let go, I had to look back. For a time, I became fixed on the fairy tale of my childhood. On finding the moral to the fable. On understanding all that my father had meant to my life.

At first, a deep sadness, an awful fear descended on me; my life kept flickering in front of me in furious flashbacks. And what I felt was the pain I must have caused him, the pain I had caused myself, the pain we had caused each other. But once I knew the pain, it all began to make sense.

I loved him so much, so illegally, that I had done everything to conceal it from him—and from myself. Meticulously, over the years I had spun a scenario that capitalized on his remoteness, propagated the fiction that he didn't love me. That he was sparing in his affections, undemonstrative, unfeeling, cold. In the words of his dummy, "an emotional hermit." So great was my investment in my fiction that it had become intractably real. It was not that I had had a distant relationship with my father, but that I had had too close a one. For my mind. For my conscience, as it was being formed as a child.

And what of him? A shy man, a remote one, a man who expressed emotion by proxy. "You were the love of your father's life," my mother had said, and suddenly I could see him whole. A man whose feelings often caught him unprepared but were no less strong for his inability to articulate them. And so we were at cross-purposes for much of our lives. Needing, rejecting . . . when everything we wanted was there all along.

What a deep sadness it gave me: the awkward attempts at affection, the armoring ourselves from too much caring, the clumsy communication. But in time, regret gave way to reflection, to a reckoning with the romance. And what a grand romance it had been. Eagerly I studied old photographs of the child who gazed at him adoringly, and thought back to when we flew away on secret weekends, soaring together into the sun . . . early morning rides in the desert. . . . "Do you know what it means to 'bill and coo'?" . . . snuggling in bed and talk of stars and musings on infinity . . . trying to still the frantic beating of the six-year-old heart.

17

One night in New York, burrowed in as usual in my snug bunker of pillows, a book that went unread propped on my stomach, I reflected idly on my life alone. Maybe Mary Ellen was right, I mused, staring out at the park, remembering that she had predicted that her friend, French film director Louis Malle, was the man I would marry. Louis Malle, she would announce again and again with simple certainty, was the perfect man for me. Her dogged insistence had become a familiar joke. But now, swaddled in my down-and-Dacron mix, I wondered if I should have listened. God knows I'd met everyone else.

In fact, I had met Louis Malle in Connecticut some years before, when Annabel and Mike Nichols took me to a Fourth of July party. He had arrived accompanied by the controversy that, like a faithful companion, seemed always to dog his heels. First, in the early sixties, with his second film, *The Lovers*, starring Jeanne Moreau; the suggestive intimacy of its love scenes had seemed thrillingly explicit to American audiences then. Again, in the seventies, with *Murmur of the Heart*, which became a movie classic; his screenplay was nominated for an Oscar, but many viewers weren't ready for a lighthearted look at incest. His seven-hour documentary, *Phantom India*, had been unanimously acclaimed everywhere but in that country, where it was banned for its realistic treatment. And he was nominated for an Oscar again, this time for Best Foreign Film for *Lacombe Lucien*. The simply told story of an innocent country boy who becomes a Nazi, it was a sympathetic look at the mindlessness of evil—too sympathetic, according to some. And now, he was preparing *Pretty Baby*, his first film in America; shooting had not yet begun and already there was trouble.

The film, set in New Orleans at the turn of the century, was based on the life of the late photographer Bellocq and his marriage to a child prostitute. The search for the girl to play her had attracted enormous publicity and ended in the casting of model Brooke Shields, who was then eleven. The mere idea of depicting a child prostitute, coupled with casting such a young girl to play the role, had provoked a violent reaction, including organized religious opposition, and people were up in arms.

A small man was Louis Malle—well-mannered, soft-spoken— but people made such a big fuss. He was brave, brilliant, gifted and daring. Seated next to him at that Fourth of July dinner, I was sufficiently intimidated by his reputation that I hardly spoke. Still, in between clutching my caftan, which kept slipping off my shoulders, and discreetly picking up the endive that had spilled into my lap, I managed to eye him intently. He was right up my alley, I had to admit: attractive, adventurous and inaccessible. But he seemed as ill at ease as I, and that first meeting was an edgy encounter, awkward and uncomfortable. There were fireworks that night—but not for me. If this was destiny, it was riding a dark horse.

We had not seen each other since, and now, returning to my book, I thought no more about it. Until the following morning when, uncannily, I received the message that Louis Malle had called. I called back; he said he was in Montreal cutting *Atlantic City*, but was coming that weekend to New York and would like to have lunch. I said that I would too.

The morning of the lunch I was nervous. If I'd been uncomfortable with this man four years before, what made me think it would be any easier now? It was okay to be nervous, I decided, nervous was acceptable. What wasn't was my old arch way of concealing it. Beforehand, as I bathed, I decided the most I could do was be myself. No more, no less.

It was a wintry Sunday afternoon, and we met for late lunch at the Russian Tea Room. He entered, breathless from the cold, burrowed deep inside a loden coat. Elegantly dressed, understated. His face was fine-featured and romantic. His softly curling black hair was shot with gray, yet he looked younger than a man in his late forties.

"Well, it's cold. That's all I have to say," were his first words as he took off his coat. But that was not all he had to say. As it turned out, he said a great deal—in a beautiful voice, a lightly musical manner of speaking, and in English that was precise, almost poetic. He had a funny, unexpected command of American idioms that, coming from his lips, somehow sounded both lyrical and literal.

He was interested and gracious—clearly a man who enjoyed and appreciated the company of women—and he spoke and listened eagerly, with a thoughtful intensity and subtle wit. He was unpretentious ("That's one of the few things I like about myself") and unpredictable. He was great.

On and on we talked—about film, painting, politics. He was extremely cultivated, intensely curious, and his perceptions were startling and astute; he did not think quite like anyone else.

He spoke with great love about his children—a daughter, six, and a son, nine, who lived in Europe. His face changed as he spoke of them, became softer, more open, and he looked very like a child himself.

And we spoke about relationships and the increasing odds against them. Odds I had begun to respect, I admitted, and I said I spent a lot of time alone and found it rewarding and productive. It sounded suspiciously like *The Nun's Story*.

It came out that we were both, by nature, loners. Confirmed bachelors. Guarded and quick to retreat into ourselves. "Basically, I don't believe in marriage," he said. "I think relationships have to be reinvented every day.

"All my life I've been searching for that *one* relationship and never really found it; something in me always held back. Probably I blame myself. Or perhaps I simply wasn't ready."

"But what were you missing?" I asked. "What more were you looking for that you didn't seem to find?"

"To belong," he said simply. "Just to feel that I belong."

When we looked up from the table, the restaurant was filling up for supper. It was six o'clock; lunch had lasted four hours.

It was followed, over a period of weeks, by lengthy dinners, concerts, evenings at the ballet. Even the opera, which, for one who had flunked it in college, was now a surprising pleasure. Yet many nights later, I was still wondering why he had called. Maybe he simply needed someone to talk to—for talk we did, often and late into the night, breaking occasionally for brandy. I was cautious, used to leapers, still not certain what he had in mind. The conversation was open, often intimate, but we kept a respectful distance and never touched. Neither of us was sure what the other wanted. And neither of us was much good at flirting, at mating dances, at making the first move.

When Mary Ellen called, like a proud parent, to ask how things were going, I told her, "Well, the thing is—we're just friends." *Just* friends. Not a bad place to begin. And maybe it was something more. For when my friend director Nick Meyer told me of the first time he had met Louis, I felt a deep sense of pleasure, an unexpected surge of pride.

It was at a birthday party in New York and the hostess asked Louis if he would cut the cake, which he quietly did, into completely unorthodox pieces: triangles, crescents, stars and squares.

And when Nick, who watched, fascinated, asked if he had anything against the traditional pie-wedge shape, Louis replied simply, "But now everyone can choose the shape they want."

"And that was the man," Nicky concluded gleefully, almost reverentially, "who made a *comedy* about *incest!*"

And here I was, in our late-night conversations, invariably curled up in the overstuffed armchair opposite his place on the sofa. Never daring, never dreaming to sit next to him on the couch. It took Louis to close the chasm. To take the risk. One night, he asked me quietly, smiling softly, "Candy, can I hold you?" And I smiled and said emphatically, "*Oh yes.*"

I felt like a small frightened animal who had spent its life curled up in the back of a cave snarling at intruders when, suddenly, someone turned on the light and said, "It's okay, it's safe—you can come out now." And from then, everything was simple, and I thought, So *this* is the point. *I understand.* Now it all makes sense.

I waited apprehensively for visits from my habitual demons, ready to club them in case they crept out to play. But they were conspicuous in their absence; and Louis—no stranger to demons himself—attested to the same strong sense of peace. The combination of two notorious long shots seemed to confuse them, to throw them off the scent. Or perhaps through loving and understanding each other's demons, we began to accept our own.

In May, we went to Europe to spend ten days in Florence. What Louis hadn't seen of the world as a cameraman in his early twenties for Jacques Cousteau, he had explored as a director since. We had both been compulsive travelers, and we had both done it the solitary way. So I wondered how it would work with the two of us. But we mined the museums and ravaged the restaurants of Florence ecstatically, and soon I asked myself how I'd done it so long alone. There we celebrated my thirty-fourth birthday. I have never been so glad at growing older.

• • •

Louis' children were coming for the summer, which we decided to spend on Long Island; we drove out and chose a house near the beach. Here comes the catch, I thought; this has all gone too smoothly. What will it be like to meet his kids? I was concerned but oddly confident—oddly confident about everything of late. There was also the particular way in which he spoke of them: some special sense of gratitude, an overwhelming love. They had helped to shape the man I wanted to spend my life with; I was grateful to them too.

He had been perfectly prepared not to have children, he said; he had not been especially interested. "But they changed my life," he said simply. "The parents are the ones who get everything; children are a gift you give yourself. I began to look at the world through their eyes, to see things differently. It's fascinating to see their instinctive approach to relationships, their perception of the world. It's very sad for me not to live with them; my happiest experiences have been with my kids."

His children arrived and I came to the house some days later, after they had settled in. I arrived at night and Louis led me upstairs. The door to the kids' room was open; they were asleep inside. His daughter was nearest the door, soundly sleeping, long, dark hair swirling around her head. Louis covered her gently, caressing her; I saw that he was very close to tears.

They were children accustomed to changes—new faces, new places—but how would they take to me? We were introduced across muffins in the morning. They watched me without speaking, silently sniffing the wind, circling me like cats, their circles slowly growing smaller, tighter—until, by the end of the day, we had begun to be friends.

They were wonderful kids, Justine and Cuote. It was hard to believe—even his kids were great—and I had never felt happier, fuller times than those we spent that summer: reading Doctor Seuss, seeing *Superman,* composing notes to the Tooth Fairy, picking strawberries, catching crabs. We searched for days for fireflies with absolutely no success until one night I went out alone to hunt them and found one—the last firefly on Long Island—and rushed upstairs to their bedroom with it cupped and winking in my hands.

Louis was at his best with them—gay, exuberant, switching back and forth from English to French, "Where are those little idiots? *Où sont les petits crétins?*"; *"Je t'ai vu,* eh, Justine; I *saw* you," as she tried to sneak a cookie. "Exquisite children," he muttered happily, as they ran in covered with jam.

On the beach, Louis is building a sand castle with his kids. Half of him is hidden—he has all but disappeared while digging out the moat. A friend from France is passing, walking storklike by the shore. Tall, sleek, impeccably bronzed, a Cartier watch and bracelet the only accessories to his tiny black bikini. He spots Louis when he surfaces for air and stops to chat, staring down at the three figures crawling round the castle. Clutching a pack of Gauloises and smoking one dispassionately, he peppers Louis with questions: When will he next be in Paris? Is he planning another film? When will *Atlantic City* be released?

But Louis is a man at work. Anyone can see he is busy— building a sand castle with his kids. He has no time for chic small talk, no interest in précis of future projects; has far more pressing matters on his mind: a part of the wall has washed away and the bridge has collapsed and requires urgent feats of engineering. Nonplussed, the man from France moves on. Louis is working furiously to reinforce the wall, repair the bridge and steady the tilting turret. Scrambling happily with his kids on hands and knees, his trim athletic body in constant motion, an ecstatic expression on his face, he seems much more a child than a parent. A man, for the moment, completely at peace.

It was an idyllic summer, and one night in the midst of it, after

the kids had gone to bed, Louis and I were sitting quietly outside
listening to the night sounds. Suddenly he said, "If I asked you very
politely, would you marry me?"

He hardly had time to finish the question. Marry him indeed.

We were married in the southwest of France in a country house
he'd owned for fifteen years. Though Louis had by then lived for
five years in America and knew the country and its people better
than I, this corner of France was the place where he felt most at
home.

The house was called Le Coual—"the raven's cry"—and looked
out over miles of rocky highlands that rolled to the horizon like the
sea. It was an extraordinary house, one of the oldest in the area,
medieval in style and mysterious in aspect, built of buff-colored
stone. To live in a house with such a long past gave faith in the
future; it seemed like a favorable place to begin our own. We decided to be married at the end of September by the mayor of the tiny
village nearby.

We wanted the wedding to be private, personal and unpretentious; we asked Pat to do her best to keep it from the press. It was
important for the kids to be there, and a few friends from Paris. We
asked Mary Ellen—who had known years before anyone—if she
would come from New York and be my witness.

France was far for my family: my brother was in college in San
Diego and I knew he couldn't take the time off from school. But,
though the trip was long and the date set at the last minute, I hoped
that my mother could come. Unlike many mothers who urged
their daughters into early marriage, mine had shown uncommon
restraint—especially when, after thirty-three years, there had been
no sign of my even coming close. She was entitled to despondence
but was philosophical instead: she simply assumed it would take
time to find the right man. Now that I had, I wanted her to be there.

"You mean my little girl is getting married?" she asked when I called her, my thirty-four years suddenly shrinking in size. She laughed lightly at her maternal reaction, her voice warm, clearly moved. "Oh, you don't want *me* there," she tossed off easily.

"Yes, I do, Mom. Please try to come."

"Well, I think I will—just to be there for 'your day.' Then I'll leave right afterward for London. I'm not going to be *that* kind of mother-in-law."

The morning of the wedding the weather was splendid—an auspicious sign in that part of France. Bad weather would have brought bad luck, but that day, as it was, we were blessed. Friends from America—Kitty, Ali, Rusty, John Calley, Mike Nichols—called to wish us well.

We'd brought the kids and Mary Ellen with us on the train from Paris, and a few more close friends followed that morning by car— Louis' brother Vincent, who would be Louis' witness; producer Christian Ferry and his wife, Basha; and Terrence Malick. David Lazer, a family friend, flew in from London. My mother had arrived the evening before and had spent the night in town an hour away; she would come by car in the morning. The wedding was arranged for eleven.

Everyone was ready early: Louis wore a tie and fawn-colored jacket, and in Paris I had found a Victorian dress of ivory silk and antique lace. Mary Ellen was hung with Nikons and Leicas— recording the day, her prescience rewarded. The scene was set: neighbors had looped the cars with pink and white ribbons, and wild cedar trees had been cut, trimmed with pastel paper flowers and placed at each side of the drive.

We waited outside for my mother to arrive and soon heard the sound of a car crunching slowly on gravel. A blue BMW pulled into view. My mother was in the passenger seat—but who was that driving? I squinted to see if it was anyone I knew. My mother got out first, and then the driver. A tall, blond man; I could see him now, but, before I could make out the face, I saw there was something familiar about the body—an easy grace, the athletic swing of the arms. The big blond head was bobbing toward me, and then I saw the eyes and the smile. I burst into tears as I hugged my brother. "Oh, pal," I gasped as I squeezed him. "I can't believe you came—oh, pal."

He explained that he had torn a tendon in football and was sidelined for the season (he hadn't wanted to worry me by telling me before now) and suddenly he thought that he should be there for his sister's wedding. How many times would I marry again? He arranged the trip, my mother approved it, and two days later, still limping from his injury, here he was in France. He had given me the happiest surprise of my life.

My mother and I held each other tightly. Then she handed me a linen handkerchief embroidered by my father's mother and an ice-blue satin garter, and slipped her diamond engagement ring on my finger "to borrow." She was tired from travel, but I'd never seen her look happier and I'd never loved her more.

We climbed into the cars streaming ribbons and drove up the hill to the village. All the local people had been invited and were waiting, dressed in Sunday suits, in the little square as we arrived.

It is a rural farming region, and on the high, rugged terrain the people earn what they need but no more. Theirs is still a world of manners, of Monsieur and Madame and courteous greetings, and they were clearly pleased that Louis—a man who moves in so much of the world—had chosen, of all the spots on its surface, to celebrate his marriage in this remote corner of France.

They had decorated the small, spare town hall, transformed it for the occasion: The traditional cedars stood on each side of the entrance, and inside, the room had been painted a pale butter-yellow. Oriental rugs carpeted the floor and the corners spilled with flowering plants. French and American flags had been crossed on the walls and over the mantel and over the portrait of Giscard d'Estaing.

The mayor, who rode his tractor in overalls, was dressed now in a suit, old but immaculate, slashed with the official red, white and blue bandeau of France. A gentle-faced man, he had worked hard on his prepared remarks and his speech was eloquent and moving. He spoke of the affection the people have for Louis—for his kindness and simplicity—and of their pride in him; of "those two great nations—the United States and France"—and "their historical alliance which has so benefited our country in the past and which is to benefit us here again today."

He read the marital contract, still in the original Napoleonic code; Louis and I signed the documents, Mary Ellen and Vincent witnessed, we kissed, my mother wept, the villagers waved their flags and cheered, and we all surged into the sunlight into a shower of rice.

At the restaurant next door, its walls studded with stuffed boars' heads, we had a champagne reception for the people of the village, then went back to the house with friends and family for lunch in the garden under the trees. At the end of the day, old Nanette, the noble donkey, was hitched up to the yellow cart, and the bride and groom went for an afternoon spin.

By evening, almost everyone had gone. My mother, true to her word, flew back to London, and my brother set off on his two-day trip back to school. I will always be grateful that they had gone to such lengths to be there.

That night, in the last light of evening, Louis and I walked outside in the cool silence surrounding the house and stared out at the night as the sky turned violet and the stars grew bright. I had never imagined it was possible to be so happy, to feel so sure-footed and at peace.

It is easy to explain what goes wrong with people; difficult, maybe dangerous, to explain what goes right, why we blended so easily into each other's lives. Louis sold his apartment and moved his things into mine. Cartons arrived crammed with clothing, china, a Cuisinart, crystal, books. Gee, I thought, he wasn't kidding. This is serious; he's really moving in. Even our tastes were compatible, and we combined our Indian miniatures, Asian and African art, Tibetan mandalas and kilim rugs.

"Do you feel like I'm invading?" he asked, smiling but concerned. I just hugged him. I'd been waiting for this invasion all my life.

We even combined our friends. Though we shared many to begin with, we soon felt friends with those new ones we met. I presented mine proudly—my friends were my dowry and I considered them my real wealth. Louis respected the closeness of these friendships and saw their importance in my life; and my friends all agreed on Louis. First they were prepared to love him for making me so happy. But quickly they came to love Louis himself. One night, at a small dinner she gave to celebrate our marriage, Kitty Hawks phrased it simply and gracefully in a toast, lifting her glass to Louis and saying, "Thank you for bringing our Bergen such happiness; you are a wonderful addition to our lives."

And so we settled in. Once compulsive travelers, we now preferred staying home. Two people accustomed to spending time alone, we lived together like two cats, making room, giving way—intimate but respectful of each other's privacy.

Before we met, I would have given anything to work with Louis. But if working apart is tough, working together, we decided early on, would be tougher. There's tension enough in making movies; having it spill over into our lives seems an unnecessary risk. Still, Louis is one of the directors actors most want to work with, one of those rare perfectionists who puts actors' needs paramount. Professional, sure of himself, confident in his craft, he leads actors beyond their limits, encourages them to exceed their abilities.

I first watched Louis work in Virginia, on *My Dinner with André,* and then in California. No one works harder on a set, and I love to watch him—eyes squeezed shut in concentration, furiously chewing gum in order not to smoke, darting around in his silver-striped "Miss Piggy" sneakers, never remaining in one place. I wonder what he tells the actors in their huddles; I watch them as they nod appreciatively, grateful for the silence he keeps for their sake on the set. I watch the casual California crews curse him for his energy, the fierce focus of this foreigner, and I grin as he surprises them with unexpected choices. "If it's sunny, we'll shoot indoors." Different ways to cut the cake.

In our lives as well, we cut the cake in different ways. We help each other, complete each other, and, while we are involved in each other's careers—discussing our work together, encouraging each other, making suggestions—it is this marriage, which Louis refers to as "a work in progress," that matters most.

"This is as good as it gets," I warned Louis early in our relationship, in case he thought he had only scratched the surface. "It doesn't get any better; you are getting the best of me. What you are seeing is not the tip of the iceberg—it *is* the iceberg. It all goes downhill from here."

Maybe not. Four years later, it only gets better, and sometimes I see glimpses of the woman I had always hoped I might be. I used to believe that marriage would diminish me, reduce my options. That you had to be someone less to live with someone else when, of course, you have to be someone more. In marriage with this man, my options have only expanded. Everything about my life has been enhanced and enriched. I used to think that when you got married your life was over, but I feel like mine has just begun.

With a new set of choices, I straddle the fence, edgy, looking anxiously at my watch: If I decide I want children of my own, it's getting late in the game. The question spins constantly in my mind. My husband gives me the lead in this decision; he has two children. The choice, it seems, is mine.

I think of the love I feel for Louis' kids. I watch them now watching television; a war movie, something with John Wayne. Cuote is riveted; John Wayne is his hero, and he is one with the man on the screen. His sister is riveted by her brother and persists in kissing him and cooing, *"Mon petit chéri."* Finally she goes too far; his manhood is offended, and Cuote, usually polite, soft-spoken, turns to her and screams, "Justine, stop it! This is an *adventure* film! This is no time to call me *mon petit chéri!"* She sits back, chastised, but flashes me a sneaky grin.

She makes me laugh; I love her. Her tiny hands fluttering. Tiny navy sneakers and almost inaudible breaths. The large, dark eyes, less impressive in size than in intensity, in their sudden changes and intelligence and humor. Their relentless fierce observation—she doesn't miss a trick. And something in her voice. Her intonation. A creaky comical quality, a singsong that we all strain to hear, remember when she's gone and imitate unconsciously when she's near.

"Has anyone around here seen a *toad*?" she asks, rounding a corner, red-cheeked and panting, hot on a scavenger hunt. Wild child. Shy child. Original, outrageous, uncertain, unself-conscious. Unaware of the magic she makes. She is generous and kind; beautiful at times; a bag lady at others. Loyal and loving but on her own terms. She captivates and fascinates me and I find myself following her dopily, devotedly. Observing her secretly from windows, smiling, delighting in her every move.

And I watch Justine with her father; how she worships him, how they rejoice in each other. The depth of love between them. How like each other they are—the shared sense of humor, the weird wisdom; it's hard to tell where one leaves off and the other begins. Will it be as hard for you, Justine, as it was for me to find someone you love as much as your father? Will it take you as long to find your way?

Justine is showing a sharp and sudden interest in fairy tales. The kind about princesses. Where the prince comes to carry them away. "Candy, would you sing me that song?" she asks as I put her to bed. "You know, the one about the prince—"

I know the one about the prince. "You mean, 'Someday My Prince Will Come'?"

"Yes, that one. I love that song."

How well I know. And I begin to sing in a voice not unlike Snow White's.

> *. . . And how perfect that moment will be—*
> *When the Prince of my Dreams comes to me. . . .*

I break off abruptly. What am I doing?

"It's just in fairy tales," I tell her, trying to cover my tracks. "You know, there's really no such thing as princes—not the kind on white horses. Not like the kind in the song." Not like your father. Not like mine.

EPILOGUE

Our apartment swells with Charlie McCarthys. You remember him. All around me are Charlie McCarthys: Charlie spoons, comics, cuff links, compacts. Charlies everywhere I turn—in enamel pins with movable mouths on my and my husband's lapels, gold profiles on cigarette cases, salt and pepper shakers, tin toys, greeting cards—spilling out of every nook and cranny, my Charlie collection grows.

Once somewhat sheepish about this bizarre background, I am now thunderstruck by its amazing uniqueness, hopelessly enamored of its eccentricity. Infinitely grateful for my past. These days, I am grateful for any number of things. Too much of my life I spent ducking gifts—unable to be grateful, too embarrassed by the conviction that they were undeserved.

I am grateful for the hug I got to give my father just before he died.

I am grateful and proud of my family now—proud of the way we look out for each other, lessen each other's burdens. I think of the love and pride I feel for my brother, the peace I've found in my mother's presence. We are open now about needing each other— she needs a daughter and I need a mom—and we take pleasure in telling each other of our affection, this time *without* counting. My mother has become my biggest booster; I, hers. I marvel at the capability with which she has assumed her place as head of the family. Will you look at my mother? I think. What a beautiful woman. What a knockout.

I am grateful for the miracle of my marriage: that we managed to find each other, that we get to begin our days together, share our lives together, respect each other, support each other and let the other be. To discover the joy of living with a lover and a friend. Sometimes, coming home at the end of a day, I worry that as in a dream it will all have disappeared. We take nothing for granted. "You know," Louis said to me once, as we spoke about our luck, "the Aztecs were terrified each night when the sun set that it would not rise again the next morning. They were grateful for every dawn."

It takes a long time to become a person. Longer than they tell you. Longer than I thought. I am grateful for my past; it has given me the present. I want to do well by the future.

Knock wood.

PHOTO CREDITS

Grateful acknowledgment is made to the following for permission to reproduce photography in this book.

1. Photo © Peter Martin
2. Collection Edgar Bergen (CBS)
3. Collection Edgar Bergen
4. Collection Edgar Bergen
5. Collection Edgar Bergen
6. Photo © Peter Martin
7. Collection Edgar Bergen (CBS photo by Pierce Grant)
8. Photo © Peter Martin
9. Collection Edgar Bergen
10–14. Photo © Peter Martin
15. Collection Edgar Bergen (CBS photo by Ben Polin)
16. Collection Edgar Bergen (CBS)
17. Collection Candice Bergen (photo by Edgar Bergen)
18. Photo by Steve Schapiro
19. Photo by Mary Ellen Mark/Lee Gross Associates Inc. © Mary Ellen Mark